WITHDRAWN

JACK I. BARDON

Professor of Psychological Foundations
Rutgers—the State University

VIRGINIA C. BENNETT

Professor of Psychological Foundations
Rutgers—the State University

School Psychology

PRENTICE-HALL, INC., ENGLEWOOD CLIFFS, NEW JERSEY

Library of Congress Cataloging in Publication Data

BARDON, JACK I.
  School psychology.

  (Foundations of modern psychology series)
        Bibliography: p.
    1. Educational psychology. 2. School psychologists.
I. Bennett, Virginia C., joint author. II.
Title. [DNLM: 1. Psychology, Educational. LB1051 B247s 1974]
LB1051.B2472 1974   370.15   73-11419
ISBN 0-13-794420-9
ISBN 0-13-794412-8   (pbk.)

© *1974 by*

Prentice-Hall, Inc., Englewood Cliffs, N.J.

10   9   8   7   6   5   4   3   2   1

Prentice-Hall International, Inc., London

Prentice-Hall of Australia, Pty. Ltd., Sydney

Prentice-Hall of Canada, Ltd., Toronto

Prentice-Hall of India Private Limited, New Delhi

Prentice-Hall of Japan, Inc., Tokyo

Contents

Foreword to
Foundations of Modern Psychology Series   *vii*

Preface   *ix*

ONE
School Psychology: A Point of View   *1*

ASSUMPTIONS FOR THE SPECIALTY OF SCHOOL PSYCHOLOGY

HOW SCHOOL PSYCHOLOGY DIFFERS FROM OTHER SPECIALTIES

DIFFERING APPROACHES TO PROBLEM SOLVING

TWO
The Development of a Specialty   *12*

A BRIEF HISTORY OF SCHOOL PSYCHOLOGY

THE CURRENT STATUS OF THE SPECIALTY

THREE

The Assessment of Children in School   27

INDIVIDUAL ASSESSMENT

GROUP ASSESSMENT

CLASSIFICATION FOR SPECIAL EDUCATION

DISADVANTAGED CHILDREN: A SPECIAL CASE

FOUR

Helping Teachers with Classroom Problems   72

BEHAVIOR MANAGEMENT

DIRECT INTERVENTION TECHNIQUES WITH PUPILS

REFERRAL TO COMMUNITY SERVICES

FIVE

Teach Consultation and Education   *116*

IN-SERVICE EDUCATION

AFFECTIVE EDUCATION

INDIVIDUAL TEACHER CONSULTATION

SIX

The School Psychologist as a Modifier of the School System   *144*

WORKING WITH OTHER SCHOOL PERSONNEL

RESEARCH IN THE SCHOOLS

SEVEN

Training for School Psychology and Prospects for the Future   *169*

WHAT DETERMINES PROFESSIONAL TRAINING?

INFLUENCES ON SCHOOL PSYCHOLOGY TRAINING

DIVERSITY OF TRAINING PROGRAMS

PROSPECTS FOR THE FUTURE

References   *183*

Index   *191*

Foundations of Modern Psychology Series

The tremendous growth and vitality of psychology and its increasing fusion with the social and biological sciences demand a search for new approaches to teaching at the introductory level. We can no longer feel content with the traditional basic course, geared as it usually is to a single text that tries to skim everything, that sacrifices depth for breadth. Psychology has become too diverse for any one person, or group, to write about with complete authority. The alternative, a book that ignores many essential areas in order to present more comprehensively and effectively a particular aspect or view of psychology, is also insufficient, for in this solution many key areas are simply not communicated to the student at all.

The Foundations of Modern Psychology Series was the first in what has become a growing trend in psychology toward groups of short texts dealing with various basic subjects, each written by an active authority. It was conceived with the idea of providing greater flexibility for instructors teaching general courses than was ordinarily available in the large, encyclopedic textbooks, and greater depth of presentation for individual topics not typically given much space in introductory textbooks.

The earliest volumes appeared in 1963, the latest not until 1974. Well over one and a quarter million copies, collectively, have been sold, attesting to the widespread use of these books in the teaching of psychology. Individual volumes have been used as supplementary texts, or as *the* text, in various undergraduate courses in psychology, education, public health, and sociology, and clusters of volumes have served as the text in beginning undergraduate courses in general psychology. Groups of volumes have been translated into eight languages, including Dutch, Hebrew, Italian, Japanese, Polish, Portuguese, Spanish, and Swedish.

With wide variation in publication date and type of content, some of the volumes need revision, while others do not. We have left this decision to the individual author who best knows his book in relation to the state of the field. Some will remain unchanged, some will be modestly changed, and still others completely rewritten. In the new series edition, we have also opted for some variation in the length and style of individual books, to reflect the different ways in which they have been used as texts.

There has never been stronger interest in good teaching in our colleges and universities than there is now; and for this the availability of high quality, well-written, and stimulating text materials highlighting the exciting and continuing search for knowledge is a prime prerequisite. This is especially the case in undergraduate courses where large numbers of students must have access to suitable readings. The Foundations of Modern Psychology Series represents our ongoing attempt to provide college teachers with the best textbook materials we can create.

Richard S. Lazarus, Editor

Preface

Most of us have spent a considerable portion of our lives in schools. For twelve or more years we learned to read, to write, to study English and history. We did homework and received grades. But school was really more than subject matter learning. It was not merely "preparation for life" as schools are often said to be; it was an important part of our lives for most of our developing years.

For many years we were told what to do and how to behave, and we were rewarded and punished accordingly. Sometimes teachers made us feel important and stimulated us to learn what they taught; there were others who caused us anguish. We were perhaps more concerned with how our classmates regarded us than with classwork. What happened in the halls and on the playground mattered to us: we remember the boy who started fights, the quiet girl who was always alone, the strange child who did not act like others. In fact, one of these descriptions would undoubtedly fit many of us. Schools certainly emphasize subject matter skills; but the concomitant learnings, the interactions, the experiences, and feelings that we remember most are what school is all about. Looking at schools in this way, we see a kind of social system that, like the family or the community, constitutes a special subculture. Schools have specific spatial, temporal, and social organizations that combine to form a distinct experience. Although schools have much in common, each school and each school system is best understood as a special case with its own problems and attributes.

The specialty in psychology concerned with how schooling affects children in general and with the pupil in interaction with a specific school is called school psychology. The specialty includes knowledge about research and theory dealing with what happens between children and others when they are together in schools; more than that, school psychology deals with how school for a child in Jackson Junior High is different from school for a child in Wilson Junior High.

Any specialty in psychology that deals with practical, everyday concerns that people present is usually referred to as an "applied psychology," as differentiated from other specialties that are more concerned with building theories and establishing basic knowledge. Practitioners of applied psychology work directly with people. As such, school psychologists work with people on problems that stem directly from schools: problems presented by pupils of all ages, by teachers, school administrators, parents, boards of education, and such community agencies as the police department, the local mental health clinics, the welfare department, or the YMCA. The school psychologist must know about how children learn and how behavior can be modified. He must be able to understand the factors that influence human behavior and to use his knowledge of psychology to facilitate the school's efforts to educate children. The school psychologist must know what forces influence schools and how those affected react and respond.

School psychology is a rapidly growing specialty. Because it is so applied, school psychology is attractive to prospective students who see psychology as a way to do something for society. The increased demand for school psychological services has resulted in an increase in the number of graduate programs designed to train school psychologists. School psychology has grown and matured in recent years; it can now be described as a distinct specialty within psychology.

Schools represent a major force in our society, second only to the home in its influence and power over the lives of people. Schools are in great trouble. It is widely acknowledged that schools are not serving the needs of many children, that they have not kept pace with changing times, and that something must be done. The school psychologist is the psychologist on the scene. While other psychologists are contributing in other ways to help us to understand and hopefully to improve education, the school psychologist is in the schools with the children and teachers, as parents and the community watch carefully and often critically. The school psychologist is part of the school system. What he does can contribute materially to the welfare of the school.

In this book the distinctive features of school psychology will be described.

We are grateful to Miriam B. Mandel, our editorial consultant, who helped us to differentiate between jargon and English. We are also grateful to our loyal and helpful secretaries, Corinne S. Henry and Charlotte Schulman, who protected us from interruptions on those days we set aside for work on the manuscript and who, in many ways, made it possible for this book to be completed.

School Psychology: A Point of View

chapter one

Every professional practitioner, regardless of his specialty, performs on the basis of certain assumptions. Some of these assumptions are explicit and fully agreed upon by all practitioners. Other assumptions are implicit and are neither clearly perceived, specifically stated, nor overtly acknowledged. Most school psychologists would agree that effectiveness depends on two interrelated factors: (*a*) what the psychologist knows (his background and training) and (*b*) the extent to which he is able to implement his knowledge. Without useful knowledge, the psychologist cannot be helpful. To implement his knowledge, the psychologist depends on his ability to get along with others and to respond to them in ways that promote their willingness to profit from his efforts. If he is perceived as disagreeable, dogmatic, or threatening, he will not be able to function effectively.

Assumptions for the Specialty of School Psychology

It is generally agreed that school psychologists must be familiar with two bodies of knowledge: (*a*) those aspects of psychology that can be related to the solution of educational problems and (*b*) knowledge of how schools teach children. Preparation usually includes work in the basic components of psychology,[1] course work and experiences that permit the psychologist to understand how and why schools do what they do (the philosophy, history, and sociology of education), and more specific knowledge about modern curriculum and school organization. In addition, the practicing school psychologist must have developed certain skills (observation, interviewing, counseling, psychological testing) that enable him to gather the information he uses when making judgments about children and schools. Even with the broadest knowledge of psychology and education imaginable, the practicing school psychologist cannot help others if they will not listen to him. The particular qualities of personality that make for effective functioning are elusive but appear to include at least several complex organizations of personality characteristics and attitudinal sets.[2]

A genuine concern for what happens to other people is important. The helping professions by their nature impart great authority to their practitioners, or "experts," who are empowered to tell others what to do. Such power is kept in check by the sincere and overriding concern for the welfare of others—a concern that should be an abiding value of the school psychologist. Not only will his concern for others serve to prevent any potential misuse of power but it will also lead the school psychologist to enjoy the personal gratification of helping others.

A second quality of personality is an attitude of positive skepticism. Skepticism reflects an understanding of the imperfections of the current state of knowledge and tools. Since the school psychologist is primarily involved with real-life situations, he must often act without the benefit or the security offered by the exact knowledge and the precision instruments available in other disciplines. If he is to remain open to change and to benefit from his own successes and failures, he should have a critical, cautious, skeptical approach to the assessment of his findings and deliberations. The adjective "positive" is added to indicate that along with such skepticism there must be a willingness to try new approaches and to persist even in the face of disappointments, lack of immediate results, apparent lack of cooperation, and sheer frustration. Anyone who

---

[1] The basic components of psychology would include virtually every area covered in the *Foundations of Modern Psychology* series, or, put another way, expanded knowledge of most areas covered in a basic textbook in general psychology.

[2] In another context researchers concerned with the interaction between psychotherapists and their clients have developed scales to measure such qualities as empathy, positive regard, genuineness, concreteness, and self-disclosure. See Truax, C. B., & Carkhuff, R. R., *Toward effective counseling and psychotherapy: Training and practice.* Chicago: Aldine Press, 1967.

has worked in the schools trying to teach or help children knows that the ability to maintain an optimistic outlook despite discouragement is a necessity.

A third personality characteristic is the capability to identify with others—to empathize. The school psychologist often works with people whose life experiences and values are very different from his. It is not unusual that those he is asked to help (not just pupils, but teachers and parents as well) may initially be extremely antagonistic toward him. Just the fact that he is a psychologist may make others perceive him as threatening. His views may be strongly opposed, or there may be preconceived and negative ideas about his role and function. The school psychologist must find ways to be useful even when those he is trying to help are determined to frustrate his efforts. It is easy to like people when they like you; it is difficult to understand how people feel and to respect their feelings when they are hostile and angry and openly trying to make your job difficult.

Less explicit but highly important in determining how the school psychologist operates is the attitude he takes toward the very nature of the problems confronting him. This issue can be clarified by posing some dichotomous questions. Is a child stupid or does he respond in ways that seem stupid under certain circumstances—but not under others? Is Albert a bad boy or does he behave in ways that offend others when he is confronted with certain kinds of situations? Is a person mentally ill or is he capable of behavior that seems to be odd, bizarre, and deviant under some conditions but not under others? John Wallace (1966) succinctly pointed out the implications of these two positions, which he called response predisposition and response capability. Response predisposition refers to man as "essence"—as having properties that describe what he really is. Response capability, on the other hand, suggests that man may respond differently under different circumstances and that it is important to examine the conditions under which certain behaviors might occur. Recently educators talked about the six-hour retardate, referring to the fact that many school pupils are classified as mentally retarded for educational purposes but, upon release from school at the end of the day, are capable of holding jobs and solving the myriad problems with which they are faced in everyday living. A phenomenon called "the self-fulfilling prophesy" (Rosenthal & Jacobson, 1968) has been cited to account for the finding that the mental ability (IQ) of children as measured by intelligence tests can be raised by the teacher's belief that children have relatively high IQ levels, whether that belief is based on fact or not. Apparently children may perform according to what others expect of them, regardless of their actual level of functioning.

It is assumed in this book that it is ultimately more useful for a school psychologist to take a response capability position with regard to human behavior than an exclusively "essence" position. It is true that it is often extremely helpful, for example, to know that a pupil attempts to solve certain kinds of intellectual problems in ways that lead him to be labeled retarded (response disposition or "essence"). It is much more helpful to that pupil if the psychologist can ascertain that in certain kinds of learning situations the pupil will be able to solve problems better than he can in other kinds of situations (response capability). This view is in accord with the earlier assumption that an attitude of positive skepticism is a desirable one for the school psychologist. To predetermine that a child *is* one thing or another is to limit one's conception of what he is capable of doing and to discourage speculation about the circumstances and conditions under which change might take place. If one believes that people are capable of change and that various properties and attributes of schools can be altered, then the number of alternatives for constructive action are increased.

One final assumption can be made. If knowledge is the base upon which the practice of school psychology rests, then school psychologists are continuously confronted with a serious and weighty set of problems. Much of what is currently known about human behavior derives from research. Most research in psychology is conducted under circumstances designed to enhance the scientific credibility of the findings. Good behavioral science research is conducted under conditions that enable the experimenter to draw specific conclusions. These conditions usually imply rigorous control of the factors to be investigated. A researcher trying to find out something about the learning process must take into account many factors (variables) that affect the learning process. With pupils these variables are almost limitless in number. Age, sex, grade, classroom climate, teacher personality, attitudes toward learning—even, perhaps, whether or not some children had breakfast before the learning task was presented—are factors that cannot be lightly dismissed. Most theories about human behavior are tested under laboratory conditions, under the best of experimental circumstances. Sometimes, however, the conditions that are controlled in the search for knowledge are the very ones that must be accounted for to understand how and why people function as they do.

Classroom conditions are literally loaded with confounding and extraneous variables. To know why Mary is two years behind in reading in the fourth grade and to help her improve her reading level, one must understand what is known about how one learns to read and the conditions that research suggests affect reading. One must also understand how reading is being taught to Mary in her classroom, how it was taught to her in her previous three years of schooling, how Mary perceives what

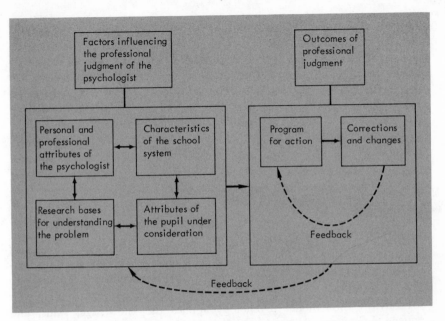

FIGURE 1. A framework used by a professional psychologist in making decisions about individual pupil problems in schools.

is happening to her in school and in other areas of her life, and what sensory, perceptual, or other special problems Mary brings with her when she tries to read.

The school psychologist concerned with Mary's reading difficulties must work from two bases at once: he must take into consideration data derived from laboratory and field studies designed to discover general laws or rules that apply to people in general (nomothetic data), and he must attempt to understand the particular event and its conditions (idiographic data). To reconcile differences and to integrate information, he uses himself as an instrument. He must weigh all evidence and come to a decision through a distillation of all he knows. To the data he must bring experience (a past history of trial-and-error behavior), the personality attributes previously mentioned, and a respect for the scientific method. As an instrument the professional psychologist is in a very real sense engaged in a scientific experiment in which he makes hypotheses, tests them, and changes his results and conclusions as new evidence becomes available. At some point he must decide on a course of action, which means he cannot always wait to know everything there is to know about a problem. When he makes a recommendation or prescribes a course of action or interprets his findings to others, he must judge the probability of the validity of his actions against his data.

To understand school psychology, or any applied psychology, it is necessary to recognize how knowledge is filtered through the person we call a professional psychologist. It is the interaction of knowledge and the practitioner himself, in a highly specialized setting, that determines how successful the practice of psychology in the schools will be. School psychology, then, is ultimately only as useful or as pertinent as its practitioner makes it. This book assumes that the content of school psychology is never far removed from its practice.

How School Psychology Differs from Other Specialties

Broadly, all psychology deals with principles and theories of behavior and is a major field of study in academic settings. Psychology is a scientific endeavor; psychologists generate theories, develop hypotheses to test the validity of the theories, and collect and analyze data dealing with behavior. Professional psychology applies the knowledge, skills, and techniques from all psychology to the solution of the kinds of problems people have—whether these problems are primarily with interpersonal relationships (as with family members), with a social situation (as with groups of people), or with the community (as with drug abuse).

School psychology is one of the professional (applied) psychologies, as are clinical, counseling, industrial, and community psychology. Clinical psychology focuses primarily on the problems of adjustment brought to the psychologist by individuals. The clinical psychologist is typically involved in the diagnosis of such problems and often offers psychotherapy to those who can benefit. The child-clinical psychologist specializes in the problems of children with emphasis on the interaction of parents with the child. The clinical psychologist usually deals with maladaptive behavior, or psychopathology.

The counseling psychologist emphasizes helping people cope with the normal problems that arise in life, especially those problems that are faced by normal adults in the world of work. Rehabilitation (helping veterans or other persons with disabilities to prepare for different vocations and to make sensible adjustments to their handicaps) and vocational counseling (helping people find appropriate occupational goals) are major considerations of the counseling psychologist.

Industrial or organizational psychology emphasizes the study of industry or business as a "complex social system which must be studied as a total system if individual behavior within it is to be truly understood" [Schein, 1970, p. 3]. Within his setting the industrial psychologist may be occupied with recruitment, selection, training, management development, improving morale, and the study of organizational effectiveness. School psychology and community psychology have much in common with organizational psychology in that all are especially concerned with understanding the settings in which behavior occurs.

Community psychology, a new specialty, is based on the recognition that problems people present to the clinical psychologist have to be considered in the context of the total community. Community psychologists have special concern for community problems that lead to social pathology, including unemployment, urban decay, and poverty. The two major emphases in community psychology have to do with (a) clinical psychology practice that emanates from comprehensive community mental health centers and involves family psychotherapy, mental health consultation to community organizations, and preventive mental health programs; and (b) social advocacy, social program analysis and planning, and the training of nonprofessionals toward community improvement.

School psychology views the school as a unique arena of life that must be studied and understood if the problems of the people who live in the school are to be solved. The "people who live in the school" include not only administrators, supervisors, teachers, and pupils but teacher's aides, cafeteria workers, secretaries, and custodians as well. The board of education, the taxpayers (to whom the local school represents the most clearly understood as well as the major drain on their tax dollar), and the parents (who are also taxpayers) are all important people contributing to the quality of life in a school.

Educational psychology is frequently confused with school psychology because both direct their interests toward the school, its personnel, and its pupils. Educational psychology, however, at least in the United States, is not an applied psychology in the same sense as is school or clinical psychology. Educational psychology studies the characteristics of students and teachers and explores such topics as learning, motivation, reinforcement, transfer, and the conditions that affect them. Typically, the educational psychologist conducts research on the many factors that influence learning with careful control of elements extraneous to the factors or variables being investigated. According to Donald Ross Green (1964), research in educational psychology can usually be conducted far more carefully in laboratory settings than in school settings. The educational psychologist is most frequently concerned with obtaining results that help us understand the processes of teaching and learning. He seeks data leading to generalizations that can be applied across educational institutions.

In sharp contrast, the classroom, the gymnasium, the playground, the principal's office, and perhaps even the school bus are all the laboratory of the school psychologist. The school psychologist is generally concerned with findings that can immediately be applied toward the solution of a particular problem. He uses the knowledge gained by the educational psychologist, among others, as part of his consideration of problems (e.g., Johnny's classroom behavior in Miss Jones's class in the new J. F. Kennedy School that serves the sprawling development area on the south side of the suburbs surrounding the city of Urba).

In short, school psychology differs from other psychological specialties in that it brings psychological knowledge, skills, and techniques to bear on the problems presented by the school as a total, unique place in which people live and work and on the problems of the people living in the school.

Differing Approaches to Problem Solving

The approaches of the differing psychological specialties to a particular problem can be explained by an example. Ten-year-old Johnnny is in Miss Jones's fifth grade but is struggling unsuccessfully to read a second-grade primer. Johnny, according to Miss Jones, is "very nervous"; he tenses up when trying to read; he giggles and squirms in his seat; he does not pay attention and annoys his classmates with unprovoked jabs and punches. Johnny appears to be unhappy in school, and Miss Jones is unhappy about her lack of success with Johnny.

How would different psychological specialists approach this problem? The following approaches are oversimplifications, but hopefully they will make certain distinctions clear.

The social psychologist will look at the demographic variables (a comparison of occurrence of various factors in a population). He will consider Johnny's socioeconomic status (the kind of neighborhood in which Johnny lives, his father's occupation, his mother's occupation, their income, the educational level of both parents, the number of brothers and sisters). The social psychologist would be interested in the kinds of appliances the family owns (or is paying for "on time") and the number and types of books and magazine subscriptions in his home. He would want to know if Johnny's father is a volunteer fireman or a member of the local tennis club and what church the family attends. He would also investigate how Johnny is perceived by his classmates, using sociometric methods designed to determine Johnny's position as a leader, a follower, or an isolate in the class. Based on this information the social psychologist could tell Miss Jones that Johnny probably has certain attitudes toward education and holds certain values. The social psychologist would be able to predict, with a reasonable chance of being accurate, that Johnny will probably vote Republican, marry at about age 24, and complete a four-year college program *if* his current school problems can successfully be alleviated. In other words, the social psychologist could offer generalities based on his knowledge of how children in general function under differing social, economic, and group conditions; he would not, however, necessarily feel that he could or should interfere in the specific problem. It should be pointed out immediately that Johnny's particular problem is not likely to be presented to a social psychologist. The social psychologist is mentioned to show how a basic area of psychology can contribute to the understanding of a problem and how important it would be to know enough about the social-psychological variables in Johnny's life to take them into consideration.

The educational psychologist (who probably would not attempt to solve Johnny's problem either) would also consider demographic variables and supply the additional generality that children who show a high level of anxiety as measured by an anxiety scale for children, and who have middle-class, achievement motivated parents, do not perform as well on tasks involving complicated thought processes (reading) as do children who do not show such anxiety. The educational psychologist might also add that verbal learning is more likely to occur when practice is interspersed with other activities. He would want to know about Miss Jones's teaching style and might very well be able to describe methods by which teacher-pupil interaction, including Johnny's reaction to Miss Jones's teaching approach, could be measured. The educational psychologist would have some cogent and useful advice to offer Miss Jones. On the premise that Miss Jones's improved instruction would benefit all the children in her classroom, Johnny might very well be helped indirectly by what the educational psychologist has to offer in this instance. Again, however, it must be pointed out that like the social psychologist the educational psychologist is not likely to be asked to help with this kind of problem.

The clinical psychologist will arrange for an interview with Johnny's parents. He will assess the family dynamics (the relationships among all members of the family). He will also interview Johnny and perhaps administer a battery of psychological tests. The clinical psychologist, whose orientation includes the use of personality theory as a base for understanding behavior, might discover that Johnny has hostile feelings toward authority figures, has not yet gained adequate control of his impulses, feels guilt and anxiety because he is not measuring up to his parents' expectations, views himself as unworthy and unlovable (low self-concept), and has great conflict in his sex-role identification because his father (an overly strong and demanding authority figure) is not providing an appropriate father image. On the other hand, because Johnny's mother is passive, weak, and dependent, Johnny cannot appropriately resolve his Oedipal conflicts and is attempting to meet his ungratified dependency needs. The extent of pathology present in Johnny's family might suggest to the clinical psychologist that his parents would profit from psychotherapy, as would Johnny.

Clinical psychologists, of course, are not confined to the psychoanalytic approach to a problem. Both clinical and school psychologists might view Johnny's problem as one to which knowledge from learning theory, especially from the work of B. F. Skinner, could be applied. These techniques, known as "behavior modification techniques," will be described more fully later.

The school psychologist considers the same data used by his colleagues but especially as they are applicable to the school situation. The school psychologist knows that Johnny's school serves a largely middle-class, professional community of young, upward striving parents and that the school reflects the community values of achievement. A high proportion of its high school graduates are accepted to colleges, and the school plans its curricula and makes demands of its pupils accordingly. The teachers expect and are accustomed to children who learn relatively easily from texts labeled to serve the grade level at which the pupil is assigned: "If Johnny is ten years old, he should be in the fifth grade and should be able to read on at least a fifth-grade level!" The school psychologist also knows that in Miss Jones's class at least half of the children are reading above a fifth-grade level and that two extremely successful classmates live on Johnny's block. The school psychologist knows a lot about Miss Jones: that she taught for several years in the city of Urba before moving back to Suburbia so that she could again teach the kind of children with whom she was accustomed to work— children who like learning and have good manners. Among colleagues and parents Miss Jones has a reputation as an excellent teacher: strict ("No nonsense in *her* class"), lots of homework, high expectations. Miss Jones is also known to be fair and consistent. Her classroom is the pride and joy of the principal ("Anyone can walk in any time, and you could hear a pin drop")—except with Johnny. The school system has no special education facilities and functions on the basis that a good teacher can handle any child. The school has classes from kindergarten through fifth grade on a campus in which children of all ages mix. All children are bused. Johnny spends thirty minutes each way on the bus, usually sitting by himself.

The school psychologist, like the clinical psychologist, will try to understand family dynamics and may administer a battery of psychological and educational tests. He may not, however, for he may have sufficient information from his prior knowledge of the school and of Miss Jones, from his observations of Johnny in the classroom, and from the information in Johnny's cumulative record folder (previous teachers' grades, comments, group achievement and group intelligence tests). The school psychologist too, may conclude that Johnny and/or his parents could benefit from psychotherapy, and he may become involved in interpreting to Johnny's parents the need for this service and he may help to expedite the referral. Whether or not a referral is made, however, the school psychologist's approach may take the form of a carefully conducted talk with Miss Jones in which he attempts to motivate her and to help her to formulate appropriate ways to modify her procedures and expectations. Ideally, he would continue to follow Johnny's school career at least for that school year and would participate with Miss Jones in making modifications in school, on the bus, and at home that might contribute to solving Johnny's problems.

There are many areas of overlap among the applied specialties in psychology, and the distinctions cited are not really as clear-cut as they have been made to appear. In practice, there are school psychologists who function in schools as would clinical psychologists. There are educational psychologists who work directly with problems of a particular school system. Community psychology is now more of an interest area than a demarcated specialty. What all applied psychologists have in common is grounding in the basic areas of psychology, a profound respect for the scientific method, and knowledge of their major tools—assessment techniques, counseling methods, and research methodology. As the world becomes increasingly complex, it is apparent that one psychologist cannot be an expert on all things. The delineations described in this section are intended to indicate how different areas of specialty serve various purposes.

The Development
of a Specialty

chapter two

A professional specialty is created by the historical factors that lead to the possibility that such a specialty can exist and the immediately antecedent conditions and needs that precipitate its creation. After a specialty is formed, it seems to have a life of its own. It is easy, even for the practitioner, to forget that his work is only the current expression of certain historical developments and present-day needs. A specialty such as school psychology needs to be put into perspective so that its practitioners and consumers can be aware of its idiosyncrasies, methods, and problems.

A Brief History of School Psychology

When primitive man hunted for his family's food and built their shelter, he also cared as best he could for their illnesses and accidents. He and his wife had to provide their children with the kinds of training and experiences that were the education of the day. Through much of man's history he has been busy clearing land so he could push a plow or hunting so he and his family could survive another day or another season.

He coped with relatively few psychological and educational problems as we think of them today. His conflicts and decisions were relatively clear-cut. Which kind of construction would afford the best protection from the elements or from his enemies? When should be plant, hunt, and fish? His household role was equally clear, as was that of his busy wife. Questions of permissiveness versus structure in child rearing, of bottle- versus breast-feeding, were hardly issues to be considered. The implication is not that people used to be free of problems: their problems were different, and they either coped or they did not survive.[1]

With the growth of communities and settlements, people began to barter goods, and the specialties related to community living emerged: the weaver, the miller, the shoemaker. As soon as some people specialized in supplying basic needs, others were freed to specialize in important but not necessarily life-sustaining activities. They became physicians, scholars, priests, and sages from whom others sought counsel.

TECHNOLOGICAL ADVANCES

As technology developed further, man became increasingly able to provide the goods (products) essential to life. More men were able to devote time to the pursuit of knowledge. Our complex technological society has decreased the need for people to be involved in the production of goods (machines do it more efficiently) and increased the need for people to consume and perform services. The more we know, the more knowledge we create. With knowledge comes complexity in virtually every corner of our existence. We appear to have reached the point at which reliance on the expertise of others is absolutely necessary.

With technology as a producer of specialists came the development of social and economic classes within society. The neurotics of mid-Victorian Vienna, whose problems helped Sigmund Freud arrive at his insights about the human psyche, were partially the result of a class system that enabled persons to seek (and thus to help develop) a specialist called a psychoanalyst. The idea that people could be helped with their emotional problems by talking could not have been accepted unless the need to solve such problems was a societal priority. Help in solving such problems was thus seen as a service that people were willing to consider to be as valuable as other services. The emergence of psychoanalysis and other psychotherapies was a function of timing. In those countries

---

[1] The late Abraham Maslow postulated an interesting theory of motivation: people who are completely absorbed with providing for physical needs and safety needs cannot be concerned with "higher need," such as actualizing their full potential for intellectual and emotional development. See Maslow, A. H., *Motivation and personality*. New York: Harper, 1954.

in which the practice of psychotherapy took hold, technology had already complicated lives: urbanization had brought educated and affluent people together, and the concept of specialized services already existed. The specialties that developed around psychoanalysis served a need unmet at that time.

THE SCIENTIFIC APPROACH

The development of what we call the scientific approach also contributed to the development of school psychology. Psychology in 1850 was primarily philosophical. It was not until the impact of work in the biological and physical sciences, especially the use of what we now know as the experimental method, that psychology began to strive to be a science. Physiologists in Europe, especially in Germany, were beginning to measure human responses. They primarily studied seeing, hearing, and the other senses. Wilhelm Wundt's first laboratory for experimenting exclusively with psychological responses (rate of learning, timing of complex mental tasks) was established in Leipzig in 1879 [Thorndike & Hagen, 1960].

In England Charles Darwin published *Origin of Species* in 1859. Although Darwin's name is associated with the theory of evolution, his major contribution to the behavioral sciences was the emphasis on variations among members of a species—his recognition of individual differences. While psychologists in Germany were focusing on similarities among human responses, in England they were studying differences among people. In 1884 Sir Francis Galton, following Darwin's ideas on the inheritance of traits, began collecting data on human characteristics for the purpose of establishing differences among individuals. Galton's interest in possible inherited characteristics led him to induce a number of schools to keep systematic records of how students performed on certain tests he devised; he tested them, for example, on keenness of vision and hearing, reaction time, and discrimination [Anastasi, 1957]. Galton's measurement of aspects of children's behavior is considered by some writers to be the first example of school psychological services [White & Harris, 1961].

The need to look at these differences scientifically led Karl Pearson, another Englishman, to refine tools and techniques that could analyze data to show significant differences among traits. Pearson's development of statistical tools that could be applied to the measurement of human characteristics put psychology firmly in the camp of science.

Application of the scientific approach. American psychologists also were interested in the possibilities of the study of individual differences, with particular emphasis on how such differences affected children's school performance. In 1896, ten years after Galton started his laboratory in London, Lightner Witmer established a laboratory clinic at the University of Pennsylvania [Levine & Levine, 1970]. Witmer's laboratory is usually referred to as the first child guidance clinic in America, one of the landmarks in the development of clinical psychology. Witmer's clinic at its inception was very closely allied with education, since Witmer's goal was to prepare psychologists to help educators solve children's learning problems.

While Witmer was establishing his clinic, city school districts in the United States were forming special classes for children who did not learn or behave well in regular classrooms. The first of these probably was a class formed in 1871 for adolescents who had been brought to the attention of law enforcement agencies in New Haven. [Connecticut Special Education Association, 1936]. Most large, eastern American cities established special classes in the 1880s and 1890s for children who seemed to learn very little of what was presented to them in school and learned very slowly—in today's parlance, the mentally retarded. The formation of special classes was a result of (a) acceptance of the concept of individual differences and (b) the demand for universal education for young people.[2]

Another landmark in the development of school psychology occurred in 1899 in Chicago, where William Healy established a clinic for a juvenile court in the public school system. The clinic began the practice of including noneducator practitioners and specialists as part of the school system [White & Harris, 1961].

THE INFLUENCE OF BINET'S WORK

The United States and England were not alone in their pioneering ventures. In the middle and late 1800s France was a leader in humanitarian and educational efforts. The British formed the Child Study Association in 1893; by 1894 the French had the Societé Libre pour l'Etude de L'Enfant [White & Harris, 1961]. In 1904 French educators appealed to psychologists for what we would now call professional consultation. The Minister of Public Instruction in Paris appointed a commission to investigate the learning potential of children who were having difficulty with school tasks. Alfred Binet, a psychologist, and Theophile Simon, a psychiatrist, collaborated to carry out the commission's charge [Binet & Simon, 1905]. Since their problem was educational, Binet and Simon carefully questioned teachers about the kinds of difficulties chil-

---

[2] A brief, readable presentation of the historical, philosophical, and literary aspects of the development of education in the United States is Maxine Greene's *The public school and the private vision.* New York: Random House, 1965.

dren had as well as the kinds of intellectual tasks most children seemed able to master at given ages. For example, most children can carry out three simple requests at age four and a half and copy a picture of a diamond-shaped figure with fair approximation by age seven. Binet and Simon developed thirty such problems and arranged them in ascending order of difficulty. Translated and adapted by Lewis Terman of Stanford University for use in American schools, the work of Binet and Simon is still the foundation of measurement of certain kinds of intellectual capacity.

Terman's first revision of the scale in 1916 "constituted a pioneering effort to apply the methods of precision which were being developed in the new science of psychology to the measurement of intellectual abilities" [Terman & Merrill, 1960, p. 5]. The Stanford-Binet Intelligence Scale, as Terman named the American version, gave answers to questions about pupils that schools wanted to know. For the most part, children who performed well on the Stanford-Binet, as indicated by an Intelligence Quotient (IQ), learned school tasks readily. Many tests were developed in further attempts to measure children's learning aptitudes, specific aptitudes, and school achievement.

During the early 1900s a few schools employed persons specifically to administer and interpret these tests. Special class placement required that someone be responsible for deciding which children should be so placed. The Stanford-Binet in particular was a valuable tool for making these judgments. Exactly when these test administrators and interpreters were given the title *school psychologist* is not clear, but it is reported that Dr. Arnold Gesell was appointed as a school psychologist in 1915 to the Connecticut State Board of Education "to make mental examinations of backward and defective children in rural, village, and urban schools, and to devise methods for their better care in the public schools" [Connecticut Special Education Association, 1936, p. v].

THE INFLUENCE OF FREUD'S WORK

While ability testing was becoming commonplace in American public schools, another growing area of psychology was contributing to the development of school psychology as a specialty. Sigmund Freud was writing on a different but allied aspect of human behavior. He was developing new and startling theories to explain the origins of emotional reactions and how people develop different personality patterns [Hall, 1962].[3] Freud's writings, shocking to many, were not immediately accepted in the United States. The conditions necessary for acceptance, however, already existed. A number of Freud's disciples promoted his

---

[3] This slim paperback is a compact and accurate overview of Freud's theories.

teachings in America; Alfred Adler, a disciple turned dissenter, lectured widely and found enthusiastic acceptance among educators as well as among psychiatrists and psychologists [Hall & Lindzey, 1965]. Adler's ideas, perhaps even more than Freud's, seemed to be relevant, useful, and progressive to educators. Freud's emphasis on the importance of events and relationships in early childhood in the development of emotional adjustment led psychologists to be concerned about the psychological health of children as well as about measurable intellectual capacities.

An equal but slightly different influence came from an aroused public. In the early 1900s, Clifford Beers described the horrors of his commitment to a mental institution [Beers, 1908]. Beers wrote compellingly and was widely read. He was convinced that concern and guidance could help prevent psychotic breakdowns, and in 1909 he founded the National Committee for Mental Hygiene, which generated public interest in mental illness. Child guidance clinics appeared in increasing numbers. With universities offering course work in psychoanalytic theories and in the use of techniques to assess personality functions, and with child guidance centers available as psychological training centers, psychologists working in the schools began utilizing the knowledge and skills characteristic of the psychoanalytically oriented clinical psychologist.

THE MENTAL HEALTH MOVEMENT

The development of ability and aptitude tests was accelerated during World War I when the armed services needed to sort out men for different wartime roles. A new breed of specialists, the psychologists, was called upon to help measure the capacities of servicemen. If World War I accelerated the testing movement, World War II accelerated the concern for emotional maladjustment. Psychologists were pressed into service, often with minimal training, not only to assess the competencies and aptitudes of servicemen but also to investigate and treat reaction to stress. Information about the large number of servicemen who received a psychoneurotic discharge or were judged to be too emotionally unstable for service heightened public awareness of and demand for more mental health services. Courses in mental hygiene, already offered in teacher training institutions, became mandatory along with the study of child growth and development.[4] Teachers became concerned about pu-

---

[4] Some misinterpretations of John Dewey's ideas of the importance of children's learning by experience plus a necessarily truncated and superficial course in psychology-for-teachers led some teachers to believe that any learning problem could be cured by complete de-emphasis of formal academic skills in favor of untrammeled and unrestrained freedom for the child to grow and develop.

pils' emotional health and turned to psychologists and psychiatrists for help in handling emotional problems. Some states that had already mandated public school education for mentally retarded children began to organize and mandate classes for emotionally disturbed children as well. Many psychologists in the schools began functioning like clinical psychologists in mental health clinics, diagnosing children's adjustment problems and sometimes offering individual therapy.

By the early 1950s the mental health movement was strong. School psychologists were being employed across the country, most typically functioning as clinical psychologists attached to the schools. After World War II the population grew rapidly. Improved medical practices made possible the birth and longevity of children with various handicaps who probably would not have survived in earlier days. The standard of living rose for many. These benefits, coupled with enlightenment and improved communications systems, allowed us to look more closely at our problems, to become more aware of the multiplicity of problems faced by children. More children were born than ever before, with subsequently greater numbers exhibiting maladaptive behavior and functioning in the schools.

The recognition by educators that a child's academic learning cannot be completely divorced from his adjustment problems was a positive step. Teachers had become more aware of the kinds of problems that interfere with a child's ability to learn. For instance, many children who show severe personality disturbance also have learning problems. A child who is constantly agitated by his anxieties has trouble concentrating on academic concerns. A child who is hostile toward adults does not readily accept teacher direction. A child who is preoccupied with his thoughts, fears, and fantasies does not even hear what is going on in a classroom. A child who has learned than any attention is better than none may engage in aggressive or annoying behavior and never sit still long enough to learn anything. It is not surprising that teachers, concerned with controlling children in their classrooms and finding themselves unable to teach all in their charge, sought someone who would either cure the child's ills or remove him from the classroom so that the other pupils in the class could learn.

One of the byproducts of the mental health movement of the 1950s and 1960s was the belief of many teachers that the mental health specialists could solve children's problems when teachers could not and that referral to such a specialist was the ultimate or only solution. The school psychologist was often the specialist closest at hand.

The school psychologist attempted to meet these pleas for help. His desk became piled high with referrals for diagnosis, with the implication that once diagnosed by the school psychologist, the child would be helped. A complete psychological examination, however, including an evaluation of cognitive and emotional functioning, usually takes about two hours. Many more hours must be spent gathering background information, interpreting results, and writing an intricate report. Bower (1969) estimated that at the very least, 10 percent of all school children present a referrable problem. In addition, most school psychologists are employed in ratios of from 1 psychologist to every 1,500 pupils to 1 to every 10,000. The demands upon the psychologist's time if he functions as a diagnostician-referrer preclude his ability to perform the job as requested by the school.

In many school districts it became commonplace for teachers to complain that they made referrals but never saw the psychologist.[5] Psychologists spent many hours in their offices evaluating children, but even if they were excellent therapists, they rarely had time to do psychotherapy. Psychologists in schools referred disturbed children to local child guidance clinics for psychotherapy, but the clinics are crowded, too, and the children on long waiting lists continued to be behavior and learning problems in school. Some parents balked at taking their children to mental health clinics; problem children often have troubled parents, and most clinics insist that parents become involved in ongoing counseling with their child.

SOCIAL PROBLEMS

Beginning in the 1960s social problems surfaced, particularly in urban centers. Delinquency, drug abuse, value differences among the generations, disenchantment with many aspects of society, rampant aggression, indifference, and apathy characterized large segments of the population. As always these problems were reflected in the schools. Teachers needed more assistance than before, but school psychologists for the most part continued to function as before. This resulted in an understandable dissatisfaction with psychology and mental health services on the part of many parents and school personnel. A state education department official shook his fist at a group of psychologists he was addressing: "Our schools are full of beautifully diagnosed kids for whom not a damned thing is being done!"

---

[5] In a small school district where we worked as school psychologists, where we smugly believed we gave more than average and better than average psychological services, we were confronted by a teacher during the preschool opening luncheon. "Oh!" she exclaimed, "You came for the big feed, and we'll not see you again for the rest of the year!"

STAGES OF DEVELOPMENT IN SCHOOL PSYCHOLOGY

The development of a specialty implies stages of development. The first stage in the development of school psychology was the use of the psychologist as a school tester, particularly as a tester of mental ability as reflected in IQ scores. The second stage was the psychologist as a clinician, diagnosing and making recommendations to teachers and others. As with many kinds of development, not all stages are reached at the same time by those involved in the developmental process. In parts of the United States some school psychologists are still in developmental stage I, the testing stage. Many serve a useful purpose at this level and perform their tasks well. Psychologists operating at stage II frequently are also gifted professionals who, despite their workloads, are useful to significant numbers of children, teachers, and parents.

It is our view that the specialty of school psychology has now reached stage III. More than 75 years ago Lightner Witmer told the American Psychological Association that plans for his newly established clinic included "the training of students for a new profession—that of the psychological expert, who should find his career in connection with the school system" [Brotemarkle, 1931, p. 346]. In 1942 Symonds wrote, "The school psychologist is a *psychologist in a school*—that is, one who brings to bear on the problems of the school and its administrators, teachers, and pupils the technical skill and insight which the science of psychology can provide" [Gray, 1963, p. 37].

The stage III school psychologist has not discarded his past skills. He is, as he has been since at least the early 1900s, a psychometrist (administrator and interpreter of tests). He still uses his clinical skills as he has at least since World War II. Over and above these functions, however, he is a psychologist with a variety of skills and knowledge who applies his knowledge broadly and in diverse ways to a specific setting—the school. It is more difficult now than ever to pinpoint the specific assignments of the stage III school psychologist, since he is likely to function differently in different situations and at different times, depending on what is asked of him by the school.

Timing is important in the development of a specialty. Although both Witmer and Symonds pointed the way to the stage III school psychologist years ago, the climate was not right for his development until recently. Disenchantment and dissatisfaction with current school practice, based on new problems facing schools, seem to have caused demands for different kinds of educational approaches and solutions. The stage III school psychologist is the outcome of the historical events that preceded him and the antecedent conditions and pressures that made his existence possible.

The Current Status of the Specialty

Today's consumer may not always read the fine print, but he is usually aware that labels tell him how much artificial preservative a can contains as well as the more usual, expected ingredients. Electrical appliances are marked "UL." Meats are "US Gov't inspected." Purchasers of aspirin may read on the bottle "5 grain U.S.P." Because we have laws to protect the public, we have come to expect that certain standards are met when we buy basic products.

Similarly, consumers of professional services ordinarily take it for granted that persons with professional titles—physicians, dentists, clergymen, lawyers, psychologists—are what their titles imply, that when the young physician or lawyer hangs out his shingle, he really is qualified to serve. If we consult a fortuneteller, we may or may not be amazed at her perceptiveness and insights, but we are well aware that her abilities have nothing to do with formal training, academic degrees, or professional standards. If we consult a psychiatrist, we know he has completed a training program of considerable duration and rigor, that he subscribes to his profession's code of ethics, and that he has successfully overcome the obstacles deliberately put in his way by his profession (examinations for licensing, for example). His accomplishments are attested to by the various framed diplomas and certificates on the office walls. We have faith that our society protects the consumer of professional services from incompetence, deceit, and malpractice.

In general, our faith is justified, in spite of the varying extent to which professions are able to police their practitioners. The long-established professions of law and medicine are perhaps the best organized to ensure standards. Even so, the public recognizes wide ranges of competence among lawyers and physicians ("I want a *good* doctor . . . not a quack!"), and we are equally aware of the occasional gross breaches of ethics that occur even in these time-honored professions. We also react with outraged indignation when the professional whose services we have engaged does not perform as well as some of his colleagues. The public assumes clearer role delineations than are true and confuses minimal standards of competence with standards of excellence [Moore, 1970]. The fact that beef is "US Gov't inspected" does not tell us whether it is good, choice, or prime.

STANDARDS, AUTONOMY, AND IDENTITY

In psychology, the problems of standards, professional autonomy, and professional identity are more complex than they are in medicine or law. Although the title *physician* subsumes a variety of specialties, we know that each physician, whether he is a pediatrician or a general practitioner, has been trained to *practice medicine*. Psychologists do not share this complete commonality of basic training. Many psychologists are not trained to be practitioners in any sense of the word: they are researchers or theorists. In the American Psychological Association in 1973 there were thirty-three divisions, each representing a different interest group, specialty, or content area in psychology. Of the thirty-three divisions, relatively few represent practitioner specialties. The coexistence of wide disparities in orientation, training, and role among psychologists makes it impossible to discern an area of specialty solely from the title *psychologist*.

Like other professions, psychology has established minimal standards for the education and training of its practitioners to safeguard the public. The American Psychological Association is authorized by the National Commission on Accrediting to accredit doctoral programs in clinical, counseling, and school psychology. Each year a list of programs and internship settings accredited by the Education and Training Board of the American Psychological Association is published in its official journal, *The American Psychologist*. Almost all states have licensing or certification laws governing the independent practice of psychology, requiring that persons who call themselves psychologists and offer their services to the public for a fee give evidence through examination and credentials that they meet predetermined minimal standards of competence. The American Board of Examiners in Professional Psychology, Inc., an independent organization cooperating with the American Psychological Association, offers diplomate status in various specialties of professional psychology. "Diplomates" are experienced doctoral level psychologists who have demonstrated superior performance and have passed stringent written and oral examinations in their specialties. These ways of ensuring basic standards, as well as providing the public with a way to determine specific superior competence, are similar in pattern to the way the American Medical Association accredits training programs, has established licensing by states, and awards diplomate status.

These standards offer considerable protection to the public, but they are by no means encompassing. For example, some training programs are not accredited by the American Psychological Association, and these programs are not in any way illegal. Even in those states where private practice in psychology is regulated through licensing or certification, institutions, agencies, and organizations can establish their own standards for the employment of psychologists. Persons can be employed at a variety of levels (postbachelor's degree, postmaster's degree, doctoral degree, or postdoctoral degree) to perform psychological services although the master's degree is generally considered a minimal requirement for most employment. The guidelines and mechanisms established in professional psychology help insure minimal standards to some extent, but as a relatively young and fast-growing profession psychology is still developing the uniformity of standards and authority that characterize the older, longer established professions.

In school psychology the problem of uniformity of standards is particularly ambiguous. Since the specialty developed from both psychology and education, it is not surprising that the problem of who is to assume responsibility for its regulation has yet to be resolved. Certainly school psychology is a part of psychology. The very title implies that its practitioners are psychologists, and the public has every reason to believe that the school psychologist comes under the same rules, regulations, and requirements as do other practitioners in psychology.

School psychology is equally a part of education, for school psychologists practice in and are employed by schools. They are subject to the regulations of public schools, but although each state requires that public school teachers be certified, not all states have certification requirements for school psychologists. A state's department of education usually develops certification standards and procedures. These standards may or may not be developed by or in consultation with psychologists. Thus school psychologists in many states are certified to practice at levels of training or by criteria that do not correspond to those used in the other major psychological specialties. As of 1970 there were forty-four states and territories that certified school psychologists through their departments of education [Bluestein & Milofsky, 1970]. They varied considerably in their requirements for certification. The minimal level typically requires a master's degree, but the required content of the degree and amount of supervised experience differ enormously.

Three interacting factors produce a confusing picture: (a) the public naively assumes that a professional title has uniform meaning; (b) psychology is attempting to protect the public by recommending and legislating standards of practice through licensing, certification, and accrediting training programs; and (c) education is attempting to develop minimal levels of competence for those who work in schools. The combination creates dilemmas that cannot be ignored in any attempt to understand how psychology can contribute to the welfare of schooling. Just as the practice of psychology in a school cannot be separated from the local sociopolitical system in which it functions, so must the forces that determine its standards and dictate its roles be taken into consideration. If parents and teachers have particular expectations about the meaning of the title *school psychologist*, if standards for school psychologists are different from those for other professional psychologists, if minimum standards and criteria for entrance to the specialty are determined by state departments of education, then certainly school psychology is necessarily surrounded by special problems that influence how it is practiced.

Standards in school psychology. The range of sophistication and competence among school psychologists is probably greater than that among other psychological specialists, due in large part to the low entry-level requirements in many states. A person may be employed as a school psychologist even if he meets employment requirements only partially, as did many teachers who were employed on an emergency or provisional basis during the 1950s. In the few states that have no certification requirements it is literally possible to appoint a teacher to the position of school psychologist even if she has had no special training whatsoever in school psychology. Fortunately, the challenges of the specialty have attracted excellent and distinguished psychologists. As the specialty has matured, the trend has been toward increased academic requirements, certificates distinguishing different levels of training, and awareness of the need for a specialized training quite different from the training of a teacher. Many states originally required school psychologists to have had teaching experience, implying teacher training. Most states have already eliminated that requirement [Bluestein & Milofsky, 1970]. The dilemma posed by low entry-level standards will become clear later; the complexity of the assignment and the demands made upon school psychologists require the highest possible standards.

Professional autonomy and identity in school psychology. The school psychologist is typically employed by the board of education of a school district just as are teachers, administrators, and other school personnel. He is part of and works closely with other school personnel. He eats in the teachers' lunchroom, attends faculty meetings, and is concerned with the same internal problems as are other professional employees of the school district. He is frequently a member of a team of specialists employed to improve pupil adjustment and learning and works with social workers, curriculum specialists, guidance counselors, and school medical staff. He is *like* everyone else in school, and yet he is *different*. Because of his title, teachers and parents attribute to him whatever it is they think psychologists are. He may be expected to have powers bordering on the occult; he may be viewed as a healer, a mystic, a charlatan, a quack, a scientist, a doctor, an educator, a therapist, a change agent, a threat, an incompetent. At the same time, he is a school employee who must be certified to work in schools just as other school professionals. Teachers, parents, and administrators are aware that many of the psychologist's activities overlap and often resemble those of other school specialists. Psychologists counsel children; so do social workers and guidance counselors. Learning disability specialists may administer some psychological tests. Curriculum specialists, as well as the psychologist, try to help teachers utilize learning techniques to influence classroom management and behavior. The school psychologist is just another school employee doing the same kinds of things that other school personnel do. Yet he is often viewed as special and potentially powerful or, occasionally, as redundant and inept.

Clinical psychologists in institutions, agencies, and clinics usually work closely with other psychologists employed by the same agency. It is characteristic of school psychology practice, however, that school psychologists do not work very closely with other psychologists. Often there is only one psychologist in a school district. Even when several are employed by the same district, they usually distribute their services to different segments of the district to afford wider coverage (psychologist A has the junior and senior high schools, while psychologist B is assigned to the Lincoln, Jefferson, and Adams elementary schools). School psychologists typically work with nonpsychologists. Consequently they are both professionally and personally isolated even when they are working with many different people.

A serious question among those with whom the school psychologist works is: "Who is the psychologist's client?" Some believe the client is primarily the individual child; others that the client is the teacher; for still others it is the parent. Some believe that the psychologist's real client is the school itself and the community that supports it.

In schools we find the psychologist functioning (or attempting to function) according to a code of ethics pertinent to psychological practice and in keeping with the knowledge and skills he acquired as a psychologist. Large and powerful groups in the schools are applying other standards or criteria to his performance. Teachers want to know how to keep Johnny in his seat and why Mary is not reading. Parents want Johnny out of Miss X's class. Principals want help in keeping teacher morale high, and administrators want to be sure all legal requirements are met to ensure reimbursement from the state. These differences in perspective, expectations, standards, and approaches to problem solving sometimes lead to heated arguments. Bersoff (1971) expressed his concern that the school psychologist who sees the school as his client and who attempts to help it achieve its goals may very well be working against the best interests of children:

> What does the school psychologist do when what might benefit the child is at variance with the stated goals of the school administration? What happens when a principal or superintendent requests that certain decisions about class placement be tendered about a child because it is in the best interests of the school system that such changes be effected? These and all other "who is the client" issues must apparently be resolved, under the present system, in favor of the psychologist's institutional employer [p. 267].

Another school psychologist (Starkman, 1966) described a crucial paradox in the practice of school psychology—namely, that after he is employed, a school psychologist is often told exactly what is expected of him and how he is to function. As Starkman pointed out:

> The school psychologist is impaled on the horns of a dilemma when his freedom to make decisions is denied, on the one hand, while on the other, he is told that he is respected and "recognized" as a psychologist, a member of a profession, therefore one who is in control of decision making pertinent to his professional activities [p. 808].

These issues and others lead to critical problems in identity and professional autonomy. The application of psychology to school problems inevitably leads the school psychologist to become embroiled in such conflicts and difficulties. These problems are important in the practice of school psychology and relevant to the two major theses of this book: (a) that the practice of psychology cannot be considered apart from the setting in which it is applied and (b) that the practice cannot be considered apart from the qualifications of the practitioner—which include being aware of the obstacles he must overcome to be useful. It is easy to idealize and glamorize professionalism and to overestimate its possible contributions to societal institutions. Without detracting from the contributions that psychology can make to the schools and hopefully without minimizing the tremendous satisfactions to be gained from working in the schools, it would be a disservice to be unrealistic. It should be kept in mind that school psychology, like other applied psychology specialties, includes the situations and phenomena that impede its implementation as well as the knowledge and skills necessary to its successful performance.

The Assessment
of Children in School

chapter three

The word *assessment* was defined by Webster as the act of determining the rate or amount (as a tax) to be imposed according to an established rate; of making an official valuation of (property) or of determining the importance, size, or value thereof. The word *assessment* has been adopted in psychology to encompass the various ways and means by which psychologists describe and measure many behavioral quantities or qualities. It is used with increasing frequency by those psychologists who wish to emphasize the difference between psychological and medical approaches to human qualities. It is a term broad enough to include situational and intrapsychic factors and to avoid the medical word *diagnosis* with its connotation of abnormality.

Individual Assessment

The primary purpose of an individual assessment conducted by a school psychologist is to gather information about a child. These data will help the psychologist, with other school personnel, to make decisions calculated to help the child function in school.

Individual assessment is usually triggered by a teacher's questions. She[1] may ask, for example, "Why isn't Jimmy learning to read?" "Why does Susie always act the class clown, disrupting the entire class?"

There are many possible reasons for Jimmy's inability to read as well as his classmates or age-mates; the school psychologist's task is to focus on just what can be done to help. To do this, he usually must make an individual assessment.

In most elementary schools the teacher spends five to six hours a day with her class and is likely to know a lot about her pupils. She may, however, have difficulty conveying the particular kind of information necessary for individual assessment. By careful interviewing, the school psychologist can help her to provide exact information about which of Jimmy's behaviors concern her, can encourage her to express her concerns about Jimmy openly and honestly, and can make sure she describes in detail the teaching methods that have been used. Obtaining this information is the first step in an individual assessment.

OBSERVATION

Usually the school psychologist's next step is to observe Jimmy in the classroom to see how he reacts to academic material, what he does when assignments are made, how he responds when called on. Many kinds of observations can be made, from the informal (simply noting what happens in class) to the more formal rating scales in which behaviors are precisely categorized and described (checked off as occurring or not occurring). The behavior rating scales need not be administered by the psychologist; a considerable amount of research with scales has been done, and the data have indicated that persons need not be highly trained professionals to use them. Frequently a short training period will enable teacher aides, for example, to observe and record classroom behaviors. A number of behavior rating scales have also been developed for teacher use (these teacher observation scales will be discussed more fully later).

The virtue of the systematized rating scale is its objectivity. School psychologists are trained observers, and their informal observations are usually based on familiarity with precise behavioral descriptions. An untrained observer making notes on Jimmy's behavior is likely to overlook

---

[1] The English language provides no third person pronoun, singular, that designates either sex, male or female. "He/she" and "he or she" are awkward. Many teachers are male; many psychologists are female; but the authors have arbitrarily decided to use "she" for teacher and "he" for other personnel. Protests may be addressed to either the male or female author.

some behaviors and overemphasize others, especially since he may already have formed some hunches about how Jimmy is likely to behave. A kindergarten teacher, for example, was concerned because during parent conferences she had difficulty in getting parents to understand that their children's behavior in school was sometimes different from their behavior at home. Parents did not seem to understand that the behavior she was reporting was directly related to the children's readiness for first-grade work. This teacher decided to invite parents to the school, a few at a time, to observe the children. The results were more amusing than definitive: parents usually commented how cute the children were and how remarkably the teacher was able to organize group activities. The teacher realized that parents needed a better idea of the kinds of behaviors to look for. In consultation with the school psychologist she prepared a list of such behaviors with directions to parents to check the behaviors if they occurred. The parents' checklist was then used as a basis for more successful parent-teacher conferences. The checklist, like the behavior rating scales, was helpful precisely because it was objective. The following is a sample checklist of behaviors directed toward observing the extent to which a young child understands relational concepts. The checklist was developed by Richard Comtois of Rutgers University (unpublished manuscript).

Check one below

_____ 1. *Extremely little*, for example, he can follow standard movements like walking and sitting which can be copied from models, but he appears to know little else.

_____ 2. *Very little*, for example, he might choose the bigger piece of food on a plate, or show preferences for bright colors, or distinguish between boys, girls, women, men, etc.

_____ 3. *Quite little*, for example, he might indicate by his responses that he knows how to match a few colors, and knows when something is to be found on top of the table versus under the table.

_____ 4. *Not much*, for example, he can name a few colors and indicate which things are smaller and larger, on top of and under, in front of and behind, when asked and in the right mood.

_____ 5. *Fairly much*, for example, he can count up to five and knows the difference between cold, cool, warm, and hot, or he has some idea of what is meant when told something will take a little while, quite a while, or a long time and he knows the names of the basic colors.

_____ 6. *Quite a bit*, for example, he can count up to eight or ten things, without understanding such things as one-half of eight or two three's; or he knows how to recognize some color mixes and knows what we mean by fat, thin, old, young, round, up, and down.

———— 7. *Very much*, for example, he can count beyond ten and knows some things such as two fives make ten; or he can draw or paint figures with parts in fairly close relationship to the way they are observed in his environment; or he can tell time to the extent of being able to recognize noon, three o'clock, or some other particular times.

———— 8. *Extremely much*, for example, he can count beyond thirty, knows two tens make twenty, draws figures in good relationship, knows circles, squares, triangles, and rectangles, and can work out the ways in which many different things are alike and different.

Another aid to observation of classroom behavior is a time sampling of the child's behavior. Teachers are very busy and usually cannot make extensive notes at the time a behavior occurs. When a teacher reports, however, that Ann never pays attention, the school psychologist may ask her to note quickly exactly what Ann is doing at 10:00 A.M. each morning for a week. It might be discovered that Ann does pay attention sometimes. A busy teacher might also be able to provide a time sampling by making a "hash mark" every time Joe is out of his seat during a fifteen-minute period, or calls out, pokes his neighbor, or does whatever has been identified as a possible behavior problem.

SCHOOL RECORDS

To return to Jimmy's inability to read—the school psychologist will also consult a source known in most schools as a cumulative record folder. This folder contains in abbreviated form a history of Jimmy's school progress, including such items as the dates of his immunization shots, his home address, parents' occupations, grades for successive years, group achievement and mental ability test scores, and teachers' comments. The school psychologist can find out if former teachers found Jimmy to be a poor or a nonreader. Perhaps information about his parents and his home might suggest if and how his background has influenced his reading problem. The group IQ scores will give the psychologist a general notion of whether Jimmy has the ability to learn reading at his age level.

SCHOOL LEARNING BEHAVIOR

By now the psychologist may have sufficient data, and he and the teacher can start to work out some educational plans to help Jimmy. Or he may believe he can be more helpful to Jimmy's teacher by finding out more about the boy's cognitive functioning—the ways in which Jimmy approaches the intellectual tasks involved in school learning. Does Jimmy know what words mean? Does his experience include certain basic knowledge that underlies reading ability? Can he remember what needs to be remembered to read? Can he concentrate long enough to learn? Does he attend to directions? Is he capable of realizing his own errors? Can he discriminate among symbols that are similar, yet subtly different? These are some of the questions about cognitive functioning that can be answered by a school psychologist's continuing, individual, psycho-educational assessment.

Psychologists attempting to assess problem areas closely allied to classroom learning frequently use the Stanford-Binet or the Wechsler Intelligence Scale for Children (WISC). These individual intelligence tests, which assess cognitive functioning, are two of the major instruments in the psychologist's repertoire. There is a considerable amount of evidence that the so-called verbal abilities (knowledge of the meaning of words, ability to use them extensively and correctly, ability to think in verbal constructs) are closely related to school success. This evidence is hardly surprising, since the world's knowledge is recorded and transmitted in words.

AREAS OF MALFUNCTIONING

The socially caused language deprivation among low socioeconomic groups is well known, but there are a number of other explanations for the inability to read. A child may have a relatively specific learning disability. Such a deficit is due to a physical or psychological abnormality and can be discovered through individual assessment. For example, a child may be the victim of some cerebral developmental anomaly that prevents or hinders his development of speech and language functions. A form of central nervous system dysfunction may impair the child's ability to organize coherently what he sees (a perceptual rather than a visual problem) so that the symbols of language are confusing and senseless to him. Social, economic, or physical factors may be involved in Johnny's inability to read.

AFFECTIVE FACTORS

Another factor that may interfere with the ability to learn is the affective or emotional factor. Just as a child's perception may be distorted by a specific physical impairment, it might also be distorted by the fact that everything going on around him is filtered through preconceptions. Just as we speak of "seeing the world through rose-colored glasses," there are those who see the world through glasses tinted with fear, anger, insecurity, or hate. There are children who seem to use *not learning* despite good abilities as a way to express resentment at their parents' nagging them to do ever better and better. These children, usually known as underachievers, are not maliciously and shrewdly planning to get even; they literally do not know why they perform poorly in school. They are using a process sometimes called unconscious motivation—an inability on the part of any human being to reach the underlying causes of much of his behavior or to change that behavior. "I don't know why I always do that, but I always do!" is common.

There are children whose anger and hostility are carefully kept under control. These children learned long ago that it is wrong and even dangerous to feel anger toward or think derogatory thoughts about others, especially important others. For example, have you ever heard a mother in a supermarket tell her child, "If you don't stop that, I won't love you"?

Children (and adults) faced with a situation that tends to bring up old angers and resentments automatically try to quash the feeling, which sometimes results in strong reactions of guilt and anxiety instead. They believe that somehow they are wrong or bad, and they are not sure why. They become anxious. Anxiety has all the physical concomitants of fear. However, when we are fearful we usually know what causes the fear response. When we are anxious, however, we feel the accompaniments of fear but are not sure why we feel as we do.

Pervasive, strong anxiety interferes with the ability to learn. All kinds of events taking place in the school can cause anxiety, and an extremely anxiety prone child reacts as though a series of small, internal firecrackers were going off. This kind of anxiety may be a basis for the behavior of some children who seem unable to sit still in the classroom or who are unable to concentrate on schoolwork and have what teachers call a short attention span.

THE STANFORD-BINET INTELLIGENCE SCALE

The psychologist has a wide variety of tools to help him make a thorough individual assessment. The psychologist's basic tool for assessing cognitive functioning is an individual intelligence test. The Stanford-Binet (discussed in the section on the history of school psychology) is one of the major instruments. Adapted for use in the United States by Terman in 1916, revised and standardized in 1937 by Terman and Merrill, and updated again in 1960, the Stanford-Binet when correctly administered is a carefully documented and reliable predictor of success in school. Its items, which consist of separate questions and problems, have been carefully selected and statistically tested for success in discriminating between children who can answer the question or solve the problem and children who cannot. It is called an age-scale because it presumes that the ability to solve certain problems increases as a child gets older. Arranging the items according to degree of difficulty results in what is known as a *mental age*. For example, most four-year-olds (chronological age) answer those items that yield a mental age score of four. Some four-year-olds, however, are able to pass only sufficient items to yield a mental age of three, and others may pass enough items to yield a mental age of five or six. It is the ratio between mental age and chronological age times 100 that we call the intelligence quotient (IQ). The four-year-old who gets enough right answers to "earn" a mental age of five is said to have an IQ of 125 (MA/CA times 100). The seven-year-old who answers enough items correctly to earn a mental age of six is said to have an IQ of approximately 86. The so-called average child obtains the same mental age as his chronological age and is said to have an IQ of 100, called the mean IQ.

Any IQ score between 84 and 116 is within one standard deviation from the mean. The standard deviation (16 for the Stanford-Binet) means that 64 percent of those who take the test derive IQ scores between 84 and 116. Persons who attain an IQ score between 100 and 109 are considered to be normal or average; those between 110 and 119, high average; between 120 and 129, superior; and above 130, very superior. Only three persons out of ten thousand (.03 percent) obtain a score of 160 or over. An IQ of 90 through 99 is considered low average; between 70 and 79, borderline defective; and below 69, mentally defective.

The derived IQ is the expression of a generality about cognitive functioning as represented in the definitions average, defective, superior, and the like. These generalities give us an overall picture of how well a child will be able to master school tasks. There are, of course, exceptions. The Stanford-Binet test by itself does not tell us *why* a child may do well or poorly. It tells us how well he does at that particular time. It is interesting, nevertheless, to note that if the test is administered to a child when he is five years old, again when he is ten, and again when he is fifteen, the results of the three tests are usually very similar. The Stanford-Binet, which originally consisted of 30 problems, has been subjected to revisions, analyses, and all the technical know-how and painstaking work of the behavioral sciences. Today's version is a carefully designed and well-researched instrument. It tells us a person's ability to perform certain intellectual tasks in comparison with others his age. How well or poorly a person performs on the test enables us to predict with a fair degree of accuracy how well he will handle the tasks of schooling.

The school psychologist can use the results of the Stanford-Binet for more than a general prediction. Individual administration enables the psychologist to observe more than right or wrong answers. He can observe how the child goes about performing tasks; the child's attitudes (tries hard, guesses, or simply shrugs without trying); whether the child is self-critical ("No, that's not right . . ."); whether the child uses a systematic or a trial-and-error approach; how he behaves under conditions of success or failure, and so on. Other information gleaned can be extremely important. An analysis of the items of the test may reveal that the child does very well on certain kinds of items, but on certain others, even on the same age level, he struggles and does poorly.

Whether the child's derived IQ score is high or low, areas of relative cognitive strength and weakness can be ascertained. Learning to read, so simple for many of us that we do not really remember how or precisely when we learned, is an extremely complicated process. Certain kinds of cognitive strengths apparently are more closely related to learning how to read than are others or are related in different ways. Although an IQ score predicts ease or difficulty in learning to read, the kinds of items that go into that score give the psychologist some insights into what approaches to reading may be most effective. The child may lack familiarity with common words, or he may have trouble with visual discrimination or with perceptual-motor organization. Indications of these problems may help answer the teacher's question about why Jimmy cannot learn to read as readily as most of his classmates. More importantly, the school psychologist can use his findings on the Stanford-Binet to help the teacher to plan kinds of learning activities that will capitalize on Jimmy's relative strengths to improve his reading.

THE WECHSLER TESTS

Depending on the age of the child and the kind of question a teacher may ask about the child, the school psychologist may select another instrument that yields an IQ score. The tests developed by David Wechsler (Wechsler Pre-Primary Scale of Intelligence, Wechsler Intelligence Scale for Children, Wechsler Adult Intelligence Scale) also predict academic success. The items are grouped by types of intellectual tasks, however, so that separate subscores can be derived for such tasks as verbal abilities dealing with familiarity with the environment, verbal reasoning, common sense judgment, basic mathematical ability, rote memory, visual discrimination, perceptual-motor organization, and ability to spot and utilize details that can be used as cues. In addition, the results of some of these subtests seem more vulnerable than others to the effect of personality functioning or to the effects of certain central nervous system disorders. The Wechsler Intelligence Scale for Children (the WISC), developed for those aged six and a half through fifteen years, eleven months, is the Wechsler test most commonly used with school-age children.

OTHER INDIVIDUAL TESTS

In addition to the Stanford-Binet and the Wechsler tests, which rely heavily on language skills, the psychologist has a number of instruments to help him discover why the child is not learning as effectively as he should.

If a child has language deficits, for example, there are instruments that require him to discriminate, make analogies, generalize, and reason purposefully without the use of any words by the child or the psychologist.

The Leiter International Performance Scale makes use of demonstrations and gestures to get the child to understand directions. The materials of the Leiter are a response frame and an adjustable card holder. Tests are administered by attaching the appropriate picture to the frame. The child chooses a block that matches the picture card and inserts it in the frame. The tasks range from matching colors and forms to completing patterns and classifying objects.

Another language-free device may or may not use language to help convey directions, but it does not require the child to respond in words. The Ravens Progressive Matrices consist of a series of designs each with a piece missing. The child selects from several pieces the one that best fits the design. The Ravens can be administered as an individual or group test.

Sometimes a child understands language fairly well but finds it difficult to organize his understanding in spoken words. The Peabody Picture Vocabulary Test requires the examiner to say a word while showing the child four pictures. The child points to the picture that best describes the word. He has to understand the word, but he does not have to define it.

One of the major advantages of these individually administered tests is that they can assess verbal concepts or verbal fluency without requiring the child to read questions or to write answers. One very minor exception is a relatively advanced item on the Stanford-Binet that requires the child to write one missing word in a simple sentence. The tests, insofar as it is possible, differentiate certain abilities from actual school achievement.

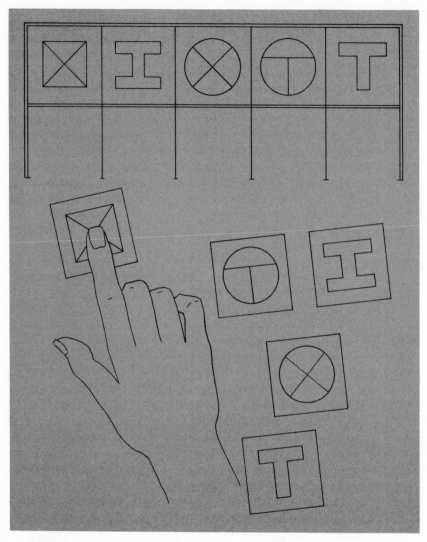

FIGURE 2. An example of matching forms similar to items on the Leiter International Performance Scale.

Both the Stanford-Binet and the Wechsler tests include some basic paper-and-pencil tasks, but these are designed to tap perceptual-motor organization and hand-eye coordination, not writing ability. A child who has difficulties with such tasks may indeed have perceptual-motor difficulties. Hints of such problems from performance on the WISC may lead the psychologist to do more testing in the area of perceptual-motor functioning. Probably the best-known and most widely used instrument in this area is the Bender-Gestalt Visual Motor Test. A child is asked to copy with pencil on paper a series of designs. If the child has great difficulty (relative to his age) in accurately reproducing the figures, the psychologist may suspect problems in perceptual-motor organization. Figure 4 is an example similar to the Bender-Gestalt designs. There is also a difference between the child who cannot seem to execute the angles and is aware of it and the child who cannot execute the figures but thinks he is doing it correctly.

There are a number of tests to tap visual-motor integration and/or perceptual-motor functions; for example, the Benton Visual Retention Test, the Rutgers Drawing Test, and the Marianne Frostig Developmental Test of Visual Perception. A psychologist may use these instruments in addition to or instead of other tools, depending on other data he has collected.

There are other tests that avoid the use of language. A number of de-

FIGURE 3. An example of a test item to show understanding of a word without defining it.

Examiner says, "Point to the picture that is a mammal."

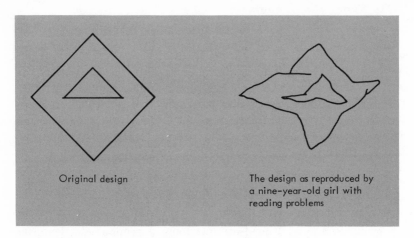

Original design

The design as reproduced by
a nine-year-old girl with
reading problems

FIGURE 4. An example of distortion on the reproduction of a design to determine perceptual-motor ability.

velopmental scales have been devised that are based on the kinds of activities children usually master at certain ages. Used primarily with
young children, such developmental scales indicate how well the child
seems able to master his environment in general, not simply in school
tasks. An example is the Vineland Test of Social Maturity in which a
parent or perhaps a teacher answers questions about whether or not the
child is able to make simple purchases on his own, use a table knife for
cutting, go about his neighborhood freely, or perform certain household
chores. The Gesell Developmental Schedules require the child to perform tasks commensurate with his age for the psychologist to observe the
behavior. A sixteen-week-old baby, for example, can be expected to put
a ring to his mouth and to show anticipation at the sight of food. A four-
year-old is expected to be able to balance himself briefly on one foot
and to engage in cooperative play with other children.

In addition to the tests that differentiate among general kinds of ability, a number of tests assess very specific learning abilities or disabilities.

Reading is the key to school learning. No matter how capable a child
may be in other areas, if he reads slowly, haltingly, or has difficulty understanding what he reads, he will sooner or later be frustrated in
school. Efforts to analyze reading problems have led to the development
of a number of tools geared to sort out the kinds of skills needed for
reading and to determine whether or not a child possesses those skills.
One such skill has been identified as auditory discrimination; a child
must be able to hear the difference among sounds to be able to read.
The Wepman Auditory Discrimination Test was designed to provide information about this skill.

The Illinois Test of Psycho-Linguistic Abilities (ITPA), based on

Charles C. Osgood's theoretical model of the processes of language function, gives information about a number of functions (auditory reception, visual sequential memory, verbal expression, and others) that are related to reading. Other such tests include the Houston Test of Language Development, the Picture Story Language Test, and a number of tests that evaluate specific oral and silent reading ability, comprehension, word attack skills (understanding letter sounds and combinations of letters), and oral and written spelling ability.

Such tests are helpful only because they enable a psychologist and the teacher to plan teaching or classroom techniques. Children can be tested or assessed ad infinitum and ad nauseam; the tests we have mentioned are possible choices for the psychologist. There are many other tests we have not mentioned. An instrument should be selected on the basis of its appropriateness. The psychologist can use any of these instruments, so long as the selection is suitable, to pin down precisely why the child is not being successful in learning. Although some instruments, like the Stanford-Binet and the Wechsler tests, are restricted to administration and interpretation by a qualified psychologist, others may be administered by other school personnel depending on their training and skill in testing. Many of the diagnostic reading tests, for example, may be administered by a teacher with special training in reading. The school psychologist frequently works with others to accumulate data for an individual assessment.

LEARNING DISABILITIES: A RECENT TREND IN INDIVIDUAL ASSESSMENT

The field of psycho-educational assessment has recently erupted as a "new scientific pedagogy" [Bateman, 1967]. Psychologists in the schools are currently trying to place less emphasis on an overall IQ score and to assess instead specific kinds of functioning related to school achievement —the child's understanding of what he hears, his ability to categorize, his visual memory—and how these abilities fit into the sequence of development. Such data should be valuable to the teacher, enabling her to decide what kinds of classroom activities will help the child learn and to determine the child's stage of development so that future tasks can be planned and organized.

As with all new approaches to old problems, the tendency has been to overextend the use of this approach to the exclusion of others. Lester Mann (1971) is very concerned about over-fractionation and about the excessive emphasis currently being placed on the bits and pieces of abilities. He warns that attempts toward differential analysis and assessment of specific learning abilities and disabilities suggest "the musty odor of

some very old bioeducational and psycho-educational approaches . . . .
Whether calipers are used on a skull or pencils on test profiles, it is still
phrenology that is being practiced when the measurements are confused
and identified as processes" [p. 5]. A comparison of the analysis of the
components of learning to the counting and labeling of bumps on the
head is a serious indictment of the learning disabilities approach to assessment.

Certainly psychologists in education must guard against premature
conclusions about the potential of new approaches, and indeed research
has not yet substantiated the claims made for some of these specific approaches to assessment [Frostig & Horne, 1962; Arciszewski, 1968].
Despite disproportionate claims of some workers in the identification of
specific mental processes and their specific educational counterparts,
many proponents of the learning disabilities approach have done careful
and useful work which has helpful implications for educators. The psychologist in the school, together with teachers, parents, and usually with
pupils themselves, is attempting to make a large, amorphous system (the
school) a meaningful experience that is helpful to the later life of each
of its students. The psychologist attempts to understand the behavior of
school personnel and of the student, and one possible approach is to
identify and label components of behavior. After behavior is identified
and understood, techniques can be developed to capitalize on strengths
and to improve weaknesses.

Trends in psychology, as in other humanistic concerns, change with
time and new ideas. Faculty psychology (based on the belief that mind
is composed of a number of discrete powers such as memory or will)
was a very molecular approach toward understanding behavior. Popular
in psychology's infancy, it was virtually discarded in favor of the more
Freudian, global approach. The global approach to personality dynamics, however, lacks the specificity needed for it to be applied to remedial
educational techniques in the schools. This has led to the development
of techniques with very precise implications for school learning tasks.
Perhaps a sensible admonition is needed now: do not throw out either of
the babies with the bath water!

PERSONALITY ASSESSMENT IN SCHOOLS

So far we have discussed methods of individual assessment of cognitive functioning, with emphasis on the measurement of abilities or disabilities closely related to school achievement. Children frequently do
not learn because emotional factors interfere with their cognitive functioning. How can the school psychologist assess such affective factors?

A number of techniques are available, and the school psychologist goes about personality assessment in a variety of ways, not depending upon only one measure. Unlike intelligence tests, personality assessment devices are not well documented with regard to their relationship to school learning or predictive validity (ability to foretell accurately what a child will do or be like in the future). Interviewing the teacher, reading the cumulative folder, and talking with the child are all useful in individual assessment of personality functioning. Many techniques for individual assessment of personality functioning could be described as particular forms of structured interviews; that is, formalized interviews wherein what the child says or does can be categorized and related to personality functioning.

The most frequently used techniques for personality evaluation are known as projective techniques. Projective techniques are based on Freud's assumption that experiences which for one reason or another are too painful for a very young child to handle are repressed or buried in the unconscious. For example, the threat of loss of parental love and care arouses anger toward the parent. The young child learns these feelings must not be expressed, so the anger is repressed and not recognized on the conscious level. Repressed material, according to Freud, strives for expression and shows itself in dreams, in slips of the tongue, in inexplicable (because it is unconscious) behavior. Repressed material can be expressed in relatively safe, unthreatening ways. Projective devices are safe in the sense that they do not directly threaten as would, for example, a direct question. "As a small child, did you get extremely angry when your younger sister was born? Was your nose out of joint because your mother seemed to pay more attention to her than to you? Did you learn to hate your sister and be angry with your mother for seeming to neglect you?" Such direct questioning would probably be answered, and quite honestly, "No," or at least, "Not that I know of." Hints at least of such reactions to one's younger sister might be revealed through the use of projective techniques.

The Rorschach technique. The most famous projective technique is the set of inkblots developed, refined, and selected by Hermann Rorschach, a Swiss psychiatrist. The Rorschach inkblots are symmetrical designs made by dropping ink in a fold of paper and pressing the folded paper, as most children have done in art class. Rorschach carefully selected ten inkblots, each reproduced on a card, that were vague enough that not all people thought they looked like the same thing, yet sufficiently structured in shape that they suggested similar concepts to many people. For example, one inkblot suggests a bat or a butterfly to most people who are considered normal in their personality functioning. Other responses to this blot are found among normal persons, but it has been demonstrated that certain responses to this card are usually associated with problems of adjustment. The responses to the cards give the psychologist an idea of how the respondent sees his world—whether he sees things pretty much as do others who have "healthy personalities" or whether his perceptions are distorted by inner anger, despair, hate, and extreme feelings of inadequacy. Rorschach responses give clues about whether the individual has a creative and satisfying fantasy life (is able to ventilate accumulated inner steam through imagination) and whether he is more a conformist or a rebel. Responses give clues as to how he views other people: is he suspicious or trusting? Does he withdraw, or is he outgoing and accepting of others? There are clues about how he sees himself: for instance, does he feel he is an adequate person, or does he have little faith in his own competencies? How the person handles the tasks and the responses per se are important clues to how he organizes his thinking, to his approach to these kinds of tasks, and by inference, to his approach to similar tasks in the real world.

Skillful users of the Rorschach can categorize persons into certain personality types. The more serious the adjustment problem, the higher the probability is that the responses to the Rorschach cards will fall into clear-cut categories. The use of the Rorschach with school-age children is less definitive, since many pupils assessed by the school psychologist are normal children with problems common to normal development. Some few children are psychotic, disturbed, and seriously malfunctioning; fortunately most are not. The child referred for individual assessment is likely to present problems of adjustment, but not in as clear-cut a way as does the adult. After all, the adult is either concerned enough to seek assessment or is so obviously in need of help that others have him referred. Schoolchildren are usually referred by teachers and parents concerned about problems that cause the child difficulty in school. The judgments the psychologist makes about personality function in such children are not based on evidence as definitive as it usually is with adults. A psychologist cannot say with certainty, based on Rorschach findings, that given a particular situation the child will behave in a particular way. He may be able to say that the likelihood is strong that the child will react in a certain way to certain situations or that he will have certain kinds of feelings about people. In addition to its lack of predictive validity, the Rorschach is a very complicated and time-consuming instrument to administer, score, and interpret. Therefore, school psychologists use the Rorschach less frequently than do clinical psychologists, who generally see people already showing some relatively serious problems of adjustment.

Other projective techniques. Another projective technique frequently used by school psychologists is the Draw-A-Person test. It consists of giving the child a standard-sized piece of white paper and a pencil and requesting him to draw a person. Adults frequently find this task somewhat difficult ("I'm no artist. I haven't drawn pictures in years"), but school children are usually comfortable producing pictures of people and enjoy complying with the request. A pragmatic aspect, from the busy school psychologist's point of view, is that it usually takes a child only a few minutes to produce his drawing.

The use of figure drawings as a projective technique is rooted in the same projective hypothesis—that unconscious material will be expressed indirectly. A number of characteristics of a drawing are related to personality dynamics, especially those characteristics concerning how the subject sees himself and how he perceives other people. Artistry or lack of it in the drawing is not a concern. Although proponents of this technique, as exemplified by Frank Buck in 1946 and Karen Machover in 1947, make very specific claims about the relationship between certain characteristics of a drawing and certain personality characteristics, the claims are probably more valid when severe and longstanding personality traits are present in the person who draws. Other workers with children's drawings indicate that a more global kind of personality evaluation, such as overall adjustment-maladjustment, is more valid than are efforts to be specific.

Another advantage of the Draw-A-Person technique is that responses need not be made in words as they must for the Rorschach. The medium of expression—paper and pencil—is common to all school children. Although psychologists find it helpful to ask the child questions about his drawing ("How old is your person?" "What does your person like to do?"), inferences can be made even if the child is unable or unwilling to respond. In 1926 Florence Goodenough found that children's drawings of a person reflected the level of cognitive development—and it is possible to score a drawing for its aspects of developmental maturity. The figure drawing is therefore useful as an indicator of personality and as a nonverbal estimate of developmental maturity.

The Bender-Gestalt Visual Motor Test, previously mentioned as a measure of perceptual-motor functioning, is also frequently used as a projective technique. The manner in which a child handles the task of reproducing geometric figures, the kinds of errors he makes, his choice of size and placement of the designs, all lend themselves to interpretation.

Another group of projective techniques is based on Henry Murray's original work with the Thematic Apperception Test (TAT). Like the Rorschach, the technique uses picture cards. However, the pictures are readily identifiable as situations and people in situations. The psychologist asks the child (or adult) to make up a story, to tell about the people, what they are doing and feeling, and how it all turns out. Using interpretation common to all projective techniques, the psychologist makes inferences from the story about how the storyteller feels about himself, relates to others, and perceives his world. A number of sets of pictures have been developed: some show children in various situations (Michigan Picture Test); some are pictures of nursery-tale animals (Children's Apperception Test); some show blacks (Thompson Thematic Apperception Test); and one shows children in school situations (School Apperception Test). A similar device is the Make-A-Picture Test, which consists of a series of small, stagelike backdrops of different scenes (home, school, outdoors); the child may populate his chosen stage with paper-doll characters. Still another projective possibility is a play kit with which a young child may arrange rooms with people and furniture and put his people into action.

Critique of projective techniques in the schools. We have presented a mere sample of the projective techniques that are available for individual assessment. The number of projective devices is so large that many psychologists have commented that what we need is not more devices but more definitive knowledge of what the existing devices actually reveal. Research directed at validation of projective techniques (to answer the question, "Do responses to projective techniques accurately tell the psychologist what many claim they tell?") is frequently equivocal. The grosser the personality disorder, the more definitive are the projectives in identification of the disorder.

There is also strong indication that the projective instrument is as valid as the psychologist who administers and interprets it is astute and knowledgeable. There is some consensus that individually administered devices provide a methodical and precise way of conducting an interview in which responses and activities of the person under examination can be compared with quantities of data collected over the years. These data provide a very good basis for norms. We know how people of differing personalities tend to respond to these tasks and can compare the subject's responses to those made by others. People who have certain kinds of problems tend to respond in characteristic ways. If the person under study says and does things characteristic of a nosological group (a group representing one of a number of classified diseases), the chances are high that in real life he functions like others in that nosological group. Some responses, for example, are typical of persons judged to be obsessive-compulsive, hysteric, severely depressed, sociopathic, or psychotic; other responses are characteristic of persons judged to be well adjusted, creative, flexible, and who are functioning very well in real life.

Judgments about a child's personality characteristics are not based on a single projective device. The psychologist is computerlike in that he absorbs a large amount of data from various sources, sorts it out, and comes to conclusions. The whole process of individual assessment begins with the psychologist's posing hypotheses (suppositions) about the child and then collecting data from various sources in an effort to confirm or reject his hypotheses. Data come from persons who work with the child (parents, teachers), from school records, from observations of the child in real-life situations, from talking with the child informally, and from the kinds of assessment devices described in this chapter. Sometimes the tools and methods used can be minimal. At other times the psychologist may feel the need to utilize many techniques.

Because of these reservations about the validity of projective techniques, especially in assessing the personality of normal children with learning problems, many school psychologists in recent years have given less credence to the analysis of personality function via projectives. Projectives are interpreted cautiously and diagnostic-type labels are avoided. An increasing number of school psychologists do not routinely use projective techniques, finding other, more realistic ways of assessing how a child thinks and feels about himself and others. Some university training programs do not even include course work or experience in projective techniques for graduate students in professional psychology.

Group Assessment

As any graduate of an American public school knows, various group tests are as much a part of school life as are the three Rs. We all remember the dire warning of testing days to come, most of us accepting with passive resignation two to three days of sitting quietly ("An empty desk between you, please"), struggling with increasingly difficult problems in those white booklets full of green words ("Put a line through the picture that goes with the one in the box" or "Circle the correct answer") or, as we climbed higher in the grades, ("Be sure to fill in the appropriate space with a heavy, dark mark made with a sharp, soft pencil"). Starting with the readiness tests of kindergarten through the College Entrance Examinations Board's Scholastic Aptitude Tests and culminating with the Graduate Record Examinations, American education is punctuated with group administered tests. With the possible exception of that first test in kindergarten, which was usually presented to us as a game, we were made aware that we were being tested. We were exhorted to do our best, not to skip any answers, and were warned not to copy from a neighbor.

As students we usually did not receive much information about how we did on these tests. Teachers quick to point out right and wrong answers on the weekly math test were vague about group tests, and most of us learned not to ask about them. Occasionally we were handed something called a profile sheet that we took home to our parents. The fact that we scored at the 70th percentile in reading comprehension but at the 60th percentile in grammatical usage rarely meant very much to us or to our parents.

CHARACTERISTICS OF GROUP TESTS

Group tests are usually administered by teachers. They are scored by teachers or by a scoring machine that produces raw scores, scaled scores, grade-point equivalents, and percentile ranks on a strip of prepasted paper to be affixed to the cumulative record folder. School psychologists are rarely involved in the administration or scoring of what schools call routine tests. The school psychologist is, however, one of the school's testing experts, with training and experience in the construction of objective tests, in the determination of norms, the standardization of tests, and the meaning of the statistics provided about various tests' validity and reliability. The school psychologist often serves on faculty committees to select group tests and to plan testing schedules. His advice is sought by teachers and guidance counselors who want to know how to interpret and use test scores and how to handle parents' questions.

Group tests, like individual tests, fall into general categories based on the area being tested. In schools the most frequently used are the group achievement tests, usually administered once a year. In the elementary grades primary level tests assess readiness for beginning reading and understanding number concepts. Tests in higher grades are usually in categories approximately parallel to subject matter. They assess reading skills in terms of grade level and specific mathematical skills. As more diverse subject matter is added to the curriculum, counterparts appear in test questions. Group achievement testing proceeds through high school, and the high school student who aspires to college usually takes a Preliminary Scholastic Aptitude Test (PSAT), which will give him fair warning about how he is likely to perform on the College Entrance Examination Board tests (CEEB).

Aptitude tests are usually geared to specific abilities. As the name implies, the College Board's Scholastic Aptitude Test is designed to measure aptitude for college performance. Aptitude tests may also be designed to predict performance in work involving clerical and mechanical skills and are frequently used in industry as well as in education.

Another category of group tests yields IQ scores and is designed to estimate general intelligence. Group intelligence tests are usually administered about every third or fourth year. Thus, most American public school graduates have been so tested three or four times between kindergarten and the twelfth grade. There are many group intelligence tests, and most can be machine scored. Those most frequently used by schools give a total IQ score and two subdivisions: a language IQ and a non-language IQ. The language IQ test deals with verbal knowledge and concepts; the nonlanguage tests are primarily in picture or design form.

The estimate of intellectual ability from group IQ tests is subject to greater variation than is the estimate from individual tests. A psychologist administering an individual test can closely observe if the child is tired and if he is trying hard and being careful. Such factors as fatigue, carelessness, or unwillingness to attend carefully to each test item cannot be discerned during group testing. Some children, bored or frustrated by the process, may go through an entire test booklet marking or circling answers at random. Despite these pitfalls, the IQ scores derived from group tests are usually surprisingly similar to those derived from individual tests, with correlations averaging about .80. The major difference between group and individual intelligence tests is not in IQ score but in the psychologist's ability to determine, in an individual test, what kinds of strengths and weaknesses go into the IQ score. Any IQ score is very much a generality.

Group intelligence and achievement tests can, when properly used, be extremely informative to the school psychologist, especially in assessing overall school problems. Group intelligence tests and group achievement tests correlate positively. Children who get high scores on group intelligence tests tend to get high scores on group achievement tests, with correlation figures averaging .60 or higher, a finding that has led to the criticism that both kinds of tests are probably measuring the same thing.

Despite a variety of criticisms about testing, which will be discussed in detail in the section on culturally disadvantaged children, schools would have few objective ways of evaluating their instructional procedures without such testing. Teacher administered grades are perhaps primarily a measure of how the teacher sees the student's progress by some arbitrary standard. If Mike is in the third grade and cannot read at third-grade level, he gets a D in reading. If Mabel, also in third grade, reads at a fifth-grade level, she gets an A in reading. It may be that Mike is working like a Trojan while Mabel's accomplishments are effortless. The instructional procedures in that third grade may actually be good for Mike while Mabel is learning despite the procedures, or vice versa. Looking at group achievement scores in relation to group IQ scores at least provides a base line for evaluation of procedures. Group testing can also be helpful in analyzing the effectiveness of new approaches to teaching certain skills.

The results of group testing should always be used with caution. A case in point is a front-page headline that proclaimed that 50 percent of a city's schoolchildren scored below average on reading achievement tests. At first glance this statement certainly seems an indictment of either the schoolchildren, their teachers, or the reading methods employed. Group achievement tests, however, are geared to the normal distribution curve. Thus it is by design that half the children taking such tests score below the average and half above, although most cluster around the average.

The relationship between IQ tests and achievement tests should also be considered. A ten-year-old child who earns an IQ score equivalent to a mental age of six and who reads at the first-grade level is not necessarily suffering from poor teachers or poor teaching techniques. A better example is a suburban school in which group IQ scores show an average IQ of 110, although achievement scores average at the 50th percentile. Investigation is in order.

Although the school psychologist rarely administers group tests, it is his function to help plan and carry out group testing programs and to serve as consultant for the interpretation and use of group test scores. School psychologists often use group test results in conducting research projects on school practices.

How group tests are used. There are other kinds of group tests, some used more extensively than other in schools. Tests purporting to yield information about personality function are published commercially for use with all ages, although fewer are available for elementary school children than for adolescents or adults. School psychologists do not often use such tests, since their results are not often definitive or helpful. They are occasionally used to categorize groups of children for research purposes; for example, to sort out children who show characteristics of passivity versus aggressiveness to see how a group of passive children reacts to certain school procedures.

Most group tests that attempt to assess personality factors operate under a serious disadvantage. Unlike the individually administered projective devices in which responses lend themselves to interpretations that may not be obvious to the test taker, group personality test items are more likely to be in the "Have you stopped beating your wife?" category. An influence called *socal desirability* also creeps into test responses. Even children are sophisticated enough to recognize the nature of items, and all paper-and-pencil personality tests are subject to the fact that most of us are unwilling to admit publicly that we may have idiosyncrasies. The most widely known of group personality tests, the Minnesota Multiphasic Personality Inventory (MMPI), has a built-in form of lie detector. The MMPI was designed for adults, however, and can therefore be used only on the high school level and only when the reading ability of the students is quite high. The use of group personality tests has received public opposition for much longer than has the use of group intelligence tests. Rarely are group personality tests used routinely.

Some group tests can be used for individual as well as group assessment. Tests reflecting vocational interests are frequently used by school psychologists and counselors and can be administered in large groups but interpreted on an individual basis. Some projective personality tests can be group or individual. For example, on sentence completion: "I am happiest when I . . ." older children can write the responses; the school psychologist can read the incomplete sentence to younger or nonreading children and record the responses.

In addition to the purposes of identification of overall school problems and research, school psychologists can use group tests as part of a process known as *screening*. Screening usually involves an attempt to locate children with special educational problems so that more detailed study can be made. Kindergarten screening is an important and usually enjoyable part of the school psychologist's job. Most kindergarten programs are noncompetitive, directed play as a form of learning; they present children with a wide variety of experiences to help get them ready for the more formal learning situations to be encountered from first grade on. Kindergarten screening is the attempt to discover those children who may need additional experiences and preparation before they can manage the chores of the formal grades. Group administered readiness tests are one source of information. When observation of the children in interaction is added and the kindergarten teacher's evaluations are considered, it is usually possible to make plans to help ensure future success. Emphasis on early childhood education (prekindergarten) and the variance in school entrance laws has led to prekindergarten screening and planning.

Another interesting use of a combination of techniques is the identification of a rather large group of children known as underachievers. A student is considered to be an underachiever when he does not do as well academically as is expected, whether those expectations are subjective (the teacher thinks he ought to do better because he seems able to do so, or his parents think he ought to do better because he will never get to college if he does not), or objective (he tests high on ability measures, but is not doing well in school). A characteristic of many underachievers is that they score in the expected ways on group IQ and achievement tests; that is, if they attain high IQ scores, they usually score well on group achievement tests, too; but they receive poor grades. Such data provide the school psychologist with an approach to the problem of underachievement by first sorting out real underachievers from pupils for whom others may have unrealistic expectations.

An example of tests in use.   Typical classrooms consist of some slow learners, many average learners, and a few rapid learners. In one small school district the administrator and teachers were concerned about an excessive number of slow learners. School personnel suspected that many of these children were mentally retarded. The school district had originally served what was largely a farming, hunting, fishing, and lumbering community with residents scattered among its hills and woodlands. New superhighways had recently made this community easily accessible to a large metropolitan area. The large expensive homes of commuter executives began to appear, along with the well-equipped barns and tack rooms of wealthy riding enthusiasts. Exclusive developments designed not to look like developments, in which trees were preserved and houses located on semicircles rather than in precise rows, were built. The school system expanded rapidly—not so much in the lower grades (young parents with young children could not yet afford to move in) but in the upper grades. The new children were from homes that provided enriching experiences; their parents were usually college graduates; and the children were characteristically academically competent and achievement motivated. They went to school with the children of the older rural community, producing a startling dichotomy in types of student.

The school psychologist, the first in the district, was presented with an array of children referred by teachers who suspected mental retardation or at least some serious learning problem. Group assessment techniques and a number of individual assessments led to the finding that the suspected retardates were, in most instances, children with average abilities. The individual assessments revealed that they attained an average IQ score (usually in the 90s) but that their level of ability was frequently lower in those areas of cognitive functioning most directly related to school achievement, such as knowledge of words, ability to use words fluently, relative difficulty in expressing abstract concepts, and concomitant difficulty in learning to read with ease. On the other hand, they showed excellent ability to conceptualize when words were not required, their sense of spatial relationships was frequently enviable; and their perceptual-motor coordination was excellent. Their abilities were also clearly evident when they talked about animals, about how to trap, how to hunt deer (in or out of season), how to run a tractor, and when to cut hay.

For most of them school was frustrating and boring. Some created discipline problems when their boredom and lack of attention led them to seek some kind of participation or relief from frustration such as talking out, engaging in horseplay, not staying in place, and other activities which, when coupled with lack of achievement, tend to worry teachers. Others sat patiently but did not participate, reinforcing by their behavior the teacher's suspicion that they lacked ability to learn. The teachers' negative perception of this group of youngsters was affected by the presence of the alert, eager-to-learn, book-minded children. The differences between the two groups were extreme.

After the general characteristics of the rural group were identified, the school psychologist, with the help of enlightened and relieved school personnel, was able to make the educational process more interesting and more successful.

In summary, psycho-educational assessment consists of a large variety of ways in which a school psychologist tries to identify both school problems and problems individual children may be having in school. Beyond mere identification the school psychologist uses assessment to find ways of helping school personnel plan educational techniques, classroom procedures, and school policies that will ameliorate problems.

Classification for Special Education

Most school psychologists spend a substantial portion of their time classifying children referred for evaluation for placement in special educational facilities. Children who seem unable to profit from regular classroom procedures may benefit from special educational procedures. These include small classes led by teachers specially trained in techniques appropriate to the types of problems exhibited by the children. Special education classes for children classified as mentally retarded were the first special classes to become widespread among public schools.

The relationship between the education of mentally retarded children and the use of intelligence (IQ) tests to determine which children are retarded was established early in the history of special education. It has influenced the ways in which psychological services are used by educators. Although most school psychologists would prefer to devote their energies to Stage III activities, as described earlier, the longstanding relationship between the use of psychological assessment instruments and special education class placement has inextricably linked school psychologists to the classification function. The psychologist is the one person on the staff who is likely to be expert in administering and interpreting individual intelligence tests.

In a number of states classification of children for special education is mandated by state laws, and the school psychologist's role is specified.[2] When the allocation of state funds to school districts is based on meeting legal requirements, the school psychologist's role in the classification

[2] An example is the following statement from "Rules and Regulations" governing classification of children for special education issued by the New Jersey State Department of Education: "A psychological examination shall be given by a certified psychologist and shall include, but not be limited to, a comprehensive battery of evaluation instruments which are intended to assess the intellectual, social, and emotional development of the child." [New Jersey State Department of Education, 1970, p. 3].

of children for special education placement is inevitably assigned a high priority.

The first laws requiring school districts to provide special education for children who could not profit from ordinary classroom procedures were passed by several states in the 1950s. Since then there has been a steady increase in the number of categories of children eligible for special class placement and special education services of all kinds. At first, deaf and blind children were provided for. Next, the mentally retarded were singled out for special attention. The recognition of still other problems, such as neurological impairment and emotional maladjustment, added to the complexity of classification. Educators began to speak facetiously of the "hardening of the categories," referring to the tendency to assign classification titles so rigidly that the titles came to represent, not merely to describe, the child. Molly became an "ED" (emotionally disturbed), and Tim was spoken of as an "NI kid" (neurologically impaired).

The very process of classification and the terms by which it is described have created problems in understanding. The terms *classification*, *diagnosis*, and *identification* cause confusion because people think of them as synonymous when in fact they represent different ways to sort out children to try to help them.

DEFINITIONS

Classification refers to the ordering of the phenomena of nature by narrowly reducing all varieties of some subset of phenomena into their components, so as to make them more understandable. One can classify plants, animals, mental disorders, or educational problems. Classification for special education is an attempt to order all the conditions requiring special educational methods and techniques that ordinarily cannot be or are not provided in regular classroom teaching. The different categories presumably sort children into groups that differ from each other in some educationally useful way.

Some states have permissive rather than mandatory legislation: a state department of education will reimburse school districts in part for the expense of setting up facilities for special education, but the state does not require such facilities. More and more states have passed laws requiring special education programming and services. New Jersey was one of the first states to pass laws making special educational facilities mandatory, and its laws are a prototype for those of many states. The categories and their definitions used by the New Jersey State Department of Education are examples of thoughtful and careful attempts to classify handicapped children with the aim of grouping those children who can probably benefit most from special teaching methods. The definitions presented below are extracted from more detailed statements and are in their original form to convey the flavor of the language used. Keep in mind that these statements are taken from state department of education rules and regulations (Rules and Regulations, N.J., 1970) which interpret how schools are to carry out a legislated, mandatory procedure. Remember, too, that these educational-legal categories and their definitions are not universal and may vary from state to state. In any state that has passed laws providing for special education, such rules and regulations define the parameters within which the psychologist is obligated to organize his thinking about the classification of handicapped children.

Categories for classification of children for special education purposes

1. Mentally Retarded
   (a) Educable
   A child shall be considered to be mentally retarded (educable) who (1) performs on a standardized clinical test of intelligence within a range encompassing approximately 1½ to 3 standard deviations below the mean; (2) gives evidence of limitation to a very low level of ability to think abstractly; and (3) gives evidence of less ability to function socially without direction than that displayed by his intellectually average peers.
   (b) Trainable
   A child shall be considered mentally retarded (trainable) who, (1) performs on a standardized clinical test of intelligence beyond 3 standard deviations below the mean and is unable to use symbols in the solution of problems of even low complexity; (2) is unable to function well socially without direct and close supervision; and (3) is unable to learn a systematic decoding process to pronounce new words in his native tongue. The child shall be capable of remembering a sequence of words, sounds, and rhythms, be able to respond to simple stimulus-response learning experiences, is aware of obvious hazard, and is able to learn to feed himself when presented with food, and gives advance notice of basic body needs.

2. Visually Handicapped
   A child shall be classified as visually handicapped (partially sighted) whose visual acuity with correction is 20/70 or poorer, or who, as a result of some other factors involved in visual functioning, cannot function effectively in a learning environment without a special educational program.

3. Auditorily Handicapped
   A child shall be classified as auditorily handicapped (deaf) when his residual hearing is not sufficient to enable him to understand speech and develop language successfully, even with a hearing aid, without specialized instruction.

4. Communication Handicapped
   A child shall be classified as having a communication disorder when

his native speech or language is severely impaired to the extent that it seriously interferes with his ability to use oral language to communicate and this disability is not due primarily to a hearing impairment.

5. Neurologically or Perceptually Impaired
   (a) Neurologically Impaired
   A child shall be classified as being neurologically impaired as a result of an examination which shows evidence of specific and definable central nervous system disorder.
   (b) Perceptually Impaired
   A child shall be considered to be perceptually impaired who exhibits a learning disability in one or more of the basic processes involved in the development of spoken or written language but which are not primarily due to sensory disorders, motor handicaps, mental retardation, emotional disturbance, or environmental disadvantage. The disabilities are manifested in the perceptual areas involved in listening, thinking, speaking, reading, writing, spelling, and the study of arithmetic.

6. Orthopedically Handicapped
   A child shall be classified as orthopedically handicapped who, because of malformation, malfunction or loss of bones, muscle, or body tissue, needs a special educational program, special equipment or special facilities to permit normal learning processes to function.

7. Chronically Ill
   A child, who, because of illness such as tuberculosis, epilepsy, lowered vitality, cardiac condition, leukemia, asthma, malnutrition, pregnancy, or other physical disabilities who are otherwise uncategorized but which make it impracticable for the child to receive adequate instruction through the regular school program shall be classified under the category of chronically ill.

8. Emotionally Disturbed
   A child shall be considered to be emotionally disturbed when his behavior is characterized by a pattern of functioning which is so inappropriate as to call attention to itself and which severely limits the individual from profiting from regular classroom learning experiences or severely hinders other pupils in the class from profiting from regular classroom learning experiences. The emotionally disturbed child further characterizes himself by a pattern of expression of emotion inappropriate to the situation in a manner of degree and quality. However, the emotionally disturbed child must give evidence of a degree of rational behavior which permits some communication with authority figures indicative of ability to profit from instruction under specially controlled circumstances.

9. Socially Maladjusted
   A child shall be considered to be socially maladjusted when his pattern of social interaction is characterized by conflicts which he can-

not resolve adequately without the assistance of authority figures, or when his behavior is such as to interfere seriously with the well-being or the property of those with whom he associates.

The socially maladjusted child exhibits his maladjustment chiefly in his persistent inability to abide by the rules and regulations of social structure.

10. Multiply Handicapped

A child shall be considered to be multiply handicapped who, after proper identification and classification according to these rules and regulations, is found to qualify in any two or more categories of the handicapped [pp. 6–11].

This classification system for handicapped children is clearly school-specific. The system refers to conditions and criteria that require knowledge of both the child's condition and the school setting in which he has been and will be educated. It is also clear that some categories require more careful attention from the psychologist than do others. The psychologist's assessment skills are especially pertinent to the classification of the mentally retarded, neurologically and perceptually impaired, emotionally disturbed, socially maladjusted, and most children who could be classified as multiply handicapped.

Diagnosis is often confused with classification. Diagnosis has been defined as "identification of disease or abnormality from symptoms presented, and from a study of its origin and course" [English & English, 1958, p. 150]. Sarason (1953) elaborated on its meaning: "Diagnosis refers to the procedure whereby one attempts to correlate observations and measurements so that predictions about the course of a presenting condition may be made and appropriate therapeutic measures taken" [p. 26]. A diagnosis, therefore, involves the assignment of a label or subcategory title based on a review of symptoms, their origin, and the course of their development so that predictions can be made about outcomes. It is a medically derived and medically oriented term.

Identification is used to describe the process of looking at a large group of schoolchildren and trying to locate those who are most likely to be included in some classification system. The methods used to identify are cruder than those used in classification or diagnosis and are often referred to as screening methods. The screening procedure described earlier, in which group readiness tests, group observation, and teacher judgment are used together to screen kindergarten children for readiness for first grade, is also a way of identifying children among the kindergarten group who have special problems. It is expected that identification on the basis of screening will later prove to have identified some children in error (false positives) and that the procedure will probably not locate all those children who should be identified (false negatives).

Identification is a screening procedure to determine, as a first step, which children should be studied or examined more carefully. Classification is the ordering of some related variety of conditions into its component parts. Diagnosis is the process of assigning a person to one of the parts of a classification system based on a careful analysis of etiology, symptoms, and course of development, leading to prediction of outcome.

Discrimination among these terms ordinarily poses no special problems in clinical work, but complications do arise when the terms are applied to the school setting. Schools want to identify and classify children to educate them. The only valid educational purposes for identification, followed by classification, are to locate and group children to offer them specialized teaching, on the assumption that the classification category tells something about how a child can profit from instruction and school management techniques. The classification category is a kind of shorthand method to describe the child's educational problems and possibilities. The classification label may not be known or may not even be pertinent to knowing how to educate the child. Classification is subject to change based on the child's ability to learn or to handle himself as a learner in the mainstream of school activity without the need for special teaching or techniques. Classification is geared toward *placement* for the purposes of improved teaching and learning. Educational classification is a very special case of classification. It is different from diagnosis, since diagnosis usually implies the cause of the condition, its etiology. As Reynolds (1971) pointed out, knowledge of etiology is not helpful in education unless it tells something about how to teach the child. Prediction is not useful unless it influences plans for learning. Diagnosis as commonly used in clinical and medical settings is not a good fit for educational purposes.

Slippage between educational and medical models and goals often results in confusion for educators and for mental health personnel. Greater sophistication is attributed to classification of the handicapped than is often true when educational classification is considered equivalent to "medical" diagnosis. Difficulty in differential determination of classification results from conflict between medical-clinical diagnosis and educationally oriented classification. A school psychologist, for example, might recognize that a child's difficulty could be diagnosed as "overanxious reaction of childhood," a term in the American Psychiatric Association's *Diagnostic and statistical manual of mental disorders* (1968), and that the best prediction for future disorder might well be the diagnosis of "anxiety neurosis." For educational purposes, however, the classification that best describes this child's current education status and behavior might be "socially maladjusted." Pointless and time-consuming arguments result from confusion among such discriminations.

One way to clarify distinctions might be to use descriptive language to distinguish more clearly between educational and medical procedures. Figure 5 shows the components of an investigation of human behavior when action is to be taken. The medical approach is traditional and well established. The educational approach is an attempt to delineate educational counterparts. The terms used reflect the spirit of the educational procedures and the differences in how one thinks about helping children in school as opposed to a medical or clinical setting. A distinction is made between research and inquiry. Supposedly, much of our knowledge about the medical-clinical process in Fig. 5 is based on research and clinical wisdom, with the implication that controlled studies, laboratory work, carefully designed investigations, and years' accumulation of knowledge have contributed to an understanding of differential patterns of deviant behavior. In the equivalent educational process it is perhaps better at this point to realize that actions are most often based on program evaluation and on seeking answers without recognition of the hallmarks of sound research and systematic data gathering. Until procedures for locating, classifying, and educating children with special problems are improved, it is far better to use terminology closer to what actually happens than to cloud the issue by using inappropriate and misleading terms.

Medical	Educational
Etiology	Causes Origin
Diagnosis	Assessment (For classification) (For description of learning pattern)
Prognosis	Prediction of educational possibilities
Treatment	Class placement Remediation Management Teaching strategies
Research	Research Inquiry Evaluation

FIGURE 5. Components of an investigation of human behavior when action is to be taken: a comparison of medical and educational terminology.

SOME PROBLEMS IN THE IDENTIFICATION AND
CLASSIFICATION OF HANDICAPPED CHILDREN
IN THE SCHOOLS

Although teaching-oriented identification and classification are an improvement over medically oriented identification and classification in the schools, sorting children for special education still presents serious and as yet unsolved problems.

Tendencies to oversimplify. It is generally accepted by community mental health workers and educators that it is a good thing to identify children. After all, if we cannot locate children who have problems or potential problems, how can we offer them help? To identify children who may need special educational programs and services, however, it is necessary to identify them as something—for instance, as having potential learning disabilities or as being educationally retarded or emotionally handicapped. Here our first concern occurs. Name calling too easily becomes labeling. And labeling, if viewed in clinical-medical terms, tends to overdefine the child. We tend to consider labeling as "bad" and identification as "good," but sometimes they become one and the same. The problem is not necessarily in the term used to describe the child but in the tendency to assume that the term *is* the child. It becomes essence thinking. A child identified as emotionally handicapped may be seen as an emotionally handicapped child, first and foremost. A child identified as educationally backward is viewed as a dumb child.

Oversimplification through labeling is even more serious once the assessment procedure has moved from identification to classification. Until recently, classification of handicapped children for education invariably resulted in placement in special education facilities. The classification title became part of the child's record and followed him throughout his school years, from grade to grade and from school to school. Also, a child placed in a special education program was not easily removed. Once a person is labeled, it is difficult to get the label removed. For example, name calling during political campaigns, whether true or not, is effective. In turn, the person assigned the classification (label) is reinforced for acting as expected and may continue to act that way as the clearest means to understand how to regard and be regarded by others.

The danger of overinterpreting the titles used in the identification and classification of handicapped children does not detract from the importance of locating such children and trying to help them. Rather, it points up the need to understand the distortions that can result from assessment in special education and to guard against them.

Consideration of the setting. According to New Jersey rules and regulations for the classification of handicapped children, a child who scores from one and a half to three standard deviations below the mean on a standardized clinical test of intelligence (an IQ of about 55 to 78), who gives evidence of a low level of ability to think abstractly, and who shows evidence of less ability to function socially without direction than do his peers of average or better intelligence is to be considered as mentally retarded, educable.[3] In the context of this definition, let us hypothesize a boy named Norman whose IQ, as determined by a well-trained school psychologist, is 70, whose scores on verbal material and manipulative performance items of abstract reasoning subtests are at about the same level as his overall IQ score, and who requires more direction and help in self-management in social situations than would ordinarily be true of the "average" child. If Norman attends a school and a classroom where the average IQ is 85 to 90, where his ability to do abstract reasoning is not unlike many in his class, and where social direction is a school-wide problem, he is not very different from his classmates. Such a school can be found in many urban and rural school districts.

Now consider Robert, whose IQ is 85, well above the intelligence range describing the educable mentally retarded child, and whose abstract reasoning abilities and social skills are at the level of his IQ, somewhat below average but not low enough to classify him as retarded. Put Robert in a suburban school where the average IQ score is about 120 and children are unusually sophisticated and, if anything, oversocialized. If the IQ of 120 is used as a mean score, Robert can be regarded as mentally retarded, educable, relatively speaking *in this school*. Whether or not he is classified as retarded, he is likely to need some kind of special services to help him to function adequately, both intellectually and socially.

Thus Norman, who is mentally retarded according to state guidelines, is not mentally retarded in his school. Robert, who is not mentally retarded according to state standards, is functionally retarded in his school. What then has happened to our definitions? They can only be viewed properly when they are used in the context of the educational situation in which judgments are being made about the child. This serves to emphasize the point that there is an important, perhaps vital, difference between an essence view of man and a response capability view. If we use essence thinking, Norman is retarded and Robert is not. Norman will be considered as retarded no matter where he is or what he does. Retarda-

---

[3] The New Jersey rules and regulations go on to warn that one must also consider health and sensory impairment and significant deprivation in growth experiences. The rules and regulations assume that competent professional judgment will be exercised.

tion describes him. Robert, on the other hand, is not retarded, and therefore we may come to believe that he does not need special educational services. A response capability view permits us to ask what each child can do in the setting in which he is being educated and what we know about him and his school that will permit us to make the best educational plan for him at the present time. A response capability view requires that we continue to assess behavior to continue to modify it.

Educational decision making. Classification for the purposes of special education is, at best, a crude means to decide what kinds of educational programs and teaching methods are most appropriate for any child. When a child is classified as emotionally disturbed, the classification tells us that he will probably succeed best in a class that gives consideration to his difficulties in expressing his feelings and in emotional control and that a smaller than average size class would be desirable. A child classified as mentally retarded, educable, may require that academic problems be presented more slowly, with greater repetition, in a variety of different ways, and as concretely as possible. Classifying a child as neurologically impaired, for example, suggests that he may need visual-motor training, specially designed equipment to utilize as many sense modalities as possible in teaching basic skills, and a classroom structure free of distracting influences and that offers opportunity for isolation within the larger classroom.

Although these are useful rough guides, they are not sufficient to help make the decisions about educational programming that are of greatest value to a school. In addition, classification based on psychological assessment will in many instances require that more than one classification category be used. Some mentally retarded children are also emotionally and socially maladjusted. Some are also neurologically impaired, and many are perceptually impaired. The decision as to which classification to use is often highly subjective; yet it may determine placement in one special class rather than another. The school psychologist needs to know the organization and composition of the classes available to the child. A very shy and anxious child may be considered to be emotionally disturbed, but he could probably learn better in a class of mentally retarded children his own age who are generally well controlled than in a class of emotionally disturbed children who act out their feelings and are difficult to control.

In schools assessment is a two-part process: assessment of the child and assessment of the available settings. To make sense of this process it is necessary to understand that the classification to which a child is assigned is descriptive of the placement in which he can best profit from the educational experiences to be offered. Classification is less a label than a match between a child and a setting, to be changed yearly or more often if some other kind of placement is deemed more suitable. The potency of the descriptive terms used to classify children for special education has contributed to the misunderstanding of this arrangement and has led to the perpetuation of the problems of labeling.

Another aspect of assessment in school psychology involves determining which available level of educational placement is most appropriate. Choosing the kind of special class best suited to the child is only one level of decision making. When sufficient data have been collected, an educational plan can be developed that takes into account how the child learns best and what his intellectual, emotional, and social strengths and deficits are. Then the school psychologist and others can decide among the various placement and service alternatives available. It makes little sense to recommend that a child be placed in a program that does not exist or that a teacher handle him in ways that are not possible. Although it might ultimately be worthwhile to describe the ideal plan for a child, to help a school think about its resources or lack of them, the school psychologist must decide what really can be done for that child at that time.

One way of considering alternatives is diagrammed in Figure 6. The tapered design indicates that there are considerable differences in the number of children to be involved at the different levels. Although most special education efforts have been concentrated at level IV, Evelyn Deno's (1970) diagram forcefully points out that most children who could be classified as handicapped will remain in the regular class.

In making decisions about special education, the school psychologist uses his assessment tools within a framework of psycho-educational assessment; he determines the level of service most appropriate for the child; and he determines, within that level, which of the actually available services will best help educate the child. It is also his responsibility to describe the child so that those who ultimately become responsible for his day-to-day education can understand how the child learns, what reinforcers can be used to encourage his interest, what attributes can be capitalized on, and what areas can be remediated.

It is not necessary to classify a child to make good educational decisions about him. What is important is to provide information that discriminates among available educational alternatives and permits the teacher to help the child learn. If classification is required by law, or if many children in a school district are identified as needing special education and grouping them would be helpful, its use can be justified provided that proper safeguards are taken to protect children from the misapplications and misinterpretations involved in identification and classification.

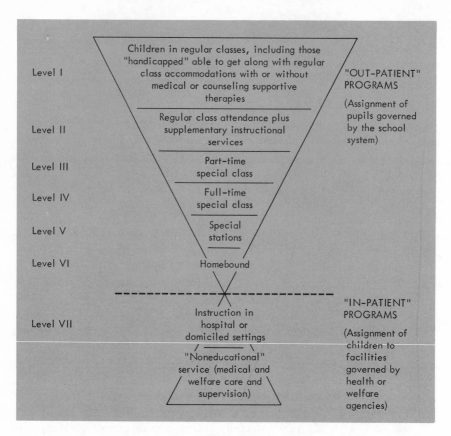

Level I	Children in regular classes, including those "handicapped" able to get along with regular class accommodations with or without medical or counseling supportive therapies	"OUT-PATIENT" PROGRAMS
Level II	Regular class attendance plus supplementary instructional services	(Assignment of pupils governed by the school system)
Level III	Part–time special class	
Level IV	Full–time special class	
Level V	Special stations	
Level VI	Homebound	
Level VII	Instruction in hospital or domiciled settings	"IN-PATIENT" PROGRAMS
	"Noneducational" service (medical and welfare care and supervision)	(Assignment of children to facilities governed by health or welfare agencies)

FIGURE 6. The cascade system of special education service. (From Deno, Evelyn, Special education as developmental capital, *Exceptional Children*, 1970, 37, *3*, 229–37. Copyright by Council of Exceptional Children.)

Disadvantaged Children: A Special Case

The recent upheavals in our society have had concomitant effects upon the efforts of the school psychologist. The struggle of black Americans to overthrow the generations old discrimination against them has led to the recognition that in the schools large numbers of Mexican-Americans, Puerto Ricans, and American Indian children have also been discriminated against. For that matter, the schools have been accused of discriminating against all children, regardless of specific ethnic origin, whose homes have not provided typical middle-class language experience.

CRITICISMS OF TESTING THE DISADVANTAGED

The recognition of such discrimination has led to a raging controversy over the use of assessment instruments that sort out some children as less intelligent than others by virtue of their scoring lower on tests that seem to measure certain kinds of language experiences as well as certain attitudes and values held by the middle class. As a result, the New York Public Schools in 1966 eliminated the use of standardized group intelligence tests to predict academic ability. At their 1969 meeting in Washington, D.C., the Association of Black Psychologists adopted a statement supporting parents who would not allow their children to take tests that, according to the association, were used to place black children in special classes. In 1970 a group of parents in Boston, supported by a number of professionals including psychologists, protested that children from a predominantly black and Puerto Rican area had been classified as retarded on the basis of scores on intelligence tests administered, according to the protesters, by less than competent examiners. In California a girl was placed in a class for educable mentally retarded children on the basis of her Stanford-Binet IQ score. When she was retested in Spanish, her score was 49 IQ points higher than that obtained on the English version. A lawsuit, Diana versus the School District of Soledad, was instituted [Leary, 1970]. Lawsuits, protests, and antitesting articles have continued to appear, implicating both testers and testing on the basis that their practice and instruments are discriminatory [Ross, De Young, & Cohen, 1971]. In 1972 a district court judge ordered the San Francisco Unified School to stop placing black students in special classes on the basis of IQ scores.

In general, the argument is that tests such as the Stanford-Binet and the Wechsler Intelligence Scale for Children cannot distinguish between genuine retardation and lack of facility in a particular form of the English language. Critics have pointed out that these intelligence tests contain items that favor some cultural groups. English vocabulary, verbal reasoning, and verbal analogies, it is argued, are taught early and well in middle-class homes. Individuals with limited or different language experience are therefore penalized by such items.

Studies of preschool children suggest that black children do well on certain test items. One study (Kamii & Radin, 1969), for instance, compared two groups of children: one consisting of three-year-old, disadvantaged black, mildly retarded children; and the other a normative group of children on whom the 1960 revision of the Stanford-Binet Intelligence Scale was based. The black, retarded children did significantly better on two items, immediate memory and ability to identify parts of the body, and significantly worse on six items (on verbal responses) of the eleven items sampled.

Tests of so-called mental ability have also been severely criticized for containing items that are considered to be culturally loaded in favor of middle-class socioeconomic status. This means that the correctness of a response is determined by the value placed on an item rather than on whether the item is adequately answered. On the Stanford-Binet, an item at the age level of IV-6 (four years, six months) asks the child to judge which of two pictures of a person is prettier. The item is called Esthetic Comparison. The child's response is judged as correct if all three of the sets are answered "correctly." Two of the sets are drawings that compare what can be described as magazine-pretty men and women with obviously white Anglo-Saxon facial features with a man and a woman with broad faces, flat noses, widely set eyes, and straight hair. One wonders how a four-year-old Mexican-American might respond, considering the strong possibility that his mother and father might look more like the "wrong" answer than the "right" answer.

Items scored on the basis of cultural values may penalize not only disadvantaged children. In our current state of rapid cultural changes, middle-class children can be penalized for their recognition of changing values. One item on an individual test asks "Why should women and children be saved first in a shipwreck?" The correct answers would include such ideas as the fact that women are needed for the care of children, children have a longer life to lead, women and children are not as strong as men. The response of a sophisticated child, raised to be aware of the struggle for women's rights, might have to be judged as incorrect. Another test item asks, "What's the thing for you to do when you are on your way to school and notice that you are in danger of being late?" A correct answer suggests that the child hurry. What does one do with a response that reflects instead the reality of rural and suburban busing, and, for the disadvantaged child, busing to another school district? For those items that appear directly to penalize disadvantaged children because of their lack of familiarity with content, there are other items that penalize middle-class children whose knowledge exceeds that required for correct scoring. In fairness, it must be pointed out that such items constitute a small proportion of the total test and account for little of the score variance.

It is generally acknowledged that a high proportion of children in special classes, especially those for educable mentally retarded children, come from low socioeconomic backgrounds. In urban areas, where there are many children from minority groups and disadvantaged backgrounds, these children are often overrepresented in special education classes. This has resulted in charges that the tests have been used to separate minority group children from the opportunities afforded by regular class instruction.

These criticisms are justified. Gross misuse of test results has resulted in discriminatory practices and has raised the question of whether the use of testing should be eliminated entirely. However, the elimination of testing in schools will not eliminate decision making or the exercise of judgment by adults working with children. Therefore, the real question is: Do we use tests wisely or do we make decisions without them? Shortly, guidelines will be given for the use of tests.

HEREDITY AND ENVIRONMENT AS
CAUSATIVE AGENTS

It is not difficult to summarize the correlates of low or high scores on intelligence tests. In general, parents of children who obtain low IQ scores tend to obtain low IQ scores themselves; they are relatively unsuccessful from a socioeconomic standpoint, have had minimal education, and have a higher than average incidence of emotional problems. Their brothers and sisters also tend to score low on these tests. At the other extreme, high IQ children tend to have high IQ, successful, emotionally sturdy parents, brothers, and sisters.

How can we account for these interrelationships? The consistency of intelligence within families is too striking to be ignored, as is the correlation of economic and social success with intelligence. Those who are most critical of the use of assessment instruments in the schools take a strong environmental position to account for such relationships, assuming that the kind of intelligence measured by the standardized tests is totally or largely dependent upon the experiences to which the child was exposed as he grew and developed. If standard English is not used in the home and neighborhood, a child has no way of acquiring skill in standard English. If a child is exposed to attitudes and values different from those of the dominant culture, he is penalized when he is asked questions related to those attitudes and values. The environmental position is explicit: the tests do not measure a child's intelligence—they measure the extent to which the child has adopted the language, attitude, and values of middle-class American culture. The environmental position also points out that economically deprived children are typically those who obtain low scores and that economic deprivation is an environmental, not a genetic, factor. Disadvantaged children may have all kinds of unmeasured abilities and should not be classified as dull or retarded.

Milton Schwebel (1968), an eloquent spokesman for the environmental point of view, summed up the optimism and spirit of the position. He gave meaningful reasons for the serious criticism leveled against the use of tests in schools:

> Who can be educated? *Everyman.* There is no known reason to set a lower estimate. For the immediate future the outlook for those who suffer from serious brain or other central neurological defects is not favorable, but on a long-term basis the current proportion of such de-

fective newborns (about ½ to 1 percent) can be greatly reduced through social change and medical advances. It is possible, too, that a combination of medical and educational intervention will activate and elevate the learning process of those who cannot now be helped. In any event, for all the rest of our children, there is no known reason to believe that they will be unable to do the work of an academic high school and of a college. That is to say, as a given society is fearless enough to welcome and encourage the emancipation of the mind, it will facilitate the heightening of man's consciousness. It will nurture every child's natural curiosity and cherish his openness to ideas. It will struggle against the forces that censor and inhibit, that make school learning a sterile chore [pp. 204–5].

There is also a genetic position on intelligence. It states that the capacity to perform in certain ways, to acquire and use complex language skills in writing or speaking, is predominantly determined by genetic endowment, transmitted from generation to generation. The genetic position asserts that just as other human characteristics (size, body type, hair color, etc.) are largely determined by heredity, so, to a great extent, is intelligence. A number of studies report the similarity of IQ scores obtained between identical twins and among siblings, even when they have been brought up in different environments. Other studies show that the IQs of children placed in foster homes are more like those of their biological parents than of their foster parents. These studies, incidentally, have been conducted primarily with white children.

These findings and other research evidence favoring the genetic position were summarized in a comprehensive report by Arthur Jensen (1969):

> The belief in the almost infinite plasticity of intellect, the ostrich-like denial of biological factors in individual differences, and the slighting of the role of genetics in the study of intelligence can only hinder investigation and understanding of the conditions, processes, and limits through which the social environment influences human behavior [p. 29].

He concluded that IQs are more a matter of inheritance than environment and that differences in intelligence exist among racial groups. Jensen stressed differences in how intelligence seems to operate among racial groups even more than differences in absolute quantity. His report, published at a time when minority groups were struggling for equal rights and opportunities, aroused considerable critical uproar.

A number of social scientists responded to Jensen's hereditarian view (Harvard Educational Review, 1969), including thoughtful psychologists who had also done considerable investigation of the factors that appear to contribute to what we call intelligence. J. McV. Hunt, David Elkind, and Lee Cronbach, for example, tempered the position taken by Jensen: they generally agreed with his claim that there probably are genetic differences in capacity, but they argued that those differences are not necessarily racial. If there are genetic differences, they also exist among individual Caucasians, Orientals, and Negroes, as well as between racial groups. Cronbach pointed out that although ceilings of innate ability may exist and vary, we do not know their exact limits. We do know that a ceiling established by the limits of environment is a false ceiling.

As is true of most nature-nurture controversies, the evidence is not definitive enough to support the extreme of either position. William H. Boyer and Paul Walsh (1968) suggested that in the absence of explicit answers to the controversy, the moral approach calls for us to address ourselves to that portion of the problem that we can control and manipulate—the environment.

THE SCHOOL PSYCHOLOGIST AND TESTING THE DISADVANTAGED

The history of school psychology and most of the psychologist's training have focused on the use of certain techniques and skills for the assessment of children's intelligence. State laws have defined his function as the assessor of children's abilities and/or disabilities via IQ scores. Teachers and parents ask him questions about children's mental ability. Although the school psychologist does not finally decide who attends special classes, he does make by far the most influential recommendations to the school administrator. Acutely aware of the nature-nurture controversy, the school psychologist makes judicious use of his instruments to provide necessary information, even though he is risking criticism from the extremists of both camps.[4]

Guidelines for the appropriate use of tests. Assessment of any child is influenced by a number of factors. The assessment of the disadvantaged child is subject to particular misunderstandings and cautions.

Many of the critics of the use of Wechsler's tests may be misinterpreting the nature of what the test is designed to tell about a person. David Wechsler (1958) wrote that, "Intelligence, operationally defined, is the aggregate or global capacity of the individual to act purposefully, to

---

[4] The school psychologist may also find himself uncomfortably in the limelight of a courtroom as he attempts to uphold his professional code of ethics, which bars professionally unqualified persons from access to confidential psychological findings and reports, while irate parents and others demand that he air his findings publicly.

think rationally, and to deal effectively with his environment" [p. 7]. Wechsler then made an analogy between intelligence and electricity. Electricity in and of itself cannot be seen or actually measured. It is measured by its effects. Similarly, intelligence is measured by what we see it doing: drawing correct inferences, solving problems, and, Wechsler goes on to say, understanding the meaning of words and solving mathematical problems.

Wechsler's quoted definition, however, does not necessarily require the use of standard American English. What is "acting purposefully"? For a school child it may be to set about getting his assignment completed in an organized fashion. Out of school, "acting purposefully" can be quite different. It may, for instance, involve planning the most efficient way to earn money to help support his family or helping to care for four younger brothers and sisters. Although both kinds of activities, in school and out, are correlated with intelligence, circumstances may hinder successful school performance while intelligence can still be expressed out of school. "To deal effectively with his environment" may mean a schoolchild's decision to study hard to master algebra because he wishes to become an engineer. Out of school, dealing effectively with his environment may consist of organizing a street gang to control activities in his neighborhood.

Wechsler's tests and especially the Stanford-Binet give information about abilities more appropriate to school situations and middle-class environments than to a rural environment or urban ghetto. As long as we are aware of what we are measuring, the administration of such tests can have value. The instruments offer valid assessment of the child's ability to function at the time the test was administered in a typical American public school that uses traditional educational techniques. Diana of Soledad, California, may have scored 49 IQ points higher when tested in Spanish, but the lower Binet score probably predicted with reasonable accuracy what Diana's difficulties would be in a classroom of middle-class, English-speaking children conducted by a middle-class, English-speaking teacher using regular teaching methods.

The justification for the continued use of tests is their accuracy in predicting school success, the key skills of which are reading and writing standard American English. There is no question that there are many kinds of intellectual functions that the tests do not measure.

Most critics of individual assessment of disadvantaged children neglect to recognize that many tests measure abilities that are not expressed in words. It is true that children who obtain high scores on verbal tests generally obtain similarly high scores on nonverbal tests, and that children whose scores are low on verbal tests tend to obtain low scores on nonverbal tests. Nevertheless, in individual instances the discrepancy between a disadvantaged child's performance on verbal tasks and his performance on tasks not requiring language can give the school psychologist important clues to that child's mental ability. In addition to nonlanguage performance scales on the WISC, a number of tests do not require the exchange of language between the psychologist and the child. Thus, possible misunderstanding of directions on the part of the child is eliminated. There are also tests that do not require a child to make any verbal response.

Another point of misunderstanding is the reason why tests are administered at all. They should not be administered expressly to label a child as retarded or as any other category; they should be administered to assess the kinds of strengths and weaknesses that are amenable to school manipulation to facilitate a child's ability to learn academic skills. As long as schools continue to operate on the principle that skills in reading, writing, and computation are basic to functioning and to upward mobility in our society, and as long as success in our society is defined as upward movement along socioeconomic lines, intelligence testing has a place in education. Perhaps the word *intelligence* is part of the problem. A better, if unwieldy, definition of what is being measured is aptitude for success as it is defined by the dominant culture of American society.

One of the points made earlier in this chapter is that individual assessment has advantages over group assessment. Most group tests do indeed penalize the culturally disadvantaged child, for as group tests are prepared for progressively older children, most of them progressively presuppose increased skill in reading. Group tests do not permit any evaluation of motivation toward working on tasks, and one of the observed major differences between culturally disadvantaged and other children is their attitudes toward school tasks.

Criticisms have been levied on the testing of disadvantaged childen on the basis that most testers, the school psychologists, are middle-class and do not understand either the culture or the language of many minority group children. Instances are common in which children define "skill" as "That's what you do when you clean a fish" (scale). "Sword" may be defined as "When you saw wood" (sawed). The problem of any kind of verbal testing with a child whose native language or dialect is other than standard English is obvious. In addition, attitudes toward the testing procedure differ among children from different cultural groups. Middle-class children from achievement oriented homes and communities are more typically motivated to try hard and to do as well as they can, frequently gratified by their own sense of accomplishment. Children from disadvantaged backgrounds may need more encouragement, patience, even coaxing from the examiner to motivate them to attempt to respond at all.

One study (Thomas, Hertzig, Dryman, & Fernandez, 1971) compared the examining style of two examiners on the WISC scores of school-age Puerto Rican children. The examiners were both female, Puerto Rican, fluent in Spanish and English, and comparable in testing experience. Significant IQ differences were found between children tested by the two examiners, with higher IQ levels related to examiner behavior that encouraged verbalization, active participation, and repeated efforts by the child.

Sensitivity to and awareness of differences among children are as much a part of the school psychologist's repertoire as is his knowledge of the instruments with which he is working. Examining style is also important and must be taken into account by the psychologist in the interpretation of his results. As Rosenthal (1966) pointed out, the intention of a researcher can be a subtle variable, influencing the outcome and direction of his experiments. So too can the intention of the school psychologist in the examination of disadvantaged children. It is assumed here that one facet of professional functioning of the school psychologist is self-awareness and that professional training includes helping the trainee to understand how he is part of his instrumentation.

Individual assessment of culturally disadvantaged children may yield an IQ score, but many psychologists in the schools avoid using the IQ numbers because they are so easily misinterpreted. An IQ score of 85 means different things even to the different professionals who work with children (psychologists, psychiatrists, pediatricians, social workers, and teachers)—small wonder that parents and the community at large misinterpret scores. However, individual testing of culturally disadvantaged children can give valuable information. If there are language deficits (deficits in the context of communication in standard English), something of the nature of the deficit is revealed, which can lead to recommendations for compensatory language experiences. If in spite of language deficit the child performs well on nonlanguage tasks, the message is clear that the child has a definable degree of learning potential. All children can learn, and the results of testing tell psychologists and teachers *how* Johnny can learn, not that he cannot.

Teachers, however, need to know that their task will not be as easy with some children as it is with others. Teachers deserve all possible help in planning educational techniques that take advantage of the level and quality of the child's learning style and potential. These educational techniques may be quite different from those learned in teacher training institutions. The results of individual assessment of culturally disadvantaged children *can* lead to educational change. When they do not, the problems are not with the instruments but with their misinterpretation and misuse. Solutions are more likely to be found in improving the education of test users and administrators, restricting test administration to those who have been trained and qualified for it, and in providing safeguards against misuse of assessment instruments and procedures, rather than in abolishing them altogether.

Helping Teachers
with Classroom Problems

chapter four

Schools vary enormously in the amount of community and tax support they receive, the kinds of buildings in which pupils are housed, and the quality and quantity of materials available for teaching and learning. Although there is much variation among schools, however, the educational experience is basically the same for each child: it can best be described as a transaction between the child and a teacher in the context of a classroom of other children. This simple truth is crucial to understanding the necessary focus of school psychology. Everything that a school psychologist does must eventually culminate in improved educational experiences for children. Central to this goal is helping the teacher cope with, teach, and motivate children successfully.

Regardless of how the school is organized—whether it is the typical classroom in a box or the more recent open school—the teacher serves as the negotiator or mediator of learning experiences, the model of how to behave in school, and the arbitrator of children's interactions with each other. Each day a teacher must make countless decisions that affect children's learning and behavior. The sum total of these decisions defines how effective the teacher is in furthering the education and growth of the children in her charge. The school psychologist's effectiveness can be judged by how much the teacher's ability to make those decisions has been improved by his assistance. The school psychologist can help teachers in a number of ways. He can help them control the actions of individual children whose behavior makes it difficult for them and for others to profit from classroom activity. He can help teachers organize classroom activity and physical space so that learning is expedited. He can help teachers by directly attempting to alter the behavior and attitudes of individuals and groups of children who appear to need assistance. He can coordinate and assist with the referral of children to agencies and resources outside the school when necessary. He can also serve as a teacher consultant and educator in areas in which he has special knowledge and skills.

This chapter will describe the more important ways in which the school psychologist can be of assistance to teachers.

Behavior Management

Jim cannot concentrate on his arithmetic problems while Ken is poking him with a pencil. Needless to say, Ken cannot be poking others with a pencil and concentrating on very much of anything else. When the noise level of a class prevents class members from hearing what the teacher or any single child is saying, subject matter learning stops. If materials needed for carrying out an assignment are misplaced, time is lost searching for them, and a teacher can easily lose control of the class.

Most teachers solve problems like these most of the time, but sometimes they find themselves unable to do so and seek assistance. The school psychologist can help teachers handle management problems in a variety of ways. He can observe and offer advice or suggestions based on his experience with other teachers. He can help teachers to understand why specific children behave as they do, thereby helping them to be more tolerant of the deviant behavior. He can support teachers in their efforts and offer them opportunities, through consultation, to work out for themselves means to solve classroom problems.

APPLICATION OF LEARNING PRINCIPLES

In recent years, one approach to solving management problems in the school has received increasing attention; it is probably the approach school psychologists use most frequently to assist teachers with management problems. Based on learning principles, it appeals to many teachers, and, perhaps more than any other approach, it seems to work.

As long as there has been schooling, pupils have been rewarded for acceptable, approved behavior and punished for unacceptable behavior. Stars and grades have been awarded for academic achievement. The use of the hickory rod is still extant in some schools, and in many others a sharp crack across a child's knuckles with a ruler is not unknown. Children have always received what we call social approval when teachers have commented, "Good work, Bill," or even "That's right." We all remember a teacher saying, "Well, if you won't tell me who started that ruckus in the back of the room, you'll *all* stay in for recess."

More specific forms of reward and punishment are not confined to recent years. Nuts, figs, and honey rewarded successful students of the Torah in the twelfth century [Birnbaum, 1962]. Erasmus in the sixteenth century advocated positive rather than negative reinforcement when he suggested that children learning Latin and Greek be offered cherries and cakes, not the cane [Skinner, 1966]. More recently students have received medals for perfect attendance, documents for making the honor roll, and graduation diplomas. The most recent innovation, however, has been a *systematized* distribution of prizes or rewards on a *frequent* basis in the classroom.

Ivan Pavlov set the stage with his well-known experiments in classical conditioning. He found that when dogs were presented with food (unconditioned stimulus) immediately preceded by the sound of a tuning fork (neutral stimulus), they soon salivated at the sound of the tuning fork alone (conditioned stimulus) without the presence of food.

B. F. Skinner's work with operant or instrumental conditioning had perhaps the most startling implications for behavioral management in schools. Hungry pigeons learned to play table tennis by being fed for pecking at a Ping-Pong ball. Food pellets were immediately supplied as the bird performed movements (successive approximation or shaping behavior) ultimately leading to a procedure similar to the playing of table tennis.

Workers in the field make a distinction between the terms *reward* and *reinforcement*. Reward is a more colloquial term and is nonspecific; reinforcement is the immediate environmental consequence of a specific performance. Operant conditioning, as exemplified by Skinner's work, refers to the effect of reinforcement upon a behavior. A positive reinforcer in operant conditioning is "any stimulus, presentation of which strengthens the behavior upon which it is made contingent" [Skinner, 1953, p. 84]. In operant conditioning, a rat presses a bar (behavior) to release a food pellet, or a pigeon approaches a Ping-Pong ball and receives a food pellet.

In both classical and operant conditioning an interesting phenomenon takes place. Stimuli originally associated with reinforcers (primary reinforcers) take on reinforcing properties. These stimuli are called secondary reinforcers, and secondary reinforcers are important in learning.

Secondary reinforcers acquire considerable power and effectiveness in shaping behavior because of their association with a primary reinforcer. Dogs in cages who have received a strong electric shock will cringe, whine, and show fear reactions when introduced to the room that contains the cages, because the room has acquired the characteristics of a secondary reinforcer. A child who has been consistently beaten by his parents will react in a hostile manner toward a teacher because the teacher is also an adult. The use of the words "Good work," is a secondary reinforcer because it is associated with a primary reinforcer, or perhaps because the pupil to whom the words are addressed has generalized from still another secondary reinforcer, approval. The primary reinforcer in many classroom or family situations is often buried, in that we cannot be sure if need for approval is based on negative reinforcement (fear of loss of love and nurturance) or positive reinforcement ("good" children receive love and nurturance).

The power of the systematic use of negative reinforcement was demonstrated in 1920 with a now famous nine-month-old baby named Albert [Watson & Rayner, 1920]. Presenting an innocuous white rat to the child just prior to the presentation of a loud noise conditioned Albert to react with fear not only to the rat but to other white, furry objects. The power of positive reinforcement was to be demonstrated by setting up procedures to eliminate the fear (counter-conditioning). Unfortunately, Albert left the hospital before these procedures could be instituted. Mary Cover Jones (1924), however, published her work with Peter, who had a severe fear of a white rat that extended to other furry materials. Peter's fear was overcome by systematically bringing a rabbit closer to the child while he was eating food he liked.

The first suggestions for systematic practical application of learning principles were probably in the field of psychotherapy, when Joseph Wolpe (1954), a South African-born psychiatrist, and Hans Eysenck (1960), a German-born psychologist working in England, applied learning principles in an effort to modify abnormal behavior.

Use of these principles in schools, however, has been relatively recent: very little work was done prior to 1960. A distinction is usually made between behavior therapy, wherein techniques are used in a therapeutic relationship (patient-therapist), and behavior modification, which generally means work done with schoolchildren in classrooms.

BEHAVIOR MODIFICATION WITH INDIVIDUAL CHILDREN IN THE CLASSROOM

Two kinds of sytematically applied reinforcement procedures have been used to modify individual children's behavior in classrooms. The first consists of direct and immediate reinforcement for desired behavior. For example: Lisa, according to her teacher, will not stay in her seat during a work period. For every ten minutes Lisa remains in her seat, she is immediately rewarded by the teacher placing a small piece of candy on her desk.

The second kind of procedure has come to be known as token reinforcement. A token reinforcement program, sometimes referred to as a token economy, includes a set of instructions to the pupil about the behaviors that will be reinforced, a means of making a potentially reinforcing stimulus (usually called a token) contingent upon behavior, and a set of rules for governing the exchange of tokens for backup reinforcers such as prizes. The best example of token reinforcement in society at large is working (the behavior to be reinforced) for money (the reinforcing stimulus contingent upon behavior), wherein the backup reinforcers are whatever money will buy.

Reinforcers used in schools can be positive or negative. Positive rewards consist of something that is considered to give pleasure or satisfaction or that meets a perceived need of the child. Negative reinforcers are punishing in nature. As has been pointed out, "A pat on the back is only a few vertebrae removed from a kick in the pants, but is miles ahead in results" [Peter, 1972, p. 194]. Many studies using animals have shown that punishment, especially some form of electric shock, is effective in shaping behavior. The effectiveness, however, is often diluted or undermined because punishment carries with it concomitant emotional responses such as fear and anger. Every parent is aware that sometimes spanking just does not work. Punishment also results in avoidance behavior, and in most school situations the desired behavior is frequently to *do* something, not to avoid doing something. There are also debatable issues about the use of punishment in schools. To deprive children of recess is one thing, but to administer even a mild electric shock is another. Therefore, most of the systematic use of reinforcers in schools utilize positive rather than negative reinforcement.

Reinforcers can be categorized in other ways. External or material reinforcers are things like toys, money, candy, or games that are awarded children contingent upon their response to some task. They are also called concrete or tangible reinforcers. They can be used directly or as backup reinforcers in a token system.

Verbal praise is also an external reinforcer, but it does not involve a material object. It is assumed that expressions such as "Good job" or "Fine work" give pleasure and satisfaction, and studies indicate that for some children verbal praise, or social reinforcement, is more effective than are material objects.

Internal, intrinsic, intangible, and abstract are terms used to describe the kind of reinforcer that consists only of giving the student information as to the correctness of his response. This kind of reinforcer assumes that schoolchildren have an internalized achievement-striving that is gratified by knowing they got the right answer. Research findings support this point of view: intrinsic reinforcers are effective with at least some children. A whole series of textbooks, known as programmed learning, has been developed on the premise that intrinsic reinforcement is effective. These texts may, for instance, present material to be learned and immediately thereafter ask questions designed to test the student's learning. The correct answers are made immediately available so that the student can check his own work and know when he gets the right answer.

A considerable amount of work has been done to try to find out what kinds of children respond to what kinds of reinforcers, but results are not definitive. In some studies lower-class children performed better when given material reinforcement than when given verbal praise; in other studies middle-class children learned more accurately and/or quickly when presented with material reinforcers. Not surprisingly, younger children respond to direct material rewards better than they do to a token system. The lack of agreement among the findings indicates that many variables must be considered when attempting to work out a behavior modification program in the school.

In many ways the program must be highly individualized to determine what kind of reinforcement is likely to be effective with any particular child. An approach known as contingency management is based on the simple notion that "For any pair of responses, the more probable one will reinforce the less probable one" [Premack, 1965, p. 132]. Following this principle, any low probability behavior may be strengthened if it can be paired with a high probability behavior for a period of time. Determining what is reinforcing to any child is an activity preliminary to the establishment of a systematic plan.

In setting up a behavior modification program for a child in school, the school psychologist must ensure that certain preliminary steps are taken. For Lisa, our fourth-grade ten-year-old who does not stay in her seat, several things must be established before it can be decided to reward her with candy for every ten minutes she sits in her seat.

First, the teacher brings Lisa to the school psychologist's attention. Miss Jones is likely to point out that Lisa is not learning to read as well as she should; that Lisa is silently sullen or openly "fresh" to Miss Jones when reprimanded; and that Lisa interferes with the rest of the class because she is always out of her seat, wandering around the room, interrupting her classmates. The school psychologist must work out with Miss Jones which of these many undesirable behaviors should be approached first. Miss Jones understandably would like all of the behaviors to be eliminated (or instituted, in the case of learning) at once, but it has been found that attempting to modify many behaviors simultaneously is likely to result in the modification of none. It becomes clear that by staying in her seat Lisa will be less likely to interrupt her classmates' work, less likely to be reprimanded, and therefore will have fewer opportunities to react with sullenness or back talk. If Lisa stays in her seat, there is a greater likelihood that she will do her own assignments. Staying in her seat becomes the behavior to be modified.

The next step, and an important one, is to establish Lisa's base-line behavior. Recording base-line behavior involves recording the frequency of the identified behavior before modification is attempted. Someone (the school psychologist, an aide, or the teacher) must record exactly how many times Lisa gets out of her seat during a specified period of time. Although Miss Jones may perceive Lisa's out-of-seat behavior as constant, it may actually occur at the rate of once every ten minutes, often enough to cause upset and distress. A simple chart can be devised so that Lisa's base-line behavior might appear as in Figure 7.

The next steps are to decide how often Lisa is to be reinforced for staying in her seat (every ten minutes) and how she is to be rewarded. The procedure must be explained to Lisa so that she understands all the rules and regulations, the contingencies upon which her behavior is to be rewarded. Another important aspect for effectiveness is to decide with Lisa what she would find rewarding. If immediate, direct, and material reinforcement is to be used, it must be something easily handled by the

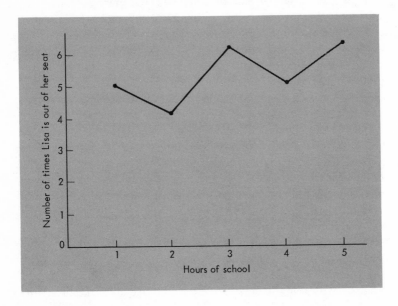

FIGURE 7. Chart showing Lisa's base line of out-of-seat behavior.

teacher or whoever is going to do the rewarding; a small, wrapped piece of candy is feasible and is perceived as rewarding by many (though not all) children.

It is important that the class as a whole understands what is going on. Some of the implications of instituting behavior modification with one class member will be discussed more fully later, but in general the rest of the class is likely to perceive Lisa's unmodified behavior as annoying and will not, at least overtly, resent the special treatment as long as they understand what is going on and why.

After it is established that Lisa is to receive a piece of candy each time she remains in her seat for ten minutes, the program must be carried out rigorously and consistently. Since the teacher has many other things to do, it would be difficult for her to keep an eye on the clock and on Lisa to ensure that Lisa gets her candy every ten minutes. An aide or even older pupils who can take turns keeping track of behavior and time are usually helpful. A kitchen timer is a useful adjunct. A chart of Lisa's behavior for the first week is shown in Fig. 8.

The chart reveals that the program is successful: Lisa is still getting out of her seat, but only one to two times per hour. At this point, the program might be adjusted so that Lisa (again with her understanding) receives reinforcement for every twenty minutes she stays in her seat rather than ten.

As continued reduction of out-of-seat behavior is apparent on the chart, several changes may now take place in the program. For one thing, after a couple of weeks the candy has probably lost some of its reward value for Lisa. The direct reward system can now be replaced by a token system: the teacher makes a hash mark on the board for every thirty minutes Lisa stays in her seat, and ten hash marks indicate that Lisa has earned her reward for the day—the specific nature of the reward to be worked out with Lisa.

Although it is not true for all children and all behavior modification projects, it has generally been found that the kind of program described for Lisa works. Not only does Lisa stay in her seat but much of the other behavior the teacher found distressing, such as her sullenness and hostility, is automatically reduced, for Lisa is now reprimanded less. Staying in her seat also prevents Lisa from annoying other children and disrupting their work.

Whether or not Lisa's ability to read will improve is less accurately predictable. Theoretically, the fact that she is now in her seat rather that out of it enables her to do more academic work. Actually, she may or may not be learning better how to read.

It is possible, of course, to set up a behavior management project in which reading per se is the behavior to be modified. A child could be directly reinforced for each word, sentence, or page read correctly, de-

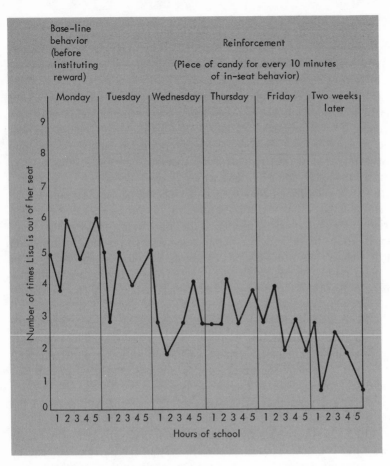

FIGURE 8. Chart showing Lisa's out-of-seat behavior before, during, and after two weeks of reinforcement.

pending on the base-line behavior, which would be the amount of correct reading the pupil can perform prior to inception of the program. A token reinforcement program can be used in which a count is kept for correct responses in reading, with reinforcement available contingent upon a certain number of correct responses.

In some instances, the pupil can become his own reinforcer. A number of inexpensive devices known as counters are available, enabling a schoolchild to keep track of his own responses. A pupil even in the primary grades can learn to chart his behavior so that he can see his own progress immediately, a process that often is rewarding in itself.

Other achievement areas can be the target of behavior modification. Arithmetic achievement, spelling, penmanship, and more complicated areas such as social studies are all subject to possible improvement by means of immediate and consistent reinforcement.

It should be pointed out that in the ever burgeoning body of research studies involving behavior modification techniques with individual children, the most successful projects, or at least the most dramatic, have been those in which children were showing an extreme of behavior.

Significant improvement has been noted in individual behavior in special schools and in classes for children suffering severe emotional maladjustment, in which behavior is usually extremely and violently disruptive. Individual programs for children considered mentally retarded have also improved academic progress, and individual work with trainable children has evoked socially acceptable behavior such as toilet training, self-feeding, dressing, and general self-care. Autistic children who have never communicated in speech have learned to speak words and in some instances to read and write. Despite dramatic results, it should be remembered that such gains do not mean that these children are behaving, talking, reading, or writing at the same rate or level as their normal counterparts.

Classes in special schools or special classes in public schools usually have considerably fewer students than regular classrooms, making individual behavior modification projects easier to plan and carry out. Classes for emotionally disturbed children may have as few as four or five children, and each child may be working on an individual management project. In regular classrooms, typically consisting of twenty-five children or more, individual projects are more difficult for the teacher to manage. Many individual projects are therefore planned for specific portions of the day. For example, a child may have a behavior modification project that his remedial reading teacher implements or a special time for a program with the speech therapist.

BEHAVIOR MODIFICATION WITH AN ENTIRE CLASS

The procedures described so far are helpful when the behavior of a single child, or even of two or three children, is of concern to the teacher. Sometimes the school psychologist is asked to help plan a program that will influence the behavior of all the children in a class.

The distinction between behavior modification in the classroom for a single child and for an entire class is a useful one in that it clarifies two major ways in which behavioral management comes about in school. Behavior modification programs for individual children involve attempts to change the behavior of a single child to conform to practices common to the other children. The child is "deviant" in that his behavior is atypical of others, interferes with the teacher's attempts to instruct the child, and probably interferes with the activities of the other children. Behavior modification programs for a whole class, however, suggest that the problem is with the teacher's ability to manage the class. The teacher has not been able to find ways to organize, motivate, or interest all or most of the children and seeks help to stop those behaviors that are out of control and to increase those behaviors that improve group instruction. A teacher may want to find ways to keep children from talking out of turn or from getting out of their seats or leaving the room without permission. Frequent fighting among the children may be a problem. Pupils may be failing to complete classroom assignments or turn in homework. A teacher may want to increase the number of work assignments that children complete each day or to improve the reading skills of the entire class.

Some classroom management problems about which teachers are concerned are best handled by helping the teacher to change her own teaching behavior. Jacob S. Kounin (1967) and his associates described what they call the Ripple Effect, in which a teacher's method of handling the misbehavior of one child may influence other children who observe the event but who are not the specific target of the teacher's attention. Related to the Ripple Effect are findings such as those of K. Daniel O'Leary and Wesley C. Becker (1968–69), who noted that disruptive behaviors in first-grade children diminished when those behaviors were ignored and appropriate behaviors praised, and that quiet reprimands were as effective as praise.

Other managerial techniques also seem to make a difference in classroom functioning. Kounin (1967) described a behavior complex he called "withitness," the ability of the teacher to know what is really going on in the classroom and by which she "selects correct deviancy targets on time, rather than reprimanding a child for whispering when two others are chasing each other" [p. 226]. Other aspects of teacher style that are amenable to change have to do with methods of inducing activity flow and movement in the classroom, the smoothness or jerkiness with which the teacher moves from one activity to another, and the amount of work and variation in work patterns that pupils experience during the school day. In other words, there is evidence that the teacher's behavior is modifiable in areas that influence how her pupils respond to her and to classroom instruction. The school psychologist working in close cooperation with a teacher can observe teacher behavior, suggest ways in which changes can be made to improve pupil behavior, and monitor changes in the teacher's style of classroom management. The use of base-line data and behavioral charting are as useful in working with the teacher as they are in behavior modification programs with individual children.

It is also possible for a teacher to institute a behavior modification program for an entire class without changing her teaching style. If Miss Jones, Lisa's teacher, had a roomful of Lisas so that talking out, interrupting others, and wandering around the room were endemic, she might consider establishing a token reinforcement program for the class. First she would decide, with the help of the psychologist, which behaviors she wanted to increase. She might decide that staying in one's seat during lessons and raising one's hand before speaking were the two behaviors most important to improvement of classroom learning. Next, she would need to select the kind of token to be used. She could consider poker chips, check marks on a card at each child's desk, stars on the blackboard—any secondary reinforcer that would be a specific cue to pupils of their success. Then Miss Jones would decide on the backup reinforcers for which the tokens could be exchanged and their relative values, as some backup reinforcers would be worth more tokens than others. In effect, Miss Jones might establish a classroom store where tokens could be exchanged at an agreed-upon time and in an agreed-upon manner for a variety of items and experiences of value to the children. The store might include tangibles such as candy, gum, baseball cards, and comics, and intangibles such as an opportunity to choose a book during recess, a special science project, or working a mathematics puzzle.[1]

If the token reinforcement system failed to work for a small number of children in the classroom, Miss Jones might add a team approach to the system, dividing the class into teams that are periodically changed. Team points would be accumulated when all its members performed the desired behavior for some preestablished period of time, and team points would be deducted whenever a member did not perform the desired behavior. Peer pressure toward the reinforced behavior would obviously tend to increase under this system. Base-line data, record keeping, and follow-up evaluation of the effectiveness of the system are assumed to be part of the formal procedures of a token economy program.

The principles involved in modification of teacher and pupil behavior in a classroom are those that have been used by competent teachers throughout time. What has been added is the systematic use of certain learning principles and the assistance, advice, and support of a professional consultant such as the school psychologist.

CRITIQUE OF BEHAVIOR MODIFICATION
TECHNIQUES IN THE SCHOOLS

The success of behavior modification techniques, especially with retarded children, children with learning disabilities, neurologically im-

---

[1] It is often noted that what children consider reinforcing has little to do with adult preconceptions. Given a wide enough choice, children may very well select school-type work, assisting the teacher, or helping other children with assignments in preference to material items. Such choices are more likely to occur after the children have become accustomed to a reinforcement system and after they have had an opportunity to choose those kinds of reinforcement they have learned they are expected to prefer, such as candy and toys.

paired children, autistic children, and emotionally disturbed children[2] has led to the school psychologist's increased involvement in such projects. Schools are pragmatic, searching for something that works and is relatively simple to institute. Schools also tend to adopt popular ideas, often before they have been shown to be effective. Unfortunately, behavior modification techniques, like programmed and perceptual training workbooks, do not always work; they are not as easy to implement in a classroom as it might seem, and there are some inherent limitations to their use.

The proponents of behavior modification techniques point out that when programs do not work, it is usually due to failure to administer them carefully and systematically. Classrooms are not typically systematic and precision oriented, and it takes extraordinary and sometimes incompatible efforts to develop such programs. There is also the possibility that if there is some unknown reinforcement for undesirable behavior, tangible reinforcers will not be successful in decreasing it. For example, if Eric receives subtle support from his classmates by giggles and other signs of approval for behavior his teacher calls "constant calling out," tangible rewards such as candy or tokens may be ineffective in decreasing his calling-out behavior. There are also indications that if the teacher does not verbally reinforce with praise as she dispenses the tangible reinforcer, it may not be effective.

Teacher expectation may also lead to failure. As part of the pervasiveness of the self-fulfilling prophecy, we have learned that if teachers expect a behavior modification program to fail, it probably will. Another reason for failure is the difficulty in pinpointing just what is rewarding to a particular pupil, although programs based on natural reinforcers determined by the pupils themselves may mitigate the problem somewhat. In one project (Charen, 1971), however, the pupils had designated the kinds of things they would find rewarding, but some of them did not bother to cash in their earned tokens. There were no significant differences in reading progress, the behavior being rewarded, between those children who cashed in their tokens and those who did not. These children were between ten and twelve, an age at which the rewarding value of a self-selected reward tends to remain stable. Younger children change their minds more often about what is or is not rewarding.

Another possible reason for failure is that there may be a physical or cognitive ceiling on the behavior to be modified. In the reading project mentioned, it is possible that some of the children were not being

[2] A comprehensive, critical review of research on "Token reinforcement programs in the classroom" by K. Daniel O'Leary and Ronald Drabman appears in the *Psychological Bulletin*, 1971, *75*, 379–98.

presented with the appropriate reading material or the necessary teaching techniques; or it may have been that they were not able to improve their reading ability above a certain level at that point. The complexity of learning in most school situations is such that it probably cannot be fully encompassed by the modification paradigm, with its one-step-at-a-time approach.

The difficulty of instituting a behavior modification program for one or several children in a class or twenty-five or more is inherent in the necessity for precise measurement of behavior and for consistent and immediate reinforcement. Many schools cannot manage the extra personnel needed to start a program. Children can be taught to chart their own behavior, and after a project is started, it can move from direct, immediate reinforcement to token reinforcement with tallies quickly recorded. Many teachers still find it difficult, however, to focus their attention so constantly and exclusively on one or two children in the class.

An important, often overlooked limitation of the use of modification techniques in the classroom is that their approach to behavior is molecular, although that of educational procedures is most often global. The proponents of modification usually point out that a particular aspect of behavior, such as Lisa's constant getting out of her seat, must be pinpointed. Yet the educational goal for Lisa is that she learn a number of complicated skills such as reading, arithmetic, social studies, and science. These skills involve interrelated sets of external behaviors, mediated by thought, that constantly change and develop. Therefore, a distinction needs to be made between modification of discrete behaviors and modification of academic performance. One can *shape* a behavior such as the number of times a pupil raises his hand; one can hope to *motivate* a pupil to want to engage in the complexities of learning to read or spell.

Another limitation is the implicit assumption in behavior modification that the basic cause of the undesired behavior is irrelevant, that the important thing is to change the undesired behavior. Lisa may be jumping out of her seat, however, because of some undiagnosed neurological dysfunction or because feelings of rejection and inadequacy propel her into activity that brings her attention. Perhaps until the fourth grade Lisa attended a private school where she was permitted to leave her seat at will, and she has not learned to sit still for as long a time as the teacher thinks appropriate in the fourth-grade class. If Lisa's problem is that of different training in private school, behavior modification would be a wise choice. If feelings of rejection are pervasive, such techniques may or may not help, depending on how well the reinforcers succeed in substituting for the other attention. If the problem is physiologically based hyperactivity, Lisa may be contained, but the basic problem remains and can be expected to show itself in other ways. As with other approaches, a blanket behavioral approach is an oversimplification of a complex phenomenon.

The example of Lisa points up another area of concern about the use of behavior modification in schools. Who decides what behavior is to be modified? Who decides what is desirable or undesirable behavior? It is one thing for a teacher to want to stop a child's constant crying or frequent soiling behavior; it is another thing for a teacher to use modification techniques to supplement her need for absolute control and power over her charges, to produce the classroom about which some teachers brag, "You can come in my room any time and hear a pin drop." As F. H. Wood (1968) commented, "Like many 'tools,' behavior modification techniques are themselves morally blind. Like a stout sword, they work equally well in the hands of hero or tyrant" [p. 14].

The response of the learning principles advocate is also cogent. Behavior is learned on a reward-punishment basis; the only difference in the use of specific behavior modification techniques is that the paradigm is planned and consistent. The reward-punishment pattern of parents is characterized by inconsistencies and lack of realization and understanding of how they are shaping behavior in their children. Similar inconsistencies and lack of understanding can also apply to teachers.

Another concern is: what happens when extrinsic reinforcement stops? Despite the work-for-pay pattern of our society, will children continue to behave in the desired ways after the M & M's or chips stop falling on the desk? Ought not children to learn in school because it is intrinsically rewarding to learn? There seems to exist in man, as well as in the other higher primates, a curiosity, a need to explore, an intrinsic drive to cope with the environment, a need to achieve. In Robert White's (1963) terms, people seem to have a drive to acquire *competence*. To some teachers, and to other persons, the very power of behavior modification techniques smacks of a Nazi-type, brainwashing approach to children, an approach that may smother intrinsic motivation. To others, it is the most sensible, scientifically based, workable means to get children to attend to tasks long enough for mastery to become intrinsically rewarding.

The school psychologist must concern himself deeply with the various problems presented by the use of direct reinforcement procedures in the classroom. He recognizes that the techniques have tremendous potential for helping children to overcome some of the behavior aberrations that interfere with their ability to learn. He knows that he can recommend a reinforcement program to some teachers but not to others. He also recognizes that the panacea to educational problems has not yet been found and that misuse of the techniques has frightening possibilities.

In practice, despite the admonitions of behavior modification experts, the school psychologist is likely at times to use the principles of operant conditioning rather loosely to help teachers and parents more clearly understand the effects of their actions on children. He might suggest ways in which the teacher or parent can change the nature and frequency of positive and negative reinforcements. He may advise and recommend new contingencies and reward patterns or how to apply consistent behavior toward preconceived goals. As an approach to helping others to manage their own behavior and control the behavior of others, the application of learning (behavior modification) principles is consistent with school functioning and is readily understood by school personnel.

ENVIRONMENTAL MODIFICATION

We are influenced by the spatial, temporal, and organizational aspects of our environment to a greater extent than many of us are aware. The kinds of behavior that occur in a classroom are a function of the interactions between teacher and child and among children. They are also a function, however, of where the children are located in relation to one another, the sequence and timing with which subject matter is presented, and the properties of the physical space in which children are taught. The history of technology in American education (Anderson, 1962) documents how the design of the classroom and the facilities available to pupils have contributed to pupil control. In the late 1800s and early 1900s fixed desks, austere surroundings within, and elaborate external architecture spoke eloquently to a philosophy in which education was adult oriented. Children were to learn and to be kept in their places.

In the typical suburban school of today, the classroom walls are decorated, the desks are movable, equipment and materials are readily available, and the outside of the building is functional and unpretentious. Such changes speak to an educational point of view that is more child centered and that permits considerably greater latitude in the behaviors that will be tolerated. With the recognition that some children do not learn in schools as they are now constituted, new organizational and architectural plans are being developed that undoubtedly will change the way children behave in school. Schools without walls, work-study programs, flexible scheduling, individual programming, learning centers, and campus schools are in operation. If successful, such alterations in the ways children are grouped or organized for learning will obviate teachers' perceived need to manage children as they now believe they should. Different organization will modify management problems to a significant extent. Of course unforeseen pupil management problems may replace the ones that now plague teachers: classroom noise level, children interfering with the activities of others, getting pupils to attend, and controlling extraneous distractions.

Although today's school psychologist may have an opportunity to contribute to change in educational system design, it is likely that he is working in a school that was designed ten, twenty, or thirty years ago. His task is to help teachers with classroom problems in settings that do not easily lend themselves to modification. Within this framework the school psychologist can serve as an environmental consultant, helping the teacher moderate, if not eliminate, those classroom management problems that are related to classroom organization and the use of physical space.

This approach to school management problems resembles the approaches taken by industrial engineers and industrial and organizational psychologists. In industry time and motion studies, task analyses, analysis of formal and informal organizational systems in operation, and the relationship between working conditions and worker morale have led to the reorganization and redesign of the system to achieve greater worker production, as Edgar H. Schein noted in his book of this series, *Organizational Psychology* (1970). Although insufficient in and of themselves, such analyses contribute to the enhancement of industrial output and efficiency.

In schools the psychologist can observe and analyze the operations of a classroom and suggest ways in which the classroom can be changed to improve instruction, student interest, and student decorum.

Examples of environmental modification. We have already established that Miss Jones has a difficult class. Not only is Lisa difficult to teach and manage but the general atmosphere in the class is frustrating Miss Jones's efforts to teach, and she is concerned that her pupils are not making the academic progress of which they are capable.

Miss Jones's classroom has twenty-eight pupils seated in neat rows in front of her desk. They are seated alphabetically from left to right, beginning with the front row of desks. The sides of the room are painted light gray and crowded with pictures, bulletin boards, and student progress reports put there by Miss Jones to increase student interest. Workbooks and visual aids are piled on a table near the door, in back of the room. Each day the schedule is the same. Children know exactly what to expect. Classroom rules are strictly enforced. Each child must raise his hand to go to the toilet, to sharpen his pencil, or to get a drink of water. No one speaks without the teacher's permission. There is one morning recess of ten minutes and one afternoon recess of ten minutes.

At Miss Jones's request, the school psychologist observes the class for a period of time, noting how children react to different assignments and instructions and how and when they use the equipment on the table in the back of the room. He observes the interaction among the children and tries to get some sense of the ebb and flow of activity, interest level, and fatigue among the children. When major disruptions occur he ob-

serves how they begin and how they are resolved. He conducts sociometric ratings and develops a sociogram that describes which children
are friends, the pattern of pupil leadership in the classroom, and which
children are essentially friendless. He reviews the children's achievement
records. Records of his observations and data are organized and, whenever possible, charted so that a record is available for comparison.

In reviewing his findings, our school psychologist notes that children
in the front row have somewhat higher achievement ratings from Miss
Jones than do children in the last row.[3] He also notices that children almost never look at the classroom walls and that use of materials usually
occurs only at Miss Jones's initiation. Pupils in this classroom are generally attentive for about half of each subject-matter lesson. The afternoons are almost always noisier than the morning sessions. In the early
morning the children tend to ignore Lisa's antics, but they become more
receptive to diversion as the day wears on. Our psychologist also observes that the alphabetical seating arrangement has distributed the
children on a random basis with regard to friendship patterns.

Based on his findings, the school psychologist recommended to Miss
Jones that she:

1. Reorganize her seating arrangement for each subject-matter period in
accordance with her educational goals. He offered to help her find those
arrangements that would group children best for the purposes of learning.
Further, it was recommended that children participate in moving furniture
after each learning period as a way to offer variety and to relieve tension
built up during work periods.

2. Remove the clutter from the classroom walls and designate special
places on them for certain purposes. One wall could be given to the children,
who could post whatever they wanted under the rotating supervision of
pupil leaders.

3. Remove materials and visual aids from the table and store them. Bring
out each day those materials appropriate to the day's activities, inform the
children of what is available, and allow them to use only those materials.

---

[3] This finding is not unusual. Although significant relationships between physical placement in class and school achievement cannot be claimed, it has been
observed (Autry & Barker, 1970) that there is a tendency for alphabetical order
of surname to correlate with high achievement, especially among girls, presumably because of the way children are preferentially grouped according to
the alphabet. Andrew Schwebel (1969), in a study of seating arrangements in
classrooms, found that children assigned by teachers to the front row were
more attentive to classroom activities than their classmates seated in the middle
and back rows.

These kinds of analyses are really part of a more complex ecological theory
and methodology of schools as behavioral settings. For a detailed presentation
of ecological psychology, particularly how school size affects high school student behavior, see Roger G. Barker and Paul V. Gump's book, *Big school,
small school: High school size and student behavior.* Stanford: Stanford U.
Press, 1964.

4. Shorten the instructional periods by ten minutes each, and develop a remedial time in the afternoon during which individual attention can be given to children having academic and emotional-social difficulty. (Lisa would get some special attention during this period and would be away from other children at the time they were most influenced by her behavior.)

5. Every month or so change the order of curriculum presentation. Every week surprise the children by including a special assignment or an extra recess period. Break the pattern only enough to introduce novelty. Keep routine within the established period.

6. Take the sociometric data into consideration in seating arrangements, so that children who "set each other off" are separated and classroom isolates are grouped for part of the time with accepting leaders who are admired by the other children.

7. Seek permission to paint the classroom a more cheerful color.

After a short period of time the psychologist would again observe, note behavior, and compare classroom patterns with his base-line information, and he and Miss Jones would continue to modify the classroom in accordance with her ability to tolerate the changes and, most important, with the actual changes in the behavior of the pupils. The entire procedure would be viewed as experimental by both the school psychologist and Miss Jones. Evidence of success or lack of success would be the basis for further changes.

After graduating from college, Mr. Roberts had as his first teaching assignment a group of children all classified as neurologically impaired. The group contained only eight children, ranging in age from nine to eleven years, but their range in developmental maturity and types of behavior was wide. Children classified as neurologically impaired have the following general characteristics: they tend to have a short attention span, they are overactive, and they seem to be triggered off by small happenings that other children can ignore. It often is difficult to keep them from leaving their seats and wandering around the room. Mr. Roberts, although he had had course work and practice teaching in special education, had a difficult assignment.

Mr. Roberts did well in establishing a warm and friendly relationship with his pupils, and his classroom ran smoothly when he had the children organized and working on specific assignments under his direct supervision. When the time came for a juice break, however, the class erupted into chaos. Mr. Roberts had established the practice of permitting the children to help themselves to juice and cookies, and the result was that all eight children charged about the room, crowding and shoving each other at the table, screeching at each other, and spilling juice on themselves, each other, the table, and the floor. The children then wandered around the room, eating and drinking. Mr. Roberts added his own rather strident voice to the melee, shouting above the children's voices, ordering them to quiet down, and issuing loud threats that he would deprive them of some desired activity if they did not settle down. If this eruptive activity had lasted for only a brief period and had served a needed function by letting the children relax—as Mr. Roberts had hoped—it might not in and of itself have been a bad situation, but such was not the case. After the juice break, the children were stimulated by their own activity into continuing activity. It was almost impossible for the teacher to get the group to settle down. Mr. Roberts knew that something about his procedures was in error, but he could not pinpoint his problem.

The school psychologist, observing Mr. Roberts's class at various times of the day, suggested that the routine of the juice break be modified as follows: (a) all children sitting down; (b) one child appointed to pour juice at each place, with a second appointed to serve cookies; (c) no one was to eat or drink unless sitting down; (d) juice break was to be followed by playground activity, permitting children free physical activity in an appropriate way; (e) playground activity was to be followed by a gradual return to classroom work, allowing a "cooling off" time. As with Miss Jones's class, the school psychologist approached the procedural design as tentative, to be modified further as it was tried.

An engineering approach to management of the classroom environment offers unlimited opportunities for teachers to change the circumstances under which they teach without direct threat to their teaching style or competence. Not only children can benefit and change as the result of alterations of their classroom environment. Alterations enable teachers to improve pupil management problems while they renew their enthusiasm for teaching by a change of pace within a framework with which they find themselves compatible.

Direct Intervention Techniques with Pupils

Direct intervention with pupils can take a number of forms, but in general this section refers to the psychologist's direct interaction with a pupil or pupils. The word *counseling* will be used to indicate one form of this interaction although there is considerable disagreement among both theoreticians and practitioners as to what precise operations occur in counseling.

INDIVIDUAL COUNSELING

Julian Rotter, in *Clinical Psychology* (1971) of the *Foundations of Modern Psychology Series*, described psychotherapy as "planned activity of the psychologist, the purpose of which is to accomplish changes in the individual that make his life adjustment potentially happier, more constructive, or both" [p. 79].

E. L. Tolbert (1959) defined counseling as

a personal, face-to-face relationship between two people, in which the counselor, by means of the relationship and his special competencies, provides a learning situation in which the counselee, a normal sort of person, is helped to know himself and his present and possible future situations so that he can make use of his characteristics and potentialities in a way that is both satisfying to himself and beneficial to society, and further, can learn how to solve future problems and meet future needs [p. 3].

The major difference between these two definitions seems to be in Tolbert's emphasis on counseling "a normal sort of person," whereas psychotherapy can include treatment of all kinds of human problems—from normal developmental problems to psychoses—and all methods that might influence human behavior—from surgery (lobotomy) to medications (tranquilizers, stimulants). Psychotherapy has been used by the practitioners of many different disciplines: psychology, psychiatry, social work, ministry, law. Only physicians may prescribe medication or perform surgery.

One of the reasons we have elected to use the word *counseling* for what transpires between the school psychologist and the pupil is that the word psychotherapy connotes *illness* that must be *diagnosed*, and *treatment* or *therapy* administered to a *patient*. The italicized words all have their origins in the profession of medicine, with emphasis on *disease*. Although it is often estimated that 10 percent or more of the nation's schoolchildren suffer from emotional problems severe enough to warrant direct psychological intervention, perhaps as many as 30 percent could benefit from assistance in solving personal and social problems that affect their behavior in school. The connotation of the existence of severe psychopathology, implicit in the term *psychotherapy*, is justified for only a very small percentage of schoolchildren.

There is another reason for avoiding the word *psychotherapy*, even though it would be difficult to differentiate what transpires in psychotherapy from what happens in counseling. Of all social institutions, the school is the most vulnerable to public scrutiny and criticism. The use of medical or clinical terminology is likely to lead the public to suspect that schools are offering treatment for illness, that a pupil must be ill if he is seeing the psychologist. The public is often unaware of the differences in training between the psychologist and the psychiatrist. Children themselves are even less aware of how helping a pupil with problems that influence his functioning in school is different from treating a child who is ill. If there is one perception of him that the psychologist in the schools usually wishes to avoid, it is that of the threatening "shrink" to whom only sick children are sent.

Educators and frequently psychologists working in the schools view psychotherapy, with its implied emphasis on serious deviation from normal behavior, as a function of the clinic or of the private practitioner. The primary purpose of the schools, however, traditionally continues to be education. From a practical standpoint the terms *counseling* or even *reeducation* are appropriately used to describe professional activities in the school setting.

The word *counseling* is similarly used to describe the kind of interaction that takes place between the counseling psychologist and his client. Although all the elements of what is thought of as therapy may indeed take place, counseling is often done with Tolbert's "normal sort of person" and deals with present and possible future situations, especially those of choice of school, vocation, or employment.

School guidance counselors frequently talk with children about suitable educational programs. In more recent years they have extended their work to include helping the counselee to understand his capabilities, goals, and needs. The counselee then can make use of self-understanding to solve such problems as college admission, relationships with the opposite sex, and getting along with others. This kind of counseling is an accepted part of good guidance programs.

MODELS OF COUNSELING

A number of the theoretical models that describe the development of a relationship between a counselor and a client apply to counseling in schools. Most models suggest that the counselor use methods based on knowledge of personality in an attempt to improve the client's mental health.[4] Julian Rotter (1971) discussed six models, and John G. Watkins (1965) listed twenty-eight procedures that he terms "supportive" and twenty-four others he terms "reconstructive." Supportive procedures aid the client in achieving some insight into problems with a view toward helping him to cope with them adequately; reconstructive procedures are directed at changing the client's characteristic ways of dealing with the stresses of life.

---

[4] Psychotherapeutic and counseling methods are encompassed by a vast and complex literature that cannot adequately be discussed in this section. For a good overview, the reader is referred to a comprehensive discussion of the various psychotherapeutic methods covering 250 pages of double-column, small print in Benjamin B. Wolman (Ed.) *Handbook of clinical psychology.* New York: McGraw-Hill, 1965, and 280 pages in Benjamin B. Wolman (Ed.) *Manual of child psychopathology.* New York: McGraw-Hill, 1972.

The approach used by the psychologist in the school will depend on his training and experience and will probably be tempered by his convictions. Equally effective intervention can result from many different theoretical bases and techniques. Like many clinical psychologists and private practitioners, school psychologists will adopt techniques believed to be effective with each particular child, whose characteristics are highly individualistic.

School psychologists are less likely than clinicians to engage in the in-depth, orthodox Freudian, psychoanalytic approach because its emphases are on understanding the dynamics of unconscious processes deeply rooted in early childhood and on working out subtle aspects of the relationship between therapist and patient (transference and countertransference). The application of such an approach is impractical as well as incompatible to the here-and-now goals of the school.

The nondirective or client-centered approach originally proposed by Carl Rogers (1951) is frequently used with schoolchildren. In this approach the counselor accepts and tries to understand and to clarify what the client says. To help the client develop his own capacity for choice and action, however, the counselor refrains from directing the client or interpreting what the client's statements mean.

Another technique, play therapy, has been found useful with individual children who either lack facility in verbal self-expression or are too young for any kind of talk session. In play therapy, a child selects a play activity or play material and is permitted to manipulate it freely. The child can act out his problems rather than state them. Puppets, doll houses, and dolls representing family members are usually part of the equipment of a play therapy room, as well as paints, clay, and dart boards.

COMMUNITY ATTITUDES TOWARD COUNSELING
IN SCHOOLS

A psychologist employed by a school is sensitive to the attitudes of the community that the school serves. Schools offer the kinds of services that parents and taxpayers want and for which they are willing to pay. Although many states have passed laws that provide partial financial support for psychological services, these laws usually state that the services should consist of psychological assessment for educational placement or the implementation of remedial or educational procedures. Counseling is not mandated by law as part of school psychological services, although many school systems require it of the school psychologist.

Community attitudes are also cogently expressed by the amount of money, beyond the legal minimum, the community is willing to spend on psychological services. Some school districts employ a psychologist part time, virtually ensuring that his time will be spent only on assessment. Large school districts may have only one psychologist on the staff, again predetermining to a large extent the psychologist's allotment of time.

In most instances, the school psychologist does have some say on how he spends his time; and time is a major factor in the decision to offer counseling, especially on an individual basis.

AVAILABILITY OF COMMUNITY RESOURCES

Many school psychologists, with the agreement of the community, administration, and faculty, refer pupils who need intensive counseling to private practitioners or community agencies, such as child guidance clinics. This solution may be appropriate in an affluent community, where private practitioners are likely to be available and where parents can afford their services. In less affluent communities, there may or may not be a public agency, such as a child guidance clinic partially supported by the county and state. In sparsely populated areas and in economically poor regions, the psychologist in the school may be the only professional available. Near the large cities, especially in the Northeast, there is a tradition of psychiatry, psychology, social work, and marriage and vocational counseling. In such areas a number of resources are usually available: community clinics, family counseling services, church-sponsored counseling services, services available through "Y" organizations, and services sponsored by parent groups such as the parents of mentally retarded children, societies for those with learning disabilities, and special schools for the emotionally disturbed, the deaf, and the blind. Despite this impressive list of possible resources, a version of Parkinson's Law seems to operate. The more numerous the facilities, the larger the demand. When outside resources are technically available, the public resources, which are relatively less expensive, are usually understaffed and oversubscribed. Long waiting lists are the rule rather than the exception.

Referral for treatment necessitates, for younger children, the cooperation and interest of parents. Most community agencies that work with children require parental participation for good reasons. Although many parents are willing to cooperate, some are not, since they do not accept the value of therapy. Young children cannot be expected to get to a clinic that may be ten miles from home by themselves.

The children on waiting lists, the children of parents who refuse to cooperate, and the children of parents who cannot or will not get their children to an agency remain in the school, their problems untouched. In those exceptional instances when the school psychologist is the only available resource, he may decide, in the best interests of the child and the school, to engage in long term counseling as the *community mental health resource*. To do so, in our view, is to step out of the role of school psychologist to perform a necessary community service. It is helpful to teachers and administrators to make this distinction: to recognize the special attributes of the school psychologist as well as the occasional need for school personnel to assume essentially nonschool functions for which they are qualified when such personnel are the only available resource.

THE SCHOOL PSYCHOLOGIST'S COMPETENCIES

The traditional training of the psychoanalytic therapist includes self-analysis, and many advocate considerable post-doctoral training to ensure competence. Psychotherapy and/or counseling training requirements are not well defined or agreed upon, but the code of ethics of the American Psychological Association clearly states that a psychologist does not perform services for which he is not adequately trained. School psychologists, because of differing state certification requirements, may or may not have had training in counseling. Those who have had such training must decide to what extent they are competent in handling varying complexities of pupils' problems.

THE SCHOOL PSYCHOLOGIST'S TIME

Very few school psychologists enjoy the luxury of being one of a large staff of service personnel, wherein many psychologists, psychometrists, social workers, and guidance counselors share the workload of assessment, consultation, remediation, and counseling. When a school psychologist decides to see a student in individual counseling, he is committing himself to a sizable time block on a weekly or biweekly basis. As his primary commitment is to the total school, he must decide whether such a large portion of his time can appropriately be spent working with a single pupil.

He must also recognize that counseling in a school situation is different from what it is in a private practitioner's office or in a community clinic, where the "patient's hour" is sacrosanct. Although Dr. Fine has scheduled himself to see Bill every Tuesday at 9:00 A.M. in the junior high school, Dr. Fine may receive a call at 8:30 A.M. Tuesday from the high school principal because there was a fracas on the school bus. Tempers are hot, and the principal needs Dr. Fine immediately to talk with both groups of students involved in the fracas. Or Dr. Fine arrives at the junior high school to see Bill and finds that Bill's teacher is unwilling to excuse the boy from class because of a very important math test. It may seem absurd, but Dr. Fine may find that the only available room that ensures privacy for his counseling session has been appropriated for the day by a photographer for taking students' pictures. Other possible interferences are the numerous holidays enjoyed by public schools, important assembly periods, group testing days, and class trips. It is difficult for a school psychologist, both from his point of view and that of the school, to set aside time for regular, ongoing, individual counseling sessions.

SCHOOL STAFF ATTITUDES TOWARD COUNSELING

Teachers may have developed negative attitudes toward counseling. Perhaps their unrealistically high hopes for a pupil who is being seen regularly by a psychologist were deflated when there were no magical or visible changes in the pupil's troublesome behavior. Perhaps there was indeed a change in the pupil's behavior, but it is one the teacher would judge to be for the worse.

Teachers also have their priorities. Miss Smith schedules her third-grade reading groups between nine and eleven in the morning. On Tuesdays, however, the music teacher arrives; on Thursdays there is a forty-minute art period. On Wednesdays Jim and Jean go for speech therapy, and Tom, Bill, and Rose go for perceptual training. Now she must excuse Leslie for counseling sessions. When are the children supposed to learn reading?

One of the facts of life in schools is that all the pupils' activities are in competition with each other for time, space, and attention. The priorities are determined through policy and through the way the school is organized for teaching. For counseling to have its place in the hierarchy of activities, it needs to be understood by staff and to be offered in ways that do not impinge on other school goals of higher priority.

Teachers and administrators usually seek any service that may help a pupil who is having or causing problems. Sometimes they expect the psychologist to produce through counseling a complete and immediate change in the way the pupil functions. Counseling is interpreted as a special secret way to get children to change. Such faith in the magic of the techniques of counseling is, unfortunately, misplaced. Teachers, although sensitive to how some of their pupils engage in self-defeating behavior, may be less aware that counseling is not a panacea. "Joe is so miserable, he wants so badly to have friends. But he teases others, bothers them, and just does everything that turns others off. Couldn't you just talk to him?" For a school psychologist to give Joe a lecture on how to win friends and influence people is no more likely to be effective than for his parents, teacher, or principal to lecture him.

INDIVIDUAL COUNSELING—SOME EXAMPLES OF WHEN IT IS APPROPRIATE

In spite of all these difficulties, the school psychologist often does decide to offer individual counseling, especially when other services are unavailable and when the particular situation makes him uniquely capable of offering help. Perhaps the aforementioned Joe, who seems to want friends but engages in behavior that antagonizes others, has talked with Dr. Fine, expressed his unhappiness immediately and directly. Finding Dr. Fine understanding and sympathetic, Joe says he would like to talk with the psychologist again. Joe also goes on to describe his parents as harried and preoccupied with the burden of a large family and small income. Although he has tried to talk with his parents, they tell him all he needs to do is stop acting like a baby, study hard, and behave himself. Perhaps Dr. Fine has determined that Joe has above-average potential to do good schoolwork, but he is failing most subjects. Joe is a sensitive boy who feels inadequate. His busy parents have made him, the eldest, responsible for a considerable amount of baby-sitting and care and control of his many younger siblings, and he has never had much opportunity to make friends. He lives in a rural area far from other homes, has never owned a bicycle, has never been able to join Scouts or Little League. His previous teachers have noted that Joe did adequate work in school and was quiet and reserved, and several mentioned that he seemed responsible but that he had no friends. Now that Joe is fifteen and in high school, he is failing and making a nuisance of himself with his teasing, inept attempts to break down a barrier that has become tremendously important to him this year.

All of these factors, plus Joe's rapport with Dr. Fine, his eagerness for help, and the inaccessibility of counseling agencies in the community might lead Dr. Fine to see Joe regularly for counseling. Dr. Fine, in making his decision, must decide what he will give up doing or not have the time to do if he is to see Joe regularly and what alternatives might be available to help Joe.

Cecily is only seven years old, and her second-grade teacher, a warm and caring person, has been completely unable to get Cecily to respond in class. Cecily is new to the school; she and her two older sisters have just moved in with their widowed grandmother. When Mrs. Grand registered the children she gave minimal information, indicating that their parents were separated and that she took in the children, perhaps only temporarily, because her son's wife "ran off and left him with the kids."

The three girls are all under eleven, and guarded comments from the two older girls have given school personnel some suspicions that before their mother left, all three girls were subject to verbal and physical abuse as well as neglect. Dr. Fine might well decide to introduce Cecily to play therapy, in which she would be encouraged to play freely with her own selection of toys and to draw or paint with no criticism. Providing himself as a warm and accepting adult, Dr. Fine hopes that Cecily will begin to feel free to express herself, first through her play. When Cecily feels safe with Dr. Fine, she will begin to express herself to him, then eventually to others. As with Joe, Dr. Fine must gauge his chances of success, the available alternatives to helping Cecily, and what he will exclude from his professional activities in the school.

A school psychologist is always faced with a dilemma, for the time spent each week with a single person inevitably represents an amount of time disproportionate to his responsibilities to the many other children, school personnel, and the community. If he knows that his intervention (individual counseling) may be critical, that he is competent to offer such intervention, and that outside avenues for such help are nonexistent, his concern will make it impossible not to offer whatever assistance he can.

GROUP COUNSELING

Working with a group of persons to facilitate the improvement of their life adjustment probably originated with the military psychologists who started meeting with groups of men occupying the Veterans Administration hospitals after World War II. Group psychotherapy or counseling started as an emergency measure, to allow limited staff to help the many men who needed psychological treatment. It was found to have considerable merit.

Group psychotherapy or counseling is usually limited to between eight and twelve persons (authorities vary) and represents a controlled microcosm of social interaction. Group members are encouraged to express their feelings about themselves and about others. In this way they can learn from feedback of other group members how they are perceived. The group leader moderates, supports, encourages, guides, and controls the situation. The emphasis in group interaction is self-awareness and awareness of one's social impact on others. The rationale is that psychological problems are based in problems of interpersonal relationships and that one can learn, in a small, controlled situation, not only how and why one behaves with others as one does but also new and more appropriate ways of behaving.

Small group interaction has its roots in the theoretical assumptions of of Alfred Adler. Originally a disciple of Sigmund Freud, Adler broke away primarily because he disagreed with Freud's ideas about unconscious motivation. Adler was impressed by the effect of social learning upon a person's adjustment and proposed ways of exploring the improvement of social interaction through group sessions.

Recently, as people have become aware of the tremendous pressures of a rapidly changing society, a myriad of techniques for working in groups has developed. Most of them are designed to help persons who are essentially normal but troubled about their life adjustment. The appeal of these groups has been enormous, and the popular press and television have made us aware of such terms as encounter groups, marathons, body awareness, the primal scream, and sensitivity training. Techniques are even marketed for amateurs to conduct group sessions with their guests for social entertainment. Many of these new groups are conducted by nonprofessionals or semiprofessionals; many psychologists have serious reservations about the possible effects of encouraging members of a group to express anger and hostility without the moderation and control of a trained professional.

GROUP COUNSELING IN SCHOOLS

For a school psychologist to meet regularly with a group of pupils rather than with each of them individually immediately extends his ability to implement direct intervention. All the earlier considerations about community attitudes, school staff attitudes, and the psychologist's own competencies are perhaps sharpened in the case of group counseling. Precisely because the long-term effectiveness of group work is not yet documented and because some of the more extreme, even bizarre, group techniques have been publicized, many thoughtful school administrators, parents, teachers, and school psychologists themselves have reservations about the appropriateness of group work in the schools.

Confidentiality becomes a serious consideration in the schools. Groups of adults may meet with their group leader and agree that what goes on within the group is confidential. Even with adults, however, this agreement is occasionally broken, with resulting publicity and occasional lawsuits. Although a group of pupils meeting with the school psychologist may solemnly agree to maintain strict confidentiality, such confidentiality is very difficult to maintain in a school setting.

It may be useful and helpful for a small group of high school students to express their anger and hostility toward the English teacher in colorful language. If out-of-context fragments of what was said get back to that English teacher, however, neither the teacher nor the students are likely to enjoy positive results. If students berate their parents, and parents get the impression that the group is being used to encourage a general attitude of hate for parents, they may, to put it mildly, object.

Some years ago, when group work was relatively untried in the schools, a young school psychologist decided to implement group techniques with a small group of adolescent boys deemed disruptive and unmanageable by their teachers. These techniques were based on work by S. R. Slavson (Schiffer, 1958) and provided a variety of materials such as workbenches, hammers, saws, and the like to be used freely as a way to release pent-up feelings. Unfortunately, the boys carried over their unmanageable and disruptive behavior from the classroom to the activity room, and the permissive attitude in the group situation gave them license to be more disruptive. Yelling invectives at each other and at the psychologist, they smashed and hurled materials with excited vigor despite the psychologist's efforts to set limits. The noise level was such that the rest of the school could hardly be unaware of the uproar. The psychologist discontinued the sessions after the third melee, probably just minutes before the school superintendent decided to order him to cease and desist. The moral is that certain kinds of techniques must be carefully used and that the participants in a school group must be carefully selected.

School psychologists have worked effectively with different kinds of groups and with pupils of varying age levels. Groups of high school underachievers—students who have good learning potential but who receive poor grades—usually have the qualities that are likely to lead them to gain from such an experience according to research in intervention techniques [Luborsky, Auerbach, Chandler, Cohen, & Bachrach, 1971]. Joe, the possible candidate for individual counseling with Dr. Fine, could also be a candidate for such a group, after or in conjunction with individual sessions. The play therapy that Dr. Fine used with Cecily could also be extended to include a small group of children, especially after Cecily had developed some confidence and sense of security from her individual sessions.

Robert Myrick and Donald Kelly, Jr. (1971) described a successful small group counseling experiment. A first-grade boy, Victor, was referred because he was restless, disruptive, and inattentive and because he was not learning. Victor shared a counseling experience with two other first-grade children, Jimmy and Linda. Jimmy was creative, likeable, and a class leader. Linda was cooperative with the teacher and well liked by her classmates, although she was a "giggler" and sometimes careless. The counselor met with the three children for a half-hour on five consecutive days. His technique focused on developing listening and attending skills; then he emphasized how the children felt about each other's behavior. At the same time, an observer recorded Victor's behavior in the regular classroom. He found that Victor's attending behavior in class increased enormously and continued to increase even after the counseling sessions were discontinued. Victor not only became less disruptive but he also accomplished more schoolwork. Such short-term group counseling has pragmatic value for the school psychologist, both in terms of his limited time and of the vicissitudes of school schedules.

Another school psychologist was working in a racially integrated high school in which violence between groups of black and white students was increasing. The psychologist at first formed two groups: one of those identified as leaders of the black students, the other of those identified as leaders of the white students. As it is generally agreed that participation in groups should be voluntary, this school psychologist, when asking the leaders to meet with him, suggested they bring a couple of friends with them, as coming alone might discourage attendance. After meeting with each group separately for a few sessions to discuss its problems and antagonisms, the psychologist suggested merging the two groups (both were small) for mutual discussion. Fantastic success cannot be claimed for this particular project, but at least the leaders of both groups were able to express and explore their anger toward each other without physical violence. Hopefully, both groups gained some understanding of each other's problems and behavior.

Eli M. Bower (1967), on the basis of his work in the California schools, suggested that school psychologists use a variety of techniques with very carefully selected groups of adolescents. A balance should be achieved so that the groups include hostile participants and withdrawn participants but not anyone who shows an extreme of either behavior. A consensus of the students' concerns is obtained; then role playing, films, and discussion of real-life needs are used to focus parent-child relationships, boy-girl relationships, jobs, and learning how to study. Bower also suggested that more severely disturbed adolescents can be engaged in a group, sometimes in addition to individual counseling. The group techniques used with more disturbed adolescents are those that encourage the expression of feelings and the gaining of insight into interpersonal relationships.

There are many ways for the school psychologist to offer direct intervention with pupils through group counseling. Although success can no more be guaranteed than it can in individual counseling, group counseling does permit the psychologist to offer direct help to more students than does individual counseling. In many instances group counseling may be the technique of choice for certain students.

WHEN CRISES OCCUR

Throughout our lives there are decisive or crucial times or events that are turning points. As a result of what happens during these critical periods or episodes, we are never quite the same again.

Sometimes these crises are so severe that they literally determine our success or failure as persons. The death of a loved one, a serious automobile accident that causes physical handicaps, a severe wound in combat are examples of such extreme events.

There are also periods in our lives that are crises in our development. Although not as sudden or as severe as those just mentioned, they constitute periods of time in which we are continually under stress, seeking new ways to handle unfamiliar situations. Examples of such periods might be the adolescent years and marriage, including the months just before and just after the ceremony and when the first child is born.

There are also events in our lives, common to many of us, that are characteristically stressful and that require us to make drastic readjustments. Entering school for the first time, moving to a new town, and starting college might be examples. Whenever we are called upon to make changes—to shift from some known means to solve problems to some unknown means—we are faced with a crisis of sorts. Whenever our behavior results in actions by others that are out of our control but that affect our subsequent behavior, we must react to what has happened. For instance, if we disobey a school rule and are given detention, we must react to that restriction of our behavior. Depending on what we subsequently do, other actions are set off, and a chain of events occurs that either solves a problem for us or creates further problems. If we accept the detention, we may get a demerit on our record; but the incident (crisis) is soon over, and life moves on, influenced relatively little by the event. If we do not go to the detention room, then we are given further detentions. Perhaps we are eventually suspended from school, and our parents are called in to meet the principal. If the issue remains unresolved, we might be expelled from school. Exclusive of the justice of such a chain of events, our behavior in this instance has precipitated a crisis of great magnitude.

Much of what happens in school has the potential to precipitate crises in pupils and in personnel. Throughout the school day, pupils are presented with new material to which they must react. A failure to complete yesterday's homework not only creates problems for today's assignments but also incurs the anger or concern of the teachers. A pending test produces anxiety that interferes with the pupil's ability to concentrate on the work of the day. A clique forms and John is not included. Al is not selected for the football team, and this matters more to him at the time than almost anything else. A teacher insensitively comments on the laziness of the poor, unaware of the financial plight of Tom's family. Mary fears she is pregnant and fears even more that others will notice and talk about her. Mr. Thompson has been told by the principal that he will not be considered for tenure unless he does a better job of motivating classes to learn. In myriad ways, crises occur throughout the school day. School is life, and life requires constant adjustment.

Most of these crises do not surface dramatically; but when they do, they present serious problems not only for those concerned but also for those around them. Schools are public places. Behavior is invariably performed in front of others. When a crisis occurs in a school, its power to disrupt other activities cannot be minimized. A child who hits a teacher sets off feelings in others that heighten the potential for them to become anxious or aggressive. A shoving match between a white pupil and a black pupil can mobilize latent reactions that are part of the crises of others, both personal and social, and thus can result in a racial disturbance. A suicide attempt can produce hysterical reactions in others.

What is most important about these crises is their potential to produce change in those involved. The resolution of a crisis can be an important experience, either for better or for worse. Having faced a difficult situation and coped with it, one gains both confidence and new skills for solving future problems; or one can suffer enormously, lose self-esteem, and be less able to handle new situations as they arise.

Gerald Caplan, director of the Laboratory of Community Psychiatry at the Harvard Medical School, has written extensively about crisis intervention and has helped to present a framework in which to understand how crises are resolved [Caplan, 1963]. He pointed out that children in temporary states of turmoil (up to four to six weeks) are certainly emotionally disturbed or cognitively disoriented, but they should not necessarily be thought of as ill or emotionally disordered. It is best to realize that they are struggling with problems that appear insoluble to them at the time. They may well show symptoms of stress: confusion, a rise of tension, and a variety of negative feelings including anxiety, anger, guilt, frustration, and depression. During crises, individuals are in disequilibrium and therefore are more easily influenced—more vulnerable—than at other times. Most often, crises are resolved in some way, with or without intervention from others. The symptoms disappear, and the individual achieves new equilibrium. What may not be immediately discernible, however, is the learning that took place during the crisis period. How the individual handled the crisis has import for how he will handle his affairs in the future. Some people solve their problems in effective ways and achieve a "reality-based, culturally acceptable pattern of adjustment and adaptation" [p. 526]. These persons emerge from their crisis better able to solve problems. During their crisis they developed better problem-solving methods and more confidence, thereby increasing their ability to master new stresses successfully in the future. Others do not cope adequately with their crises. They emerge less able to handle problems. As successive crises occur, as they inevitably must, the history of resolution of previous crises becomes noticeable.

> The previous history of a mentally healthy individual shows that he has passed through a succession of crises . . . . At each of these crises a more or less significant development of his personality occurred. The improvement in his capacity to deal with life in healthy ways has occurred in a series of spurts, and during each crisis a personality enrichment took place.
>
> In contrast, the history of a mentally unhealthy individual shows a series of crisis way stations, at each of which wrong paths were taken, so that his personality developed more and more significant weaknesses, until a "straw broke the camel's back," and he emerged from a particular crisis with an overt illness. Looking back at his life, it can be conceived that on a number of occasions it might have been possible for him to have chosen different coping mechanisms and to have taken a healthier path in his life trajectory [Caplan, 1963, p. 527].

The school psychologist may be asked to assist with personal crises as they occur in school. Although the school may want no more at the moment than to "put out the fire," the psychologist views each opportunity to intervene in a crisis as a way to influence personal development positively and to prevent further breakdown in the ability to cope successfully. Successful intervention during a crisis period has a higher "payoff" than at other times. What might take months to accomplish in counseling or in remedial efforts during less stressful times may be acccomplished relatively quickly in successful crisis intervention.

METHODS OF CRISIS INTERVENTION

There is no one way in which crises are best handled in the school. As in psychiatry, where emergency psychotherapy is used in hospitals and in mental health clinics to deal with immediate emotional problems (Bellak & Small, 1965), the immediate goals of crisis intervention are to provide the quickest possible relief, to ameliorate or to remove specific symptoms, and to permit the person to continue to function. In schools, there is the additional goal of helping the pupil to deal with possible infractions of school rules, with the reactions of others toward the crisis behavior, and with other reality-based considerations related to attending school. In situations in which crises have excited the interest of others, the pupil must be removed to a place where he can "cool down." William Morse pointed out (1971), however, that a pupil can "cool down" so much that the opportunity to help him resolve the crisis may be lost. In situations where the crisis is internal and not made known to others through acting-out behavior, it is important to identify those pupils most likely to be in crises and make time available to them so that their concerns can be aired. The child entering his first year of high school in an academically oriented community, who is two weeks late, and who comes from another community 2,000 miles away with a mediocre grade record may not have a temper tantrum in class; but it is highly probable that he will be in a state of crisis for at least some time.

To educate teachers to be familiar with crisis theory and to identify those most likely to be in crisis states is one excellent way for school psychologists to locate these children with whom they might work. Consulting with teachers to help them to handle crises is also possible. In this section, attention will be given to approaches which can be used by the school psychologist or others who have training in direct intervention in crisis situations.

THE LIFE-SPACE INTERVIEW

The approach to crisis intervention most applicable to the schools is called the life-space interview. It was developed and described by Fritz Redl (1966), based on work in residential facilities for emotionally disturbed boys. (Its application to other kinds of school situations has been described in a volume edited by Ruth G. Newman and Marjorie M. Keith, 1963). It is Redl's contention that a child in trouble cannot wait until his therapy hour five days hence, but that he needs therapeutic attention on the spot. He differentiates two categories of goals for life-space interviewing and then describes a number of tasks that are necessary for these goals to be accomplished. Redl's goals and tasks are most appropriate in residential facilities where student/teacher ratios are favorable and where a therapeutic atmosphere exists. Still, they can be applied with modifications to regular schools.

Clinical exploitation of life events. Here the goal is to pull out of a life experience (such as one that might take place in a classroom, the lunchroom, or the halls of a school), whatever clinical gain might be possible:

a. Reality rub-in refers to helping children to understand what is really happening around them at the time, so that misinterpretations and actions based on misinterpretations can be minimized.

b. Symptom estrangement is concerned with helping children to let go of their maladaptive symptoms by providing insight and support.

c. Massaging numb value areas is Redl's way of describing attempts to help children to use positive values that they are not using for various reasons, such as peer-group pressure or erroneous notions of manliness.

Appeals to "fairness," for instance, may be acceptable to children within their value system but may not be used to solve problems. Life-space interviewing might be aimed at helping a child to use values that would not otherwise be available to him for problem solving.

d. New tool salesmanship refers to attempts to point out to the youngster the inadequacy of his defenses and to help him to substitute and try out better mechanisms that increase the chances of adaptation.

e. Manipulation of the boundaries of the self includes all those attempts in the interview to encourage trying out new roles, roles that increase feelings of worthiness and pride in self and that permit the child to engage unfamiliar people and groups.

Emotional first aid on the spot. There are problems that children cannot manage well on their own and that may call the children to the attention of the teacher or the principal. Crisis theory as developed by Gerald Caplan probably has more pertinence to this goal than to the one already described.

a. Drain-off of frustration acidity is Redl's graphic description of those aspects of the interview that are cathartic; that is, they permit the child to talk about his negative feelings or discomfort in the safety of the interview so that expression will, in and of itself, relieve the feelings and lessen the chances that the child will need to act them out.

b. Support for the management of panic, fury, and guilt refers to having an adult with the child when he is experiencing panic, having a temper tantrum, expressing his anger, or being anxious. The attending adult offers support toward management by his presence, tries to help the child "put things back into focus and proportion" (Redl, 1966, p. 49), and helps him to get back to the day's activities.

c. Communication maintenance in moments of relationship decay is an attempt to keep the child from breaking off communication with others and retreating to the use of fantasy as a means to handle his concerns.

d. Regulation of behavioral and social traffic refers to the adult's keeping the child aware of the rules to be followed, the consequences of his behavior, and the structure of the life he will lead.

*e. Umpire services—in decision crises as well as in loaded transactions—*refers to assisting the child in choosing with discretion among the choices available to him. Redl likens the role to that of a good friend "whom we ourselves might take along shopping, hoping he would help maintain more vision and balance in the weighing of passionate desire versus economic reason than we might be capable of in the moment of decision-making" [p. 51].

The goals and tasks of life-space interviewing may vary from interview to interview. The tasks are also applicable to situations that can only be loosely considered as interviews, such as a brief encounter in the hall or a short conversation in a classroom. The techniques needed in life-space interviewing are as complex as those required of therapists and professional counselors, despite the seeming simplicity of the tasks to be performed.

THE PSYCHOSITUATIONAL INTERVIEW

Psychosituational assessment is another approach that can be used in crisis intervention. A crisis may be precipitated by the actions of others toward a child. Expectations of him and impressions as to the meaning of his behavior may create intolerable pressures on a child, to which he may react badly. The crises, in these instances, are crises of helplessness in which the child can find no way to meet the demands made upon him. Unless those around him, teacher or parent, can be persuaded or helped to relieve the pressure, the child virtually has no choice but to use ineffective coping mechanisms, moving him further and further toward unsuccessful patterns of response to stress.

An interview approach has been developed to deal expressly with instances in which the situation in which someone finds himself leads him to behave in particular ways. Donald N. Bersoff and Russell M. Grieger (1971) described an interview approach to the psychosocial assessment of children's behavior in which the focus is on the analysis of behavior and the antecedent and consequent conditions that produce, reinforce, and perpetuate that behavior. They are also concerned with an analysis of the expectations, attitudes, and emotions of others who are concerned about the child's behavior. The interview strategy requires the interviewer to pinpoint the actual behaviors about which concern is expressed, the environments and situations in which the behavior appears or does not appear, and the consequent contingencies that may serve to perpetuate the behavior. The approach is data oriented and behavioral and leads to the detection of beliefs that are not supported by facts (irrational ideas) and eventually to practical recommendations for changing the situation, again in very specific behavioral terms.

Bersoff and Grieger (1971) cited a case that is quoted here in its entirety to give the flavor of the psychosituational approach to crisis intervention:

A 13-year-old child was referred because of academic difficulties. He was in the sixth grade, doing poorly, and had already experienced one retention. Both parents were seen together in the initial interview. Three times in the first ten minutes of the interview the father suggesed that the root of the problem lay in his son's laziness. After the third assertion to this effect, the interviewer stated, "I cannot treat laziness, but I can work with the behaviors that lead you to say that he is lazy. Please tell me what he does that causes you to say he is lazy." The father responded, "Well, he never does his homework."

Such a specific behavioral response in place of what seemed an overgeneralization was quickly and strongly reinforced: "Good, what else does he do that makes you say he is lazy?" The interviewer was prepared for a long list, but neither the father nor the mother could think of anything else that could be labeled as "lazy" behavior. The issue was pressed, but no further indications were forthcoming. The interviewer then pursued the statement, "He never does his homework." The word "never" denotes frequency quite explicitly, but because that determination was somewhat suspect the statement was questioned further:

INTERVIEWER: In the course of the week, how often does he fail to do his homework?

FATHER: Maybe once or twice.

I: So, once or twice a week he doesn't do his homework at all. Does he complete it the rest of the time?

F: Well, it's not that he doesn't do it all. It's just that he doesn't get it finished before he has to go to bed.

I: And, how often doesn't he get it finished?

And so the interview proceeded. The final specification of the statement that the boy was lazy came down to the fact that on about two nights a week he did not complete his homework before bedtime, that about once every two weeks he did not do his homework at all, and that on all other nights he completed it [pp. 485–86].[5]

This kind of interviewing not only defines the target problems but offers the possibility that the perceptions of the interviewees might change sufficiently to moderate the stress that their attitudes and expectations are creating in the child.

THE ECLECTIC APPROACH

It has often been pointed out that no one set of rules or procedures will apply to all school psychologists. Not only do their training and theoretical orientation vary but they tend as a group to be eclectic and experimental in their approaches. Some school psychologists report the effectiveness of intervention based on Redl's exploitation of life events, reality rub-in, with an overtone of Caplan's crisis intervention and Albert Ellis's rational-emotive therapy.

For example: Jim, a high school junior, has a history of suspensions for his provocative "talking back" to teachers in socially unacceptable language when being reprimanded for any number of offenses, such as not doing his work, talking to others, and starting fights. Sullen and muttering imprecations, he sits in Dr. Fine's office. Dr. Fine might confront Jim directly with, "Jim, what do you really *want*?" Jim may well reply that he would like nothing better than to perform an intricate series of tortures upon Mr. Jones, his history teacher. While he's at it, he might introduce a few other faculty to the rack, including the vice-principal (in charge of discipline). Dr. Fine would then attempt, by direct confrontation, to get Jim to state what his goals in life really are and what the alternative ways to reach these goals are.

If Jim really wants to remain in school (and many Jims really do) and to get certain faculty off his back, what can he do? Such interviews, sometimes with further intervention by the psychologist with teachers, frequently help the student come to terms with the inevitable consequences of certain behaviors. Sometimes a form of contract can be set up: Jim will agree to attempt to curb his language if Mr. Jones will agree to stop certain sarcastic reprimands.

Another technique that is sometimes effective in a crisis situation is role playing. Dr. Fine could, for example, take Jim's role, asking Jim to play the role of Mr. Jones. Together they could reenact the incident. Or, the two girls who have just been separated from a slapping, hair-pulling fight in the hall could be asked to reverse their roles and reenact the events that led to the fight. These techniques, oversimplified for the purpose of brief presentation, are based on the assumption that the reversal of roles will enable the disgruntled student to gain some insight into how his behaviors and feelings cause certain reactions in others.

When a student is referred for an academic problem, it is frequently helpful for the psychologist to institute direct intervention immediately following a psychological assessment. The psychologist can give the student some immediate feedback about the way he approaches cognitive tasks and about the areas of his relative strengths and weaknesses. The psychologist can do some planning with the student about ways to go about mastering academic tasks.

When the family situation seems to be an important element in a student's problem, a family conference is sometimes helpful. The psychologist carefully and sensitively leads the discussion to areas of difficulty in an effort to help parents to see how their actions are perceived by their son or daughter. This kind of conference also often leads to a kind of contract between parents and child.

VARIETY OF CRISES

As inevitably happens in school psychology, crisis intervention by the school psychologist takes on almost as many forms as there are problems to be resolved. Although crisis-oriented interviewing would be the choice of the psychologist faced with a child in immediate difficulty, it is necessary in schools to intervene in ways that cannot be confined to any one set of techniques. The school psychologist may find himself talking to several students together who all are antagonistic to one another. He may be asked to meet with irate parents and a frightened child in the principal's office, with the principal present. He may find himself at one end of a telephone with a child threatening suicide at the other. A teacher and a pupil may have reached a point at which neither is rational about a situation, both wanting to punish the other for supposed injustices. There is no end to the kinds of crises that occur in schools in which the school psychologist may become involved. In each instance, his background in individual and group counseling and in crisis techniques and his knowledge that each of these situations leads to either positive or negative change guide his professional behavior.

Referral to Community Services

Some children have problems that cannot be adequately handled by their teachers, even with the resources of special services and supplementary instruction. The number of problems that are *best* handled by referral to an agency, institution, or practitioner outside the school is probably smaller than many teachers think and greater than can be accommodated by existing community and state agencies and facilities. As already indicated, a substantial proportion of teachers request psychological services to have children "treated" by someone else or to remove troublesome children from the classroom. These teachers may not be satisfied with attempts within the school to modify the child's behavior and may believe that experts can change the way the child acts or that the child would be better off elsewhere. The belief in the curative powers of nonschool professionals, particularly mental health professionals, and in the restorative qualities of residential schools and institutions often is greater than is justified. Most community agencies, such as child guidance centers, social service agencies, and residential and day-school facilities for children with problems and special needs, are oversubscribed and have waiting lists. If a referral is made, there is little assurance of prompt attention. If there is prompt attention, there is no assurance of success if success means the child is changed in drastic ways.

Therefore, a child with a complex problem, the nature of which may indicate out-of-school assistance, poses a dilemma of great magnitude. The school psychologist may find himself caught between the ire of a teacher who has reached the end of her patience with the child and is no longer willing, or perhaps able, to work with him, and the lack of adequate facilities in the community. Yet the child is a pupil in the school. Even if community facilities do exist and can be of immediate assistance, it is not very likely that out-of-school assistance will change the child's behavior rapidly, if at all. Unless a child is removed from the school and sent elsewhere, there is little choice for the school but to cope with and to try to help the child. Referrals do not offer relief to teachers. They only offer hope that complex problems may eventually be mitigated. It is for these reasons that this book concentrates on how to help children in school and how to help teachers and administrators to better understand and to handle that which cannot be wished away.

INVOLVEMENT OF PARENTS

Let us suppose that it is determined that a child can benefit from referral to a community agency or resource. The school then contacts the child's parents to suggest referral, to help them to understand why a community service can be helpful, and to arrange for it to take place. On the surface a recommendation to parents that their child needs help may appear to be an innocuous procedure, relatively simple to arrange. In actuality it is a sensitive and difficult process for both parents and psychologist.

For the school psychologist, the task is to convince the parents that help is needed and to make them want to seek assistance. As William J. Ruzicka (1967) pointed out, *initiating* parental cooperation is not the same as *developing* or *maintaining* ongoing relationships. The assignment involves selling oneself and community services before any beneficial results can be seen by the parents. The psychologist makes recommendations based on facts about the child and knowledge of community resources, and he helps parents to see potential, practical outcomes without inspiring false hopes. At the same time he must recognize and deal with the anguish, concern, or perhaps indignation and anger generated by the referral. This complex counseling function is often handled in only one counseling session. Failure to sufficiently motivate the parents to cooperate usually means the end of a promising source of assistance for the child. The considerable effort leading to the decision to refer is blocked, and the school must seek alternative ways to help the child. Under these circumstances it is easily understood that the psychologist is under pressure to achieve results.

For the parents recommendation for referral means many things. For some it is a kind of open acknowledgment of parental failure or bringing family concerns to the fore that were not previously shared with others. It generates anxiety and guilt. It arouses defensiveness; some parents may criticize the school for its failures and their child's teachers for "making trouble," and others may rationalize the seriousness of the situation.

There is evidence that the nature of the referral also influences the outcome of the referral process. Anthony Conti (1971, 1972) has demonstrated that parents tend to respond favorably to referrals to clinics and/or schools for special evaluation and education for the severely mentally retarded, the physically handicapped, for children with multiple learning disabilities, and for severely emotionally disturbed children who require residential placement. They tend to respond unfavorably to referral to counseling services within the community. In other words, when the child's problems can be viewed primarily as his own and the child is visibly deviant (as with severe mental retardation or physical handicap), parents tend to recognize the need for out-of-school assistance, to accept referral, and to follow through. When the problem is less manifest and involves not only the child but parent-child relationships as well, parents are less inclined to accept the initial referral. If they do follow through and make contact with a community service, often because of school pressure, they tend not to maintain contact beyond more than one or two interviews. Further, in cases referred to counseling services, contact is less likely if the family is described as coming from lower socioeconomic strata (low educational level and manual employment). In these instances, it is extremely difficult to involve both parents in the referral and actual treatment. According to Conti's surveys, given the most favorable circumstances possible, it can be anticipated that about half of all referrals made by the school psychologist for counseling or psychotherapy will not be accepted by parents or will terminate before real assistance can be offered.

It is no wonder then that Milton Kornrich (1965) can offer these examples of parental responses to recommendations to accept a psychotherapy referral:

"(a) Maybe it's just the stage he's in. He'll grow out of it; (b) We can't afford it; (c) I hear your tests aren't that good; (d) My religion is against it; (e) Won't this stigmatize him? (e.g., college, job); (f) I know someone who went. It didn't help; . . . I'll 'think about it' " [p. 275].

Although there is just a grain of truth in each of these responses, the point being made is that parents are uncomfortable with assistance that has implications for their manner of functioning and child-rearing practices. If it is beneficial for them to accept such assistance, careful attention should be given to helping them to deal with their defensiveness and to methods for expediting referrals.

INVOLVEMENT OF SCHOOL PERSONNEL

It should also be noted that school psychologists spend a considerable part of their time counseling families to contact and to use services offered by outside agencies [Hoedt & Farling, 1971]. When families fail to follow through, a substantial portion of the school psychologist's time may have been wasted. Although it has been argued that failure to follow through is not the psychologist's fault (Roberts & Solomons, 1970), the fact remains that the precious little time the psychologist has to give to the many problems presented to him has been ill-used if he seeks to make a referral and parents decide not to cooperate. Not only have his efforts come to nothing, but ways the school may have been able to help to moderate or to contain the problem may not have been given attention.

When a recommendation for referral to an outside service is made, particularly for psychotherapy, the teachers and the administrator must know that such referral will not offer immediate relief to the school. As his special contribution to differential assessment leading to referral, the school psychologist should consider an estimate of the probability of follow-through by the parents and the receptivity of the service to the problem the case presents. Thought must be given to means to help the parents to accept the referral, with consideration for their needs and concerns as well as for the concerns of the school.

What appears to be a simple procedure—the referral of a child to a clinic, agency, or practitioner for help that cannot be offered easily or at all by the school—is a profoundly complicated matter, requiring compassion and skill. School psychologists and other special services personnel can do a great service for local agencies and private practitioners by seriously, thoughtfully, and painstakingly screening and preparing children and parents for referral. Our society, sadly enough, has not yet given high priority to the care of its children, particularly to the psychological aspects of child care [Joint Commission on Mental Health of Children, 1970]. Community services are typically in short supply, understaffed, and oversubscribed. Careful preparation of referrals by school personnel can help improve both the caseload and the efficiency of community services. In any event, schools find themselves responsible for the education and welfare of all but a small percentage of children who can truly profit from education and treatment out of the community as in a residential treatment center.

Most referrals should be seen as ways to increase the opportunities for helping children, *coupled* with the school's attempt to do the same. Community services are not alternatives to action by the school; they are resources, as is the school psychologist himself. There is virtually no way for school personnel to delegate full responsibility for a child to others in the community. Understanding this fact helps to explain why it is so important that teachers and school administrators accept the charge that schools serve all children and youth. As former President Harry Truman used to say, "The buck stops here."

Teacher Consultation and Education

chapter five

Consultation with teachers is the single most important function of the school psychologist. This point of view is consistent with the belief that preventive effort in mental health (prevention of pathogenic occurrences and preparation for the solution of critical problems) is ultimately the best approach to problems that beset people when they become adults in a fast and ever changing society; it is consistent with the belief that schools are influential in determining how children learn, grow, and develop; and it is consistent with the belief that teachers have unique opportunities to help children solve problems. The school psychologist can, through consultation with teachers, help to improve attitudes and promote techniques that are helpful to children.

Gerald Caplan (*The theory and practice of mental health consultation*, 1970) pointed out that the term *consultation* is generally used to apply to almost any activity carried out by a profession. In England the office of a physician is known as his "consulting room," and to be told by any professional's secretary that he is "in consultation" means that he is engaged in any one of a variety of activities: college faculty with colleagues, a lawyer with his client, a pediatrician with a mother. As Caplan suggested, mental health consultation can also be defined in a more restricted sense. Teacher consultation can be used to define a process of interaction between two professional persons, the school psychologist and the teacher. Such interaction consists of the consultant's (the psychologist) helping in regard to a current work problem in which the consultant has specialized competence.

In this chapter the word *consultation* is used to mean that the school psychologist is the specialist, and the teacher (or other school personnel) is the consultee. As Caplan (1970) wrote:

> The consultant engages in the activity not only in order to help the consultee with his current work problem in relation to a specific client or program but also in order to add to the consultee's knowledge and to lessen areas of misunderstanding, so that he (the consultee) may be able in the future to deal more effectively on his own with this category of problem [p. 20].

Caplan's discussion included some characteristics of mental health consultation that are particularly appropriate when the school psychologist is consultant: the consultant must have expert knowledge in the areas of consultation; the consultant has no administrative responsibility for the consultee's work; and consultation does not focus overtly on the personal problems and feelings of the consultee—it respects the privacy of the consultee. Although the aim of consultation is to improve the consultee's job performance and not his sense of well-being, the two are linked; and a consultee's feelings of personal adequacy will probably be increased by successful consultation. Thus, consultation may have the secondary effect of being therapeutic to the consultee.

Despite its ultimate goal (to eliminate the need for consultation in specific problem areas), successful consultation is expected to continue indefinitely as other problem areas are identified. As teachers become more competent and sophisticated, they are also likely to recognize an increasing number of problems and to ask for additional consultation. It has been noted, for example, that when a school psychologist functions effectively, more problems are referred to him.

The basic relationship between consultant and consultee is that of two professionals with different but coordinate specialties. The consultant exerts influence, not authority. If the consultant attempts to be authoritarian, there are two possible unsatisfactory results—depending on the nature of the authority-subordinate relationship. If the consultant is subtly authoritarian, exuding supreme confidence and issuing his dictates in a kindly and winning way, he is likely to foster the consultee's dependence on him. Such dependence negates the possibility of the consultee's ability to deal effectively with problems on his own. On the other hand, if the consultant is overtly and directly authoritarian, he negates the influence of his ideas; for a man convinced against his will remains unconvinced still. Psychotherapists have long recognized that their clients do not improve simply because the therapist orders them to change behavior or attitudes. The consultant school psychologist must be aware of the dangers of both types of authoritarian attitudes.

In general, consultation (as the term is used in this book) includes awareness of teachers' differing ways of coping and differing personality assets and liabilities; but it does not focus directly on these characteristics or problems. Rather, the consultant school psychologist focuses on the professional problem, even if the consultee is displacing his personal problems onto the work setting. The school psychologist does not ignore the feelings of the consultee, but he does distinguish between direct discussion of a teacher's personal problems and taking such problems into consideration when dealing with a work problem.

The school psychologist as a consultant performs this service in a variety of ways and reacts to the particular problem or kind of problem presented by the school or by some of its personnel. Donald L. Williams (1972) suggested four role dimensions for the consultant: the use of substantive material in the area of the consultants' expertise; his unique qualities as a person; his ability to model the behavior he wishes to have emulated; and his skill as a catalyst or facilitator. Consultation can be individual or group, direct or indirect, formal or informal, spontaneous or planned. The first type of consultation discussed is the prearranged, relatively formal approach.

In-Service Education

Mental health consultants often make a distinction between education and consultation. The kind of teacher education to be discussed, however, is really a form of consultation in which more traditional educational methods are deliberately used to provide background information as a basis for more direct interaction with teachers and to set the stage for regular, preplanned meetings of groups of teachers with the school psychologist. In-service education should not manifest itself with teachers sitting passively in a classroom, listening to a lecture. Such didactic tactics are rarely effective. In-service education as a form of consultation usually involves considerable teacher participation.

EXAMPLES OF IN-SERVICE
EDUCATION-CONSULTATION

One school district has a "Tuesday Afternoon Program." During the entire school year the students are excused on Tuesday afternoons, and a variety of teacher activities take place. This particular school district has a number of self-selected (teacher) groups in which administrators, custodians, secretaries, cafeteria workers, board of education members, and teachers participate. Some teachers participate with selected pupils in nondirective play activities supervised by the psychologists. This enables teachers to gain insight into children's behavior in a nonschool-type nonauthoritarian setting. One-way mirrors, permitting observation of the playroom, are part of the school facilities. These play sessions are first conducted by the school psychologist, with teachers observing through the one-way mirror. Later, as individual teachers start working with children, the school psychologist and other teachers observe. Group discussion follows the play activity.

Other school psychologists in this progressive system work with other groups: one meets with a group of high school teachers to discuss ways of handling the incidence of drug abuse; another group discusses racial tensions. Still another school psychologist meets with a group planning curriculum changes in the elementary schools.

Child study groups. A well-established format for teacher groups is the outgrowth of early work by Daniel Prescott (1957). Although child study groups, as they have become known, have been used throughout the United States, New Jersey has had a wide dissemination of this kind of teacher group through the efforts of Julia Weber Gordon (1967), a student of Prescott's. Dr. Gordon, as Director of Child Study for the State Department of Education in New Jersey, promulgated the use of this teacher group technique throughout school systems in the state. The groups were originally formed in schools among interested teachers who selected their own teacher-leader, but Dr. Gordon worked with school psychologists from all over New Jersey to train them to become leaders of child study groups in their local districts.

Child study groups are task oriented, as their name implies. Teachers volunteer to participate, and occasional efforts by administrators to insist that certain teachers join "because they need it" are discouraged, on the principle that only persons interested in volunteering are likely to profit. Each teacher in the group selects a child in her class for study. A system of objective observation is outlined; teachers record brief anecdotes on the selected child, even if only one or two anecdotes a day. At the weekly group meetings, teachers take turns reading their anecdotes aloud. They learn to discriminate fact from opinion, and discuss implications. As the anecdotes accumulate, the teachers begin to form hypotheses about why the child behaves as he does; they use the data from the anecdotes to support or reject their hypotheses. All teachers in the group contribute to this process. Since teachers from various grade levels participate, the behavior of children from different age groups is discussed.

Eventually the teachers learn to translate their supported hypotheses about the child's behavior into a series of insightful statements that delineate how the child sees himself, how he sees the world around him, how he characteristically interacts with other children and adults, how he handles academic tasks, and what his behavioral goals seem to be. From these statements the teachers work together to find ways to help the child to improve his way of functioning. The children selected for study are carefully kept as anonymous as possible, and one of the group's early discussions revolves around the need to respect the child's privacy. The children selected for study are not necessarily those the teachers find troublesome, since the purpose of the group is to enhance understanding of all children. As discussions continue, it is inevitable that although the focus is on the child, child-teacher interaction becomes the hidden agenda: many teachers derive insights into their own classroom behavior as well as into that of their pupils. The school psychologist as a leader can prevent such insights from becoming threatening to a teacher, can protect the sensitivities of one teacher from the probing or criticism of another, and can be supportive and encouraging of the group's increasing awareness of the subtle interplay between child and teacher, child and other children.

Measurement and evaluation as content.   School psychologists also organize teacher groups on a subject-oriented basis. Teachers usually spend more time than they find desirable on the administration, scoring, and recording of the group tests that most school districts have them administer every year. The batteries of achievement tests usually consume two to three days near the end of the school year. Some schools administer achievement tests at the beginning and end of each year. Group intelligence tests are frequently administered three to four times during the pupil's twelve to thirteen years in public school. Teachers often administer additional standardized tests of achievement in specific subject areas. They are also constantly engaged in the process of evaluation of pupil progress, whether by observation, teacher-made tests, or report cards.

Most teachers have had only a very basic introduction to evaluation procedures and are usually interested in knowing more about measurement and evaluation. They are often unable to make sense of the results they are required to enter on a pupil's permanent record folder. Thus, some teachers record raw scores, some record scaled scores, and some record grade-level equivalents. When these series of discontinuous numbers appear on a permanent folder, they are virtually useless because no one looking at the folder is sure what the numbers represent.

A school psychologist can serve as a leader-imparter of knowledge to teachers interested in knowing more about measurement and evaluation. Perhaps this kind of group seems more purely educative than consultative. However, when a school psychologist is working with a group from a single district (as opposed to a college professor offering a class in measurement to teachers from various districts) the psychologist becomes a consultant. He is making it possible for teachers sharing a problem to get help toward the solution of practical, here-and-now problems as well as toward learning something to apply to future problems. Consultation may take the form of leading discussion on the issues of group testing, especially if the school district has minority group pupils. The problem may be how to interpret the various numbers entered on a pupil's permanent record folder or how to record data consistently. A curriculum study group may be searching for appropriate testing programs. The consultation may deal with the teachers' concerns as to how to interpret group test results to parents.

Controversial issues. In recent years many schools have begun to offer drug education and sex education. Both are areas in which teachers are likely to believe themselves ill-equipped through their teacher training. Teachers may feel ambivalent about attitudes and values they are supposed to hold when dealing with such subject matter. The ambivalence felt by the teachers is frequently even greater in the community the school serves, and school systems need support and guidance in dealing with such controversial issues. The school psychologist may find his services useful not only to teachers but to administrators and other school personnel. Sometimes the school psychologist serves as a consultant to a board of education considering the advisability of dealing with controversial issues.

A workshop in sex education was offered to teachers in a school district that had to comply with a mandate from the state department of education to offer sex education, grades kindergarten through twelve. The purpose of the workshop was to enable the school psychologist to offer consultation to a large group of teachers, school nurses, physical education teachers, and administrators. The psychologist surveyed the group and found the anticipated concern on the part of school personnel about how to handle certain aspects of sex education without causing unfavorable reaction from religious and other community and parent groups. The school psychologist's survey also revealed an unexpected amount of ignorance about the anatomy and physiology of sex on the part of those who were to teach sex education, even among school nurses. The psychologist then engaged an obstetrician and gynecologist to give instruction on the anatomy and physiology of sex as well as basic medical information about contraception and venereal disease. He also engaged other consultants: representatives of religious groups, of psychiatry, psychology, and such organizations as Planned Parenthood and SIECUS (Sex Information and Education Council of the United States) to present differing points of view about sex education.

The school psychologist arranged smaller meetings after the more formal presentations. He employed role playing, in which one teacher assumed the teacher's role, while the other teachers were pupils. The "pupils" badgered the "teacher" with every conceivable question and comment, such as "What does rape mean?" or "Is it bad to masturbate?" Older "children's" questions were likely to center around premarital intercourse and the use of contraceptives. The consultant role of the psychologist was to be supportive as well as specifically helpful. It was clear that a lot of anxiety was generated because teachers had no idea of how they should respond to such questions. They were also worried about how to handle pupil's questions or comments put in four-letter words. The role playing enabled the teachers to practice responding to questions accurately and without making value judgments that might be offensive to some religious or parental beliefs. Many teachers hold traditional middle-class values and find the use of slang terms for sexual functions and the reproductive organs shocking and offensive. Once they had practiced saying, "That's a slang word that means sexual intercourse" in response to the question "What does fuck mean?" their initial shock reaction and anxiety generated by the question decreased, at least overtly.

It should be apparent that although these teacher groups are usually labeled "workshops" and are primarily educational in nature, they are a form of consultation. The psychologist helps school personnel to deal with problems specific to the particular school system: he uses his mental health expertise to enable personnel to function effectively and comfortably on their own when dealing with the specific problem.

In schools where racial issues are causing bitterness and disruptions or where it is becoming apparent that racial issues may cause problems, school psychologists may form teacher discussion groups to explore ways of circumventing or handling disruptions. The school psychologist does not have definitive answers to such problems, but he can be supportive of school personnel's efforts to cope with racial issues.

Teacher-selected topics. One school psychologist, selecting an elementary school, instituted a carefully planned series of teacher consultation sessions on a variety of subjects. This particular workshop was designed to try out a model that calls for a school psychologist to train teachers to build the mental health of their pupils through individualization of the curriculum [Walker, 1972]. Prior to instituting the workshops, the psychologist asked teachers to contribute topics they considered relevant for discussion, and the principal was asked for his aims and objectives. Dates were selected, and the topics were prepared and circulated in advance among participating teachers. The workshop included such topics as learning principles, behavior modification techniques, the identification of learning disabilities, and a number of innovative teaching techniques. The underlying assumption of the didactic format was that helping teachers to find a number of ways to build academic competence in children is an acceptable and workable approach to positive mental health in those children. It is well known among educators that the children who have difficulty in mastering academic skills are the children who show a number of problem behaviors.

Teaching operant learning techniques. The use of behavior modification techniques in the schools has increased in the last several years. Many school psychologists consult with teachers to implement such projects in the classroom. The principles of behavior modification can be discussed with teachers as a group. Ogden Lindsley (1971), a former student of B. F. Skinner, offered a very concisely defined model that the school psychologist can use as a consultation technique. Lindsley encouraged teachers to teach their pupils how to chart their own behavior. For example, a pupil can count the number of words he reads correctly and record this number on a chart with a dot to indicate the frequency. The next day the pupil can again record the frequency of correct words read and so on, until he is able to see a profile of his success or failure by connecting the dots. Most children enjoy keeping track of their own progress, and the process of charting is reinforcing by itself. The same procedure can be used to plot the frequency of certain behaviors before, during, and after an extrinsic reward (the charts are very much like those in Fig. 8, p. 80). The school psychologist is again working toward autonomous behavior on the part of teachers in classrooms. Teachers and pupils themselves can carry out the procedures with, eventually, only occasional consultation from the school psychologist.

Thomas M. Stephens (1970) described a form of consultation with teachers of learning and behaviorally handicapped children. The consultation uses a behavioral model in which the school psychologist works with teachers to select appropriate instructional strategies, schedules of reinforcement, and instructional materials. Teachers work with the psychologist to establish criteria for evaluating success among their pupils and can thus evaluate pupil performance readily and can determine when to teach new tasks.

Joseph K. Andrews (1970) reported the results of a program to train teachers in the classroom application of behavior modification techniques. Teachers who volunteered to participate were permitted to leave their classes one day a week. The school and the teachers each contributed 50 percent of the time. In this project a textbook dealing with the theory and application of social learning was used. Although Andrews was able to conduct only six hours of training sessions, he demonstrated that even such a short-term program in the application of operant techniques can be effective in bringing about behavior change in students as well as in teachers.

Other examples. In another school, primary grade children are assigned to homerooms traditionally labeled grades one, two, or three, but the children in all three grades receive reading and mathematics instruction at their level of progress, rather than at their designated grade level. Some first and second graders, for example, may be reading at a third-grade level, whereas some third graders may be receiving mathematics instruction with second and first graders. This modification of the "ungraded classroom" procedure results in several different teachers interacting with the same children. These teachers had identified shared problems and wanted to discuss them with the school psychologist.

The administrator made it possible for a series of such consultation groups to take place during regular school hours. The teachers were asked to write an anonymous description of the problem behavior. The school psychologist served as a consultant and also as a moderator and expediter of discussion, for the teachers, a wise and sophisticated group, freely volunteered explanations and possible approaches to remediation.

In this same school district the teachers of the upper grades requested similar group consultation. In this group an eighth-grade girl was identified as a source of concern to a number of teachers. Susan had always been rather quiet and academically competent, but during the year she had undergone a metamorphosis. Besides attaining obvious physical maturity in that year, Susan suddenly became alternately sullen and rebellious, breaking school rules and causing uproars in the cafeteria and in the gym. She no longer did her schoolwork. The teachers were most concerned about the fact that Susan was unhappy. They admitted that because of Susan's previous exemplary behavior in school, they were reacting not only with surprise and distress but also with considerable annoyance and exasperation because "Susan should know better." They began, as they discussed Susan, to recognize that they had all been reacting with frowns, disapproval, reprimands, and a certain amount of sullenness. Discussion with the school psychologist, based on his suspicion that positive reinforcement was absent and that little in the school was presently rewarding to Susan, resulted in a decision for all teachers to "be nice to Susan." Teachers agreed to make a point of smiling at the girl, of speaking pleasantly to her when passing her in the halls or in the cafeteria. In addition, a plan was worked out for two of her teachers to work with Susan in planning the annual school sport show. Susan, an ardent young horsewoman, was to be given the responsibility for working out a junior horse show as part of the annual sports day. Whether what worked was the horse show or the "Be nice to Susan" cannot be definitely evaluated, but the teachers reported almost miraculous success. Susan resumed her interest in schoolwork and behaved more maturely. Her parents spontaneously contacted the school to report that something good must be happening, for they had been distressed about similar sullenness at home and had noted the same miraculous change. Reports from the high school a year later indicated that Susan continued to do well, socially and academically.

These examples of successful in-service education formulated and conducted by school psychologists do not exhaust the possibilities for offering and promoting knowledge, skills, and insight that allow teachers to improve their ability to educate and help children. Nor should it be assumed that in-service education is a foolproof road to preventive mental health intervention. Evaluation of the effectiveness of such programs is typically not available; and, like much of what happens in school, precise knowledge of effects of educational efforts is lacking. Research in the schools is a difficult and frustrating task. At this time, the best that can be said, according to reports and informal follow-up by participant psychologists, is that in-service education as a form of consultation with teachers appears to be effective.

Affective Education

It is commonly accepted and reasonably well documented that the teacher's characteristics greatly influence pupil behavior and learning. Whether a teacher is child-oriented or subject matter-oriented, her willingness and ability to accept a wide variety of pupil behaviors and attitudes, to be empathic, open and honest, fair, enthusiastic, and genuine are all related to her success in teaching. In some large measure consultation with teachers is aimed toward enhancing those aspects of their personalities or teaching styles that will increase their success in helping pupils to respond positively to efforts to teach them. As anyone knows who has tried to change himself or to help others to change, the process is arduous, slow, and often unsuccessful. It requires the willingness to change and/or some evidence that the new behavior or attitude will be more satisfying and acceptable than that which it replaces.

It is no wonder that school psychologists, and others concerned with helping teachers to interact more beneficially with pupils, have become interested in group approaches and methods that have become popular as ways of helping people to rapidly develop sensitivity to others, to improve human communications, and to increase self-knowledge. Affective education is a rubric that includes a bewildering array of techniques, gimmicks, theories, styles, and approaches.[1] As mentioned in the section on group counseling methods, many readers have probably heard about or participated in T groups, encounter groups, touch-and-feel groups, bioenergetic workshops, Gestalt workshops, body awareness groups, nude marathons, rap sessions, etc.

The development of the movement to reestablish contact with non-intellective aspects of one's personality and to help people to learn to relate to one another in more open and honest ways is undoubtedly a reaction to the increasing complexity and technological sophistication of our society. Its unfortunate concomitants are loneliness, feelings of alienation, and superficial relationships with many persons in the absence of strong relationships with a few. For some people one or another form of affective education has taken on the properties of a cult.

Affective education has found a respectable place in industry and business and on some college campuses in courses and counseling service programs; it has been promoted by competent mental health professionals as well as by charlatans and quacks; it has taken on quasi-religious properties; it is sold in kits for home use, and it is a parlor game. Affective education has a long and illustrious history in social psychology in its development as a laboratory method by the National Training Laboratories. The history of its development from philosophy and existential psychology as a movement within humanistic psychology is equally respectable. It has in recent years, however, fallen prey to gimmickry and gamesmanship so that its dangers have increased through misuse, and its potential to improve group relationships may have been lessened. Its popularity is undoubtedly related in part to its provision of a format that quickly promotes the circumstances for exposing feelings and attitudes that are not usually spoken or even thought in words and because it sanctions behaviors and contacts not ordinarily allowed in typical group relationships.

DIRECT METHODS

Affective education methods have been used in teacher consultation and education as a *direct* method to influence teachers and other school personnel to change their behavior toward one another and as an *indirect*

---

[1] An excellent, brief review of sources of information about one major form of group experience is Banks, G. & Carkhuff, R. R. Sensitivity training: A brief annotated bibliography, *Professional Psychology*, 1972, *3*, 93–95.

means to change their behavior and attitudes toward the children in their charge. Confrontation approaches in all forms have been tried, both by school psychologists and more often by outside consultants brought to the school to help improve intergroup relationships. Evidence for success, other than anecdotal, is hard to find. As with psychotherapy, self-reports by participants vary: some believe they have improved their ability to communicate with others and are better teachers as a result of their experience; others report no changes; and some report having suffered psychological distress that has made them less able to function well. It is likely that reported success is related to many factors: community acceptance of teachers' participation as part of their assignments and responsibilities, the degree to which teachers are forced to participate against their will, the skill of the group leader, and the tolerance of the school system for changed interaction by teachers after participation. A survey of research on group attempts at behavior change in industry (Wohlking, 1971) strongly suggests that attitude change unaccompanied by structural change will not lead to behavior change. If applicable to schools, the survey can be interpreted to mean that attempts to change teachers through group approaches without changes in the organizational structure in which they work will not be successful.

Further, schools must be willing to suffer some casualty rate if they encourage teachers to participate in intensive group experiences. Although little evidence is available on either beneficial or harmful effects of affective group experiences, one study by Irvin D. Yalom and Morton A. Lieberman (1971) reported that of 209 college-age students who entered encounter groups, 170 completed participation with 16 suffering considerable and persistent distress. In this study the type of group had little relationship to the production of casualties. Rather, the style of the leader did. Those whom the researchers called "aggressive stimulators" accounted for 7 of the 16 harmed by encounter experiences. The least harm-producing leader was the one who created an accepting climate.

SKILL TRAINING METHODS

Other kinds of group experiences deliberately try to help teachers to become more sensitive to children, but without the intensive and highly personal interactions just described. These programs offer training in human relations skills using such methods as simulated classroom experiences, supervised training in one-to-one therapeutic intervention with children, observation of children's behaviors, role playing, and practice in modifying classroom style.

The "C" group. One approach directly involves the teacher in exploring her own feelings and attitudes. It is not as all-encompassing as sensitivity training or encounter approaches, and it does include skill training. The "C" Group (Dinkmeyer, 1971; Dinkmeyer & Muro, 1971), based on principles of Alfred Adler's Individual Psychology, attempts to combine didactic and experiential procedures that emphasize the teacher-child interaction and tries to help teachers to understand how their own life-styles and characteristic patterns of response interact with the life-styles of the children they teach in the classroom. The "C" Group serves as a kind of social laboratory in which the teacher may gain insight about how children respond in groups and may develop skills in working more effectively with children. The appellation "C" Group is used to reflect the factors that are believed to make such a group effective: *collaboration*, in that teachers are consultants to each other; *consultation*, whereby the teachers in the group provide and receive ideas about how to apply the new approaches they are learning; *clarification*, as each group member clarifies for the others what she really believes and how congruent her behavior is with what she believes; *confrontation*, in which each group member must be willing to try to see herself, her purposes, and attitudes and to confront others to do so; *communication*, in that not only content but feelings are communicated; *concern and caring,* meaning that group members show they care for children and one another; *confidentiality*, indicating the privacy of the group; and *commitment*, in that the group members commit themselves to try to change.

Dinkmeyer's approach is firmly based on a point of view about the psychological foundations of human behavior attributable to Alfred Adler's theories of personality development. The following assumptions are the basis for helping teachers in "C" Groups to understand themselves and their pupils:

1. Behavior is understood on a holistic basis and comprehended in terms of its unity and pattern.
2. The significance of behavior lies in its social consequences.
3. Man is understood as a social being whose behavior makes sense in terms of its social context.
4. Motivation is best comprehended by observing how the individual seeks to be known or become significant.
5. Behavior is goal-directed and purposive.
6. Belonging is a basic requisite for human development.
7. Behavior is always understood in terms of the internal frame of reference of the individual, his perceptual field [Dinkmeyer, 1971, pp. 67–68].

There is an elegant simplicity about these assumptions that immediately appeals to many teachers. The premises are not far removed from what many teachers already believe. They furnish a readily adoptable set of "rules" by which to guide one's behavior. In "C" Groups, composed of a leader-consultant and no more than five teachers already committed to these principles of behavior, teachers are furnished the opportunity and climate for improving their styles of behaving and interacting in the classroom.

Human relations training. Another skill training method that appears especially promising was developed by Robert R. Carkhuff [1971]. Based on an approach that he and Charles B. Truax (1967) developed for improving training and practice in counseling and psychotherapy, it emphasizes three bases of human relations training: the experiential, the modeling, and the didactic. Carkhuff attempts to focus in training on those conditions that have come to be regarded as common elements in effective human interaction: empathy (the ability to grasp accurately the meaning of another's behavior and feelings on a moment-to-moment basis); genuineness (the ability to be nondefensive, authentic, and integrated in encounters with others); and nonpossessive warmth (the ability to provide a safe, secure atmosphere by showing positive regard and acceptance). By use of a variety of scales developed by Carkhuff and his associates, it is possible to assign levels of functioning to each of the conditions the approach attempts to improve. The trainer himself must rate high on the scales of the qualities he wants to impart. By involving the helpee (teacher) in homework and exercises involving expression of these conditions, by modeling the desired behaviors, and by presenting information about what is known to be effective for others, the program aims to improve the teacher's ability to relate to pupils. The rating scales provide feedback on how well learning is taking place. Carkhuff and others (Berenson, 1971) reported data that indicate that the approach is effective in helping teachers to improve interpersonal functioning, to use more positive reinforcing behaviors in their teaching, and to perform more competently in the classroom.

Filial therapy. Bernard Guerney, Jr. and his colleagues (1964) developed an approach to training parents to conduct play sessions with their young emotionally disturbed children. The parents receive the same kind of orientation and supervision in conducting client-centered play therapy that might occur in the training of clinical or of school psychologists. The parents are trained to play with their children at home for predetermined periods of time and in the clinic under the observation of the psychologist-trainers. The process is called filial therapy. Recently, Guerney adapted filial therapy to the school situation (Andronico & Guerney, 1967; Guerney & Flumen, 1970) with the following goals: to extend the school psychologist's efforts in therapeutic intervention by utilizing teachers as direct therapeutic agents; and, more important here, to help teachers apply therapeutic principles in the classroom.

As adapted for teachers, filial therapy training involves after-school training groups for about fourteen weeks. The ninety-minute meetings may be devoted to such topics as client-centered (Rogerian) play session techniques, demonstration of play techniques by the school psychologist, and practice play sessions with children that are observed by the school psychologist and by other participating teachers who offer constructive criticism. Evidence so far suggests that withdrawn children seen by teachers in filial therapy show improvement in assertiveness in the classroom, as compared to similar children without filial therapy. Teachers report that they have gained insights into how to deal with children in the classroom.

To extend the principles of filial therapy to the classroom, Guerney and his associates (Guerney & Merriam, 1972) developed what they called a Democratic Teacher Training project. Its specific goals were to train teachers to use reflective listening (to understand students' feelings as well as their words and to accept their feelings and ideas without judgment); to "own feelings" (to give verbal answers in which the teacher identifies and expresses his feelings as his own); and to conduct classroom group meetings in which personal and interpersonal decisions are made through democratic procedures. Evaluation of the project suggested that the teachers considered the democratic group discussions to be valuable. It was noted that the more the teachers used democratic procedures, the more the children modeled this behavior and used discussion methods to solve their problems. Children also began to use reflective listening: the teachers reported an increased trust in their pupils' ability to solve their own problems and to make intelligent decisions. The project, which took seventeen weeks to conduct, was not considered by its developers to have lasted long enough to allow teachers to learn the intended skills at high efficiency. Yearlong projects are planned.

INDIRECT METHODS

Still another level of affective education for teachers is concerned with teaching them how to involve children in classroom experiences designed to promote the children's character and emotional development. Although the teacher is not directly involved in her own emotional education, learning to help others indirectly provides her with opportunities to develop new learning styles and to improve her relationships and interactions with pupils.

Reality therapy. An approach with wide appeal for school personnel is that of William Glasser (1969), a psychiatrist who promoted what he calls reality therapy (1965). According to Glasser, the need to love and to be loved and the need to feel worthwhile to ourselves and to others are the two basic psychological needs. However, one cannot be lovable or worthwhile to others if he does not maintain a satisfactory standard of behavior. Therefore, responsibility is a key concept for Glasser. People who have not learned to lead responsible lives behave so as to fulfill their basic needs, but their behavior is inadequate and unrealistic. They are "irresponsible."

Reality therapy differs from conventional therapy in six ways: (a) it negates the concept of mental illness on the belief that the patient who has no responsibility for his behavior cannot become involved in therapy; (b) it works from the present to the future rather than from the past to the present; (c) the relationship with patients is natural, rather than that of doctor-patient; (d) patients are not permitted to excuse their behavior with unconscious motivations; (e) the morality of behavior is emphasized, with issues of right and wrong faced directly; and (f) patients are taught new and better ways to fulfill their needs.

Glasser has used reality therapy principles as the basis for organized classroom meetings in which the teacher leads the entire class in discussions about what is important and relevant to the pupils. Three kinds of classroom meetings have been described: the social problem-solving meeting in which pupils discuss problems of living and working together in school; the open-ended meeting in which the teacher and class deal with intellectually important topics where stimulation to thought is more important than correct answers; and the educational-diagnostic meeting concerned with topics and subjects the class is studying, in which the teacher tries to learn what the class has *really* learned from previous exposure to subject matter.

The class meets in a circle so that all participants can see one another. The teacher-discussion leader must understand the philosophy of reality therapy and must be prepared to help children to confront reality with understanding. When a child makes a commitment to change his behavior, no excuse is acceptable for not following through, based on the premise that teachers who care do not accept excuses. Children must make their own value judgments and learn to accept the consequences of their behavior. In helping children to do so, one can help them to gain a sense of self-worth and identity and to learn the skills necessary to solve their problems in a responsible manner that is acceptable to others.

Glasser's approach to working with schoolchildren is generally well received by teachers. Like behavior modification approaches, the "theory" makes sense. It corresponds to the kinds of goals teachers tend to have for children, and it provides concrete methods that are not too difficult to learn and that fit what ordinarily goes on in a classroom. By working with children in the ways Glasser describes and by working with a consultant who models the approach and who offers encouragement and support, teachers can learn better ways of interacting with pupils in *all* their efforts.

The magic circle.   A curriculum approach to affective education of children in classrooms was developed by Harold Bessell and Uvaldo Palomares [1970]. Their Human Development Program is intended to facilitate the affective learning of elementary level children through a cumulative, sequential set of daily activities presented in lesson guides. Presentation of the affectively oriented curriculum is through a method known as the "magic circle." Eclectic in conception and borrowing from existential, behavioral, Adlerian, and nondirective approaches to human behavior, the "magic circle" attempts to put the teacher and pupils in a different relationship to one another for some part of each day. The teacher, as leader-facilitator, helps her pupils to explore their ideas and feelings through participation in predetermined activities furnished in the curriculum guide. For twenty minutes each day, the teacher seats her pupils in a circle of which she herself is a part. In an atmosphere of acceptance, children are encouraged to share feelings, to learn to listen to others, and to observe others. The teacher explains the topic for discussion and may demonstrate by taking the first turn. After each child has had a chance to participate, the teacher helps to review and to summarize what has been learned. Examples of topics are: "I made someone feel bad when I . . ." "It made me feel good when . . ." "Something I can do very well is . . ." The program is aimed toward enhancing feelings about one's ability to handle his environment, to build self-esteem, and to make affective aspects of functioning allowable. The consultant participates by demonstrating to the teacher how the program can work and by helping her feel comfortable with such an approach in a classroom setting.

These examples of affective education that directly and indirectly influence the teacher to change are just that—examples. They are not offered as the sole approaches possible or necessarily as the most useful or desirable ones. They do give some idea of the ways school psychologists and others can consult with teachers to help them to improve their relationships with pupils and to acknowledge and handle feelings and attitudes as indivisible parts of teaching and learning.

Individual Teacher Consultation

Any kind of consultation with teachers must be based on a knowledge and understanding of the uniqueness of being a teacher, especially a public school teacher. There has been considerable documentation of the characteristics of teachers as a group. Fifty years ago most teachers came from middle-class, "WASP," rural and small-town families and attended two or three years of normal school to attain a teaching certificate. More recently teachers have come from lower middle-class or first generation, upper lower-class families who viewed teaching as a first step up the professional status ladder. A Bachelor's degree is now required; a few states require a Master's degree for permanent certification. It has been demonstrated that teachers score better than average on IQ tests, but as a group not as well as most other professionals. "If you can't do anything else, teach" is a cruel and unrealistic comment, but it has its roots in the fact that the public does not regard teaching as a high-status profession. One obvious explanation is that teachers comprise the single largest professional group in the nation, representing a wider diversity of talent than is typical of other more select professional specialties. Like the school systems that employ them, in a nation of compulsory education, teachers are highly visible to the public and susceptible to public criticism. Every parent of a schoolchild is a self-appointed expert on whether a particular teacher is good or bad.

As is usually the case, particularly among large groups of people, generalities seldom hold in single instances. Teachers vary almost as widely in intellectual potential and personality characteristics as does the population at large. They also vary in their amount of training, and there are variations in the programs of the colleges that produce them. A survey by the National Education Association (1972) indicated that some of the differences in attitudes toward teaching seem attributable to the amount of training teachers receive and to the type of school district in which they are employed.

Seymour Sarason (1971), a community-oriented clinical psychologist, has worked for many years in schools and with teachers, and he makes some interesting general points about the uniqueness of teaching. A public school classroom is frequently a highly structured, very routinized place. Year after year teachers deal with essentially the same lesson plans and the same routines. The same amount of academic material must be covered each year. Despite initial enthusiasm, young teachers frequently find themselves inadequately prepared for the problems they face. Experienced and mature teachers, even those considered to be excellent teachers, begin to feel that they lack the time to give special help to the children who need it. Combined with their frustration about the lack of time is a growing sense that they, as teachers, have inadequacies in knowledge and techniques.

A typical public school class consists of twenty-five pupils: twenty-five different personalities, achievement levels, and developmental maturity levels; twenty-five different sets of abilities, interests, and behavior patterns. Tradition, parental expectation, and sometimes school administrative edict has passed down to the teacher the expectation that each one of those twenty-five pupils should be achieving by the end of the school year, in a variety of subject areas, at least at the grade level to which the child is assigned. This expectation exists, despite lip service given to individual differences. Even in so-called open classroom organizational plans in which children supposedly progress at their own level, *progress* is expected. As Sarason pointed out, teachers must cope with both professional and personal dilemmas created by the expectations for progress. One way to reduce the range of individual differences in a classroom and thus to increase the chances of success of any one teaching approach is to remove those who are most different academically and behaviorally. Since the teacher's effectiveness may be judged by the progress and decorum of her pupils, she may decide that some children cannot be accommodated in the ordinary classroom—some children need special help that the teacher cannot provide in a regular setting. Therefore, these children should be put in a special class, in a special school, or be assigned to a mental health professional for part of each day. Sometimes the rationale is to help the individual child; sometimes it is to prevent interference with the progress of the rest of the class. Regardless of the rationale, the decision involves an attempt to reduce the range of deviation in the group so as to achieve the goals established for academic progress.

The school psychologist has an extremely potent role in helping to determine which children should be placed in a special class or program. From Sarason's analysis it is clear why school psychologists are so frequently overwhelmed with referrals from teachers who think that referred children (or their class) would profit from their removal from the regular class. Such removal resolves a major problem imposed upon the teacher: she is no longer accountable for the child's failure to learn.

POINTS OF DIFFERENCE BETWEEN TEACHER AND PSYCHOLOGIST GOALS

The school psychologist usually tries to respond to a teacher's referral with suggestions about how to change the teacher's behavior with the child within the regular classroom. Even though teachers ask the psychologist for assistance, they are not always receptive to being told things *they* should do with the child. They want the *school psychologist* to do something. Teachers have too often been told that all Johnny needs is some individual attention and some tender loving care. To the teacher these suggestions are vague and unrealistic. She has tried being nice to

Johnny, she has praised him; but Johnny still disrupts the class or refuses to participate.

The teacher sometimes resents the various specialists, including the school psychologist, who see Johnny for an hour or so in an individual assessment situation, then return Johnny to her and to the class with statements to the effect that there is no reason why Johnny should not learn if he is properly motivated; but that he should not be expected to progress at the same level as the other children and that he needs help to develop more adequate feelings of self-worth. These suggestions tend to make a teacher feel that she has received no help at all; she has simply been told to fall back on her own resources that she already is aware are not adequate.

If the school system is characteristic, the school psychologist has an ever-increasing number of individual referrals on his desk. A frequent criticism of psychological services by teachers is that they hardly ever see the psychologist. The help they get is too little and too late. This state of affairs tends to confirm a pervasive feeling among teachers—that nobody really cares about their problems. Teachers resent being subjected to criticism when they are unable to solve unsolvable problems.

It has been commented by a number of observers that teachers as a group feel lonely, isolated, misunderstood, and unappreciated. Elementary school teachers especially are frequently confined to their classroom of children without a break for the entire school day, starting with playground duty in the morning and continuing through lunch period. Most states have laws that make it illegal for a teacher to leave her class unattended. The reasons are understandable, but such laws create a tense and confined situation for many teachers.

The situation described makes it difficult for a school psychologist, or anyone else, to be perceived as a consultant to whom a teacher can appeal for constructive help. The teacher's need for assurance, for relief, and for reduction of dissonance and variability in the classroom is greater than any immediate assistance a consultant can offer. A teacher's hopes are high and often unrealistic; disappointment is often inevitable.

INFORMAL APPROACHES TO CONSULTATION

It is the nature of schools that they start fresh each September. Teachers have new pupils and renewed optimism. Teachers are usually willing to "see how things go" before asking for help. The school psychologist can use this period of the year to try to establish a realistic relationship with teachers.

The school psychologist, even if he is new to the system, will find a number of referrals from the previous year that were not acted upon. The child whose referral was not acted upon has probably been routinely promoted and now has different teachers. The school psychologist can approach the new (at least to the child) teacher and mention the referral, requesting her reaction to it and her advice as to its current relevance. This approach immediately involves the teacher in a way that tacitly assumes her expertise; she is not asking for help but giving it. Since children tend to present problems from one year to the next, it is likely that the teacher has already developed some concerns about the child and will share them with the psychologist.

The next step is for the psychologist to explain his conviction that a child must be understood in context, not just in a one-to-one situation in the psychologist's office. He can point out his awareness that children can behave differently in a group setting than when they receive the undivided attention of an interested adult. The teacher usually responds positively to this recognition that a child as one of twenty-five or thirty is not the same as a child alone. Few teachers object to a request to observe a child in the classroom after they understand that the psychologist appreciates what is involved in group management and teaching. After an observation period the teacher will almost invariably ask the psychologist, ostensibly in the classroom to watch Johnny, "Did you happen to notice what Susan was doing during the reading lesson? I'm very concerned about her, too, and . . ." The psychologist will probably respond with more questions and is likely to get a flood of concerns from the teacher. The psychologist, depending on the situation and his evaluation of it, may respond with a few suggestions then and there; he may make a few sympathetic and understanding comments; he may promise further investigation. Whatever he says, he is providing a sympathetic ear; he is beginning to establish the image of a realistically helpful person. He is setting the stage for future consultation.

Changing teacher's response set. Karl Pribram (1972) pointed out that as the structure of an organism achieves homeostasis by absorbing a stimulus, so does a social system like a school tend to absorb any impact made upon it for change. Pribram pointed out that the most effective way to change an organism is to change its response set. He continued the analogy by suggesting that the way to change a school is to change its response set. Pribram's remarks are appropriate here because the school psychologist, in his initial informal contacts with a teacher, is attempting to change the teacher's response set to him as a psychologist. Her preconceived notions of his profession and her previous contact with other school psychologists form her response set toward him. If he can change her preconceptions, he can begin to be effective in his efforts to provide helpful consultation.

Again, school psychologists do not have all the answers to school problems. Perhaps a past mistake has been that psychologists have been presented not only as possessing advanced academic degrees and years of graduate training but also occult, mystic powers. No psychologist, no matter how well trained or how intuitively perceptive, can possibly live up to such expectations. It is hardly surprising, then, that teachers, other school personnel, and parents are critical of the psychologist's relative ineffectiveness. The particular response set, or preconceived notion of omniscience, is all too quickly destroyed and replaced by the notion of impotence. The psychologist must work carefully and painstakingly to achieve a realistic response set among those with whom he works. Hopefully, the response set will yield a view of him as one who can sometimes be very helpful but who at other times may be as baffled as the teacher, someone who, when unsure, will continue to seek answers. Most important, he will engage the teacher in a process of mutual learning and mutual trial-and-error behavior on behalf of the teacher and her pupils.

Examples of informal consultation. The psychologist informally visits as many teachers as is possible. He becomes familiar with the ebb and flow of school life. He knows that between 8:30 and 9:00 A.M. most teachers are at the doorway of their rooms, greeting children as they enter. The psychologist walks down the hall, stopping to ask Mrs. Jones how Joseph is doing, saying "Hello" to the children. Sometimes teachers will approach the psychologist: "Oh, Dr. Fine, could you stop in for a minute?" Most gratifying is the request that proclaims friendliness and trust: "Dr. Fine, come in and see what we've been doing in our unit on Africa. The children want to show you their projects."

Because teachers are lonely and isolated, they seek each other's company whenever possible. Playground duty usually consists of the rotating assignment of a few teachers to stand guard when the children are on the playground in large numbers, such as the time between arrival at school and the bell that signals the time to enter the building or during lunch period after the children have eaten. Teachers tend to dislike this watchdog assignment, but the school psychologist notes that they use the opportunity to seek each other's company. The two or three teachers on duty are usually found in a small group, their eye on the childrens' activities, but talking shop. Observing children in a free-play situation is also a useful source of information about how children relate to each other, so the school psychologist joins the teachers and their shoptalk. In such situations the psychologist is often a listener or an information seeker, not an advice giver.

One of the simplest yet most effective ways to offer consultation informally is to join teachers during lunch periods. Teachers use their lunch hour to congregate, and of course a wide range of topics is discussed. Inevitably they talk about their pupils and teaching responsibilities. As Stanley Newman (1965) commented, teachers who may want consultation but are uneasy about making a formal request for it seem to feel that less emphasis is put on the request if it is made in a less formal atmosphere. "I know this is lunchtime, but could I ask you about Sarah? I don't think there is anything seriously wrong, but . . ." Such a request leads quite naturally to an offer by the psychologist to observe Sarah in the classroom.

During one lunch period with elementary school teachers, a first-grade teacher commented to the psychologist, "I'm a little worried about Jennifer. She's always been immature, according to her mother, but I thought she might begin to catch up during the year. Here it is April, and she's so timid and quiet; and she isn't keeping up academically with the other children. She's a sweet child, and I don't think there's anything seriously wrong; but I worry about what will happen if she goes on to second grade. She's still having trouble handling the first primer in reading, and the other children pretty much ignore her."

The school psychologist responded, "Yes, it's always a problem deciding whether it is better for an immature child to repeat an early grade or to go on to the next and feel swamped. How old is Jennifer? When is her birthday?"

"She's young in the group—won't be seven until late in August. She entered school just under the admission age deadline."

"How do her parents feel about Jennifer's school placement?" asked the psychologist. "Sometimes parents unwittingly can make it difficult for the child if she is retained."

"I'm not too sure. When we had a conference last month they recognized Jennifer is young, but they—and I too—kept thinking she'll catch up eventually."

At this point a second-grade teacher, Judy Smith, joined in. "Our rooms are next to each other, and I see Jennifer quite a bit. She's timid, but I think she's gotten to know me. And you know I wouldn't put a lot of pressure on her to keep up with those who are already reading on a second-grade level."

The first-grade teacher looked relieved. "I was hoping you'd say that." She turned again to the psychologist. "Can you help Jennifer get placed in Judy's second grade? Then I'd feel more comfortable about letting her go on."

The psychologist said he would certainly recommend the placement.

A week later, the school psychologist joined the first-grade teacher on the playground. The physical education instructor had organized a game, and two first-grade teachers were watching. Jennifer hung back;

the physical education teacher made an effort to get her to join the group, but Jennifer refused.

"She is tiny, isn't she?" the psychologist commented, noting as he had many times before that Jennifer was by far the smallest child in the group.

"Yes," responded her teacher, "and I just found out something else. Judy Smith isn't going to teach second grade after all next year. They've had to do some changing to make a new section in first grade and decided Judy is going to teach first grade."

The school psychologist made no comment, thinking about the personalities of the two possible second-grade teachers.

The first-grade teacher, less inhibited, blurted out, "I really think Mary Brown is too . . . uh, cold. She'll terrify Jennifer. And as for Mildred Simms, you know she expects every second grader to be doing second-grade work."

"Well," said the psychologist, "if Judy Smith is going to teach first grade, how about having Jennifer repeat first grade, but with Judy? If you prefer, I can talk to Jennifer's parents about it. I think we can help them realize that Jennifer will really fit better in first grade than in second next year. From what you say about her and what we're watching right now, it seems that socially as well as academically she'll be more comfortable and secure. And she knows and likes Judy Smith, and some of her classmates will be only a month or so younger than she is chronologically. What do you think?"

Superficially, this exchange may seem relatively inconsequential—but not in the life of Jennifer. Jennifer's parents were agreeable. They recognized her immaturity and did not feel guilty or defensive, since the immaturity could largely be attributed to the accident of a late summer birthday and to a rigid admission pattern for school entrance.

Jennifer did well the next year in first grade. Although she will probably never become an aggressive leader among her classmates, she became comfortable and unafraid, made reasonable academic progress, and developed a few good friends among her new classmates.

This example, in which the conversation has been considerably condensed, also shows how the psychologist and teachers interact as co-professionals, not as an authority and subordinates. The teacher has the important part in decision making; the psychologist serves to clarify and support. The example further illustrates how the psychologist can develop the teachers' trust in him. Even if the ultimate decision is not exactly as the teacher originally proposed, if she believes her recommendations have been given just consideration and have been meaningful to the final decision, she begins to perceive the psychologist as a person who respects her, understands her, and responds to her needs.

Making informal procedures effective. Leonard Handler, Allan Gerston, and Barbara Handler (1965) described the areas of conflict and confusion that arise when psychologists make general recommendations that are of little help in classroom management or are physically impossible to implement. Such recommendations add to the teacher's sense of inadequacy and frustration. These authors listed very specific suggestions for improved communications and cooperation, most of which would be carried out in the form of informal consultation:

1. The psychologist should relieve the teacher's uneasy feelings by sympathetically reviewing the problem with her.
2. The psychologist and teacher should both help to define the various aspects of the problem or problems.
3. The steps to be taken should be planned together, be it observation, interviewing, testing, etc.
4. The information available should be pooled; the total amount of information will thus be increased, and additional insights may be gained.
5. The psychologist should prepare a specific plan for the teacher, taking into account her capabilities as well as her limitations.
6. The psychologist might well supplement the written report to the teacher with an oral report. This would help insure that the teacher does not place exaggerated value in the written psychological report. To do so might result in the teacher shunning her responsibility, and placing the entire matter into what she feels are the omnipotent hands of the psychologist. She may feel that the problem will now be magically solved; this attitude will lead only to frustration and disappointment on the part of the teacher.
7. The psychologist should explore with the teacher the ways in which the personnel, the resources of the school and community may be advantageously used.
8. The teacher should be relieved of the responsibility for behavior of the child over which she has no control. She might be reminded that the home should share such responsibility.
9. It is the responsibility of the psychologist to make certain that the teacher does not expect immediate results. Such unrealistic expectations would only prove frustrating and disheartening for the teacher.
10. The teacher should be encouraged to adopt a variety of methods in dealing with her students; flexible procedures should be stressed.
11. It is the psychologist's responsibility to remain available for help in future consultations, when they are requested [pp. 80–81].

There is no one way to offer consultation; nor do all psychologists in the schools emphasize informal consultation. Marvin Fifield (1967) delineated two distinct schools of thought on the function and responsibility of the school psychologist. The first maintains that the major responsibility of the psychologist should be to lead teachers and other staff members to a better understanding of the child and of his problems. This approach has been termed "Child Study and Consultation." The second approach, according to Fifield, emphasizes diagnosis, holding that the unique skill the psychologist possesses is his ability to engage in differential objective assessment in learning and personality.

Fifield pointed out a developmental trend that seems to operate in defining the two schools of thought; most school psychologists start their professional careers essentially as diagnosticians, followed by gravitation toward increased emphasis on child study and consultation. He noted that psychologists with the master's degree tend to spend much more time in diagnosis than do those with the doctorate and suggested that professional security, professional maturity, and better acceptance by the school staff may account for the trend toward consultation. Fifield is in agreement with the authors of this book when he says, "General acceptance of psychologists in the schools will come from educators only when psychologists (1) present an acceptable image, and (2) can demonstrate their contribution to the education of children" [p. 68]. The authors add that acceptance of psychologists in the schools means willingness to trust the psychologist.

DYNAMICS OF THE CONSULTATION PROCESS IN SCHOOLS

We have indicated that teacher consultation is probably the single most important role of the school psychologist. It has been emphasized that the effectiveness of consultation depends on the extent to which the teachers feel accepted and comfortable, valued and valuable contributors to the consultation process. It has also been documented that teachers, as a professional group, need to feel that they are important in schooling while they struggle with external factors that tend to downgrade their importance, their status, and their concept of themselves as valuable professionals. Perhaps the single most important aspect of consultation is that it can be used to communicate to teachers that somebody *cares*— cares about them as important professionals trying to do a good job, cares about and understands their problems and obstacles, cares about trying to make their job not easier but more likely to be accomplished more effectively, and cares about the education and welfare of the children in their charge.

During World War II a classic research project was carried out in a production plant. The results of this study are so well known that the term "Hawthorne Effect" has become part of psychological jargon. The project consisted of changing working conditions in the plant; lighting was changed, and production increased. Music was piped in, and production increased. Various other changes were implemented with the same result—increased production. Then still another change was instituted—all the innovations were removed. Interestingly enough, production again increased! One possible explanation for this may be that change eliminates monotony, therefore increasing production. Another explanation, based on the results of other projects, is also feasible: that when people have some kind of evidence that someone cares, they try harder.

In an intensive review of experimentation on specific administrative factors in schooling, J. M. Stephens (1967) noted that the vast majority of these research studies reveal differences that are not statistically significant. Whether the factor studied was attendance, the effects of television on classroom performance, class size, individual or group counseling, time spent in study, size of a school, teacher load, ability grouping, or a host of other factors, no special case could be made for the effectiveness of any of them. Rather, Stephens holds that background factors (such as the maturation level of the child, out-of-school influences, and the importance of the school in the community) and the "spontaneous tendencies that are always at work whenever the teacher is in the classroom" (pp. 84–85) are the forces that influence success or failure to learn in school. Stephens commented, "Whatever the truth or persuasiveness of our statements about what to teach, for instance, the teacher's minute-by-minute actions will determine the actual curriculum" [p. 13].

In numerous projects schoolchildren have been assigned to experimental and control groups in which the experimental group received special instructional techniques or approaches while the control group did not. Variations in results were found on the basis not of instructional techniques but of the classes within the project. That is, some of the classes in the experimental groups showed significant progress, and others did not. Similarly, some of the control classes using conventional methods made significant progress, and others did not. Informal conversation with some of the teachers whose class progress was significant led to the realization that if the teacher had faith in the method—whether that method was experimental or conventional—the method was more likely to prove effective. These findings are similar to those in medical research that suggest that if the physician or the patient has faith in a medical technique or medication, the patient is more likely to improve. In such a "double-blind" experiment neither patient nor physician is aware that the medication is a placebo (an innocuous substance of some sort).

The now famous Rosenthal and Jacobson study (1968) supports the ephemeral but potent notion that faith can move mountains. In this study teachers were told that certain pupils had "academic promise," and those pupils did show gain in measured mental ability scores. In subsequent studies, however, the same enhancing effect has not been found. In one (Fleming & Anttonen, 1972) the teachers who were told that certain pupils showed "academic promise" stated flatly that they did not believe the accuracy of the information (inflated IQ scores) they had received.

It has been suggested that some of the difficulty in pinning down the efficacy of certain techniques such as counseling or psychotherapy is due to the difficulty of assessing specifically the relationship of the therapist to the patient. One of the first principles of client-centered therapy (Rogers, 1951) is that the helping person must truly accept the helpee to be effective in the helping relationship.

Teachers are in contact with pupils for six or more hours a day, five days a week. Children usually attend school for twelve or thirteen years at least. It is hardly surprising that teachers' personalities, expectations, and attitudes have a strong effect on the children in their charge. Indeed in some instances, teachers exert a stronger influence than parents do, a thought that may have a frightening or consoling effect depending on the teacher, child, and parents in any specific instance.

Recognition of the possible ramifications of teacher influence on children is the basis for the school psychologist's role as a consultant. Handler et al. (1965) quoted Eloise Cason, who as long ago as 1945 commented:

> School psychologists cannot operate in an ivory tower. Whenever the welfare of a child is at stake, several individuals share the responsibility. The school psychologist's value depends not only on the keenness of his diagnosis, the adequacy of his predictions about future behavior, and his own therapeutic work, but also on his ability to stimulate in the school personnel an understanding of the child and a willingness to bring their best efforts to bear upon his needs [p. 137].

The School Psychologist
as a Modifier
of the School System

chapter six

Virtually everyone is critical of schooling, particularly schooling as it is practiced in public supported systems. Schools provide an arena in which political, economic, and philosophical differences are aired and argued. Issues related to religious practice, to racial prejudice, to local, state, and national autonomy and control, to censorship, to invasion of privacy, and to taxation determine how people view public schooling in general and their community school district in particular. Education is a huge bureaucracy. Its budget represents a large proportion of our total national resources. In political and economic terms schools are viewed as producers of products. They are judged by their efficiency and cost as they are related to certain national, state, and local priorities. When all goes well, we tend to praise our political know-how and the moral fiber of the family. When all does not go well, we blame the schools.

In fact there is much to blame. Reflecting as they do the values of the community, subject to powerful currents of national concern, and almost always understaffed and operating on marginal budgets, schools tend to change very little over the years. They tend to maintain a conservative and cautious approach to almost everything, giving high priority to survival and stability.

Yet to any pupil enrolled in any school these large problems are not what school is all about. For a school-age child, school is an important part of his life. Schools are personal. They are made up of experiences involving other children and adults in positions of authority. Schools, like homes, are places with distinct physical properties, sounds and smells. They are populated by people who do things for and to you. Schools are testing grounds for growing up. As much as anything else in a child's life, his experiences in school can propel him forward or ensure his failure as an adult.

The school psychologist is part of both school worlds. As an employee he is part of the system, caught up in policies, practices, and pressures that influence school functioning. He is also a spokesman for individual differences among children, offering services that hopefully will help individuals to improve their ability to function within the system. As Emory L. Cowen (1971) pointed out, school adaptation is a challenge that all children must face. It requires that the pupil achieve some minimal learning objectives established by his school and by his teacher and that he function within some preestablished framework of acceptable behavior. So far, emphasis has been given to the school psychologist's efforts to strengthen the child's ability to adapt and the teacher's ability to improve conditions under which that adaptation can take place. What remains to be discussed is how the psychologist can assist the school to adapt—to modify its behavior—so that it can educate its pupils more effectively and become the kind of place that works for the child rather than against him.

William Clark Trow (1968–69) said that nothing short of participation in educational reform will allow the school psychologist to function effectively. He proposed two ways in which the psychologist can participate in reform: renovation and innovation. By renovation he means participation in those areas of schooling that can improve school conditions, such as improvements in plant and equipment, student morale, curriculum (subject matter content), and teaching (how the teacher presents the curriculum). By innovation he means participation in the development and implementation of new ideas. He singled out for consideration changes in grading and marking, provisions for differential teaching so that teaching styles and roles are made more suitable to different educational purposes, development of more effective educational media and techniques, and participation in the development of better educational objectives for the school.

Trow's desire for renovation and innovation as goals for the psychologist are appropriate as long-range goals. In the short run on a day-by-day basis, the school psychologist's influence depends in large part on how he works with other people in the school and the community. Just as trust is a prerequisite to his usefulness to teachers, his being able to influence policies and practices in a school district depends on how he is perceived and valued by those with whom he works.

Working with Other School Personnel

Administrators. School systems have been compared to big business, the board of education to corporate boards of directors, the school superintendent to the president of the corporation, the assistant superintendents to vice-presidents, and the principal to middle-management personnel. As with most analogies, the similarities break down at some point. Rarely, for example, do all the shareholders of one company live in the same community and participate directly in the company's process or product.

School superintendents. The school superintendent is the senior executive of his school system and is responsible to his board of education, which usually selected him for the position. Like his corporate counterpart, the superintendent rarely has tenure. Unlike his corporate counterpart, his success or failure is not measured in company profits, but in relative intangibles. In some communities, success is measured by the number of high school graduates accepted by colleges. In others, it is keeping a school budget trimmed so that taxes are not raised. Some communities view educational innovation as educational success; others equate success with a traditional, hold-the-line approach to education.

The school superintendent walks a tightrope across an abyss. One end of the rope is secured by his board, usually elected by the community and frequently representing different interest groups in the community. The other end of the tightrope is secured by his school personnel. No superintendent survives if the morale of his faculty is low, whether because of perceived low salaries, poor working conditions, or lack of support for desired educational practices. In the abyss waits the community with protests about busing and concern about split sessions, the tax burden versus the cost of new school buildings, rising salaries, and rising costs in general.

School superintendents are a vigorous breed. To survive and succeed, they need the resiliency of a politician, the perennial optimism of a high-powered salesman, the diplomacy of an ambassador, and the expertise of a labor-management negotiator. Needless to say, turnover is rapid, particularly in school systems in communities that are undergoing change.

These men (and by far most of them are men) have reached their positions through the ranks of teaching, usually via graduate school. Most superintendents have had at least a year of graduate training in school administration, and many have had two years or more. A doctoral degree is often held by superintendents in large city districts or in affluent districts. Their graduate course work has typically been in supervision of instruction, administration of budgets, the planning and running of school plants, community relations, school law, and more recently, in labor relations. By the time they reach superintendency, most of them have served as principals as well as teachers. On the average they are ten years older than the average male teacher.

The school superintendent, as the chief executive of the school system, is the ultimate authority to whom everyone on the staff is responsible, including the school psychologist. The channels to this authority vary. In large districts there may be a number of assistant superintendents whose authority derives from the superintendent. One assistant superintendent may have sole responsibility for school plants and their operation; another may be in charge of personnel; still another responsible for curriculum and another for special services. In large districts the school psychologist may have been hired by an assistant superintendent and may have contact with the superintendent only briefly, infrequently, and from afar. In small districts, the superintendent probably has his principals report directly to him and meets with them and other key staff regularly.

A school psychologist must know to whom he is responsible when he joins a school staff. Although this seems to be self-evident, the channel of administrative responsibility is often unclear for the school psychologist. Mary Alice White and Myron Harris (1961) have given criteria for a good relationship between the school administration and the psychologist:

1. There should be a definition of the school psychologist's functions.
2. The school psychologist's scope of authority and its limits should be clear to him, the superintendent, and all other school personnel.
3. The lines of communication between the school psychologist and the superintendent, or other supervisor, should remain open [p. 39].

David G. Salten (1964–65), former superintendent of the New Rochelle (Long Island, N.Y.) schools, pointed out:

> I take the view that all the personnel in the school are trying to meet the same overriding purposes of the schools, and we must not permit our own short-term or idiosyncratic objectives to get in the way of the over-all purpose of the school. We are all trying to get to the same place, but everyone uses a different road according to the discipline he is practicing. In this respect I think that school psychology resembles the school superintendency in that it is really a constellation of positions . . . There are a few large systems in America in which a school psychologist can be employed to carry on some narrow specialized ac-

tivity, but in practically 99 percent of the cases he is working in an area where he should be a generalist. Just as the superintendent of schools has to be interested in curriculum, instruction, finance, law, supervision and personnel, the school psychologist, too, must contend with many school problems [pp. 29–30].

There are school superintendents who authorize the employment of a school psychologist only because the state law requires psychological services and hope this new staff member does not do anything to inconvenience the administrative staff. However, many superintendents, like Salten (1964–65), see psychologists as

a great group to have in the school system for several reasons . . . in almost any school system, and almost without exception, they tend to be the people with the most vigorous intellects. Psychologists today are very much brighter as a rule than teachers and brighter than most supervisors. This, of course, creates a problem but it is something which is very, very valuable to the administration. Also, school psychologists are less conforming than teachers. In some respects, they are uncomfortably uncomforming. They are more adventuresome; they are not quite as wedded to all the vested interests . . . which surround the public schools [pp. 28–29].

Along with these words of praise (which many school psychologists would regard as atypical of school superintendents), Salten pointed out that although the word "gutless" applied to psychologists may be unduly harsh, he sees them as only moderately self-assertive. He attributes this lack of pugnacity to the fact that many psychologists work in relative isolation.

Salten argued that although school psychologists are doing many things well, they are not doing enough. His advice to them is to concentrate on essential matters and leave the less essential to others. For Salten the essential matters are those that deeply affect school functioning, and he lists a number of these to which he feels school psychologists could contribute: the improvement of relationships with community mental health centers; assistance with admission of children to schools; grouping of children to increase opportunities for intellectual growth, academic achievement, social and emotional development; reform of the marking system; assistance with educational technology; sensitization of teachers to children's needs; development of the rationale and curriculum of special classes; psychosocial analysis of those groups that affect the schools; study of faculty morale including the factors that underlie teacher expectations and the teacher reward system; and evaluation of changes in school programs and procedures. In other words, Salten believes that the school psychologist should act, as Trow recommended, as an innovator and renovator who serves the entire system as a behavioral scientist-consultant.

There are as many differences among superintendents as there are among school districts. It is probably true that most school executives see their school psychologists primarily as testers and handlers of psychological crises among children. School systems have become increasingly beset with a myriad of problems, however, and a number of superintendents are beginning to recognize the need for a behavioral expert who can consult with teachers, help to evaluate school programs, and generally help and advise on complex school-related issues. Superintendents agree, however, and psychologists should recognize that although psychologists in the schools can be useful, the school system will not collapse without them. This puts the school psychologist in a different category than the teacher.

School principals. The administrator with whom the psychologist will have the most direct contact is the principal. Whether the school psychologist is ultimately responsible to the superintendent, an assistant superintendent, or a director of special services, he is also responsible to the principals of the buildings in which he works. The principal is in charge of *his* school, and in many ways the functioning of the psychologist depends on the extent to which the principal supports his activities. The principal is the school leader. His ability to organize and direct and his style of leadership profoundly influence how teachers in his building function and how the children learn. Without the principal's support and understanding, psychological services in a school will at best be fragmented and piecemeal.

The principal considers the teachers in his school to be *his* teachers, and he usually wishes to help them to function more effectively. Although principals technically are responsible for teacher supervision, they do not actually spend much time supervising teaching. Principals are busy people: they are responsible for scheduling, for assignments, for building maintenance, for supplies, and for custodial, cafeteria, and secretarial services. Even in large schools, where assistant principals may take on some of these responsibilities, the principal directs all operations. Principals see the many visitors who come to a school each day. Pupils transferring in and out must have their records checked. The bookkeeping involved in attendance records and budget keeping is the responsibility of his office. It is the principal who must meet the emergency when school bus number 9 breaks down on the highway or when the antiquated heating system refuses to warm classrooms to more than 48 degrees on a February day. He must see to it that state laws concerning number and quality of fire drills are met. In addition, as every person who has attended public school in the United States knows, his office is the repository for children "sent to the principal's office" for infraction of rules. The principal must attend every meeting of the Parent-Teacher Association, participate in meetings of principals in the school district as well as his own faculty meetings, is supposed to be involved in the development of educational programs, and should supervise and consult with his teachers. He also meets with community organizations, sees to it that the Cub Scouts have a room for their Thursday afternoon meeting, and finds himself trying to track down two trombones missing from the music room.

All principals have come through the ranks in that they have all been teachers. Some small schools still have a "teaching principal" who has a regular classroom assignment in addition to his many other duties.

Most principals cannot afford to spend much time visiting classrooms. Some schools have curriculum supervisors, and high schools usually have department chairmen who assume responsibility for working with teachers in the classroom. Principals are sometimes not welcome in classrooms because of their evaluative role in teachers' lives and because principals' schedules do not permit visits frequent enough to make their presence routine. To add to the principal's dilemma, many new teachers, eager for help and direction, complain that they cannot get the principal's help.

It should be clear that it is the principal, more than anyone else, who establishes the atmosphere of a school. His authority and wide-ranging activities tend to influence all phases of school life.

Principals are likely to eye the psychologist with a mixture of irritation and relief. The psychologist, because his avowed purpose is to help teachers with classroom management, can do things that the principal may recognize as a necessarily neglected portion of his, the principal's, job. The psychologist, however, may encourage teachers to request services or materials, which adds to the principal's already heavy burden. The psychologist may unwittingly cause negative reactions from parents with whom the principal then must deal.

On the other side, the principal seldom has anyone with whom he can discuss school matters who is also knowledgeable about what is happening in the school. The principal who is concerned with how well his school is functioning and who is faced with pressures from parents, teachers, and higher echelons of administrators can use the services of a consultant. A psychologist who can participate in sensitive and difficult meetings with parents or community agency representatives can relieve the principal of sole responsibility for difficult decisions. Reviewing decisions out loud with the help of someone who is objective and informed can prevent rash decisions and improve planning. By acting as a consultant who can represent the school in matters relating to community services, child development, and mental health, the psychologist can relieve the principal of some of his responsibilities as well as he can expand and enrich the school's resources.

The psychologist must be willing to try to understand the responsibilities and problems faced by the principal, and he must be sincere in his efforts to help him solve school problems to the extent that he can. Trust and acceptance come only with time, and a relationship of mutual trust and acceptance is necessary before a principal can make effective use of the school psychologist or permit him to function in ways that will improve school operation as well as the functioning of individual children.

Other specialists. In schools psychologists are considered part of pupil personnel services, the services and functions in elementary and secondary schools "which aim to adapt the school program to the needs of the learner and to help the learner adjust to the school program" [Ferguson, 1963, p. 5]. Although there is no accepted, inclusive designation of pupil personnel workers throughout the United States, certain specialties are generally considered to be within their ranks. They include school psychology, child accounting and attendance services, school social work, guidance and counseling, and school health services. Speech and hearing clinicians and remedial personnel are sometimes considered to be pupil personnel workers. Most recently the specialty of learning disabilities has developed.

Requirements for practice and job specifications vary enormously from school to school and among states, but each of the pupil personnel specialties has come to include certain functions and responsibilities that distinguish it from others.

Attendance officers. Child accounting and attendance workers were the earliest members of the pupil personnel services. They were introduced into the school after the passage of compulsory attendance laws during the late 1800s and early 1900s. The "truant officer," whose task was to enforce school attendance and labor laws, became the prototype of the school attendance enforcement officer. Comic strips still include the truant officer as a stock character although the present-day attendance worker is no longer a punitive law enforcer. He is instead a mental health-orienated worker who tries to determine the causes of attendance problems and to assist the school in taking remedial steps. He also fosters cooperation between the school and the home and is sometimes called a "home-school counselor." This specialty is less common now, since the functions of the home-school counselor have been incorporated into more sophisticated specialties.

School social workers.   School social work appears to have developed from efforts to make attendance services more effective. Like the truant officer, the teachers assigned to tutor pupils who were unable to attend school became the school's contact with the home. These visiting teachers helped teachers to understand the child's out-of-school experiences and interpreted to parents the school's efforts on behalf of the child. It is not clear at what point the visiting teacher came to be considered a school social worker, but certainly the similarity between her functions and those of the graduate social worker in community agencies must have been apparent. Each was concerned with the influence on the child of the home and of the community, and each was involved in providing a variety of direct services aimed toward increasing the ability of the home to support and nourish the child. Schools and state departments of education have a long history of adapting the titles of nonschool specialists to suit their needs, regardless of professional qualifications established by the particular specialties. Thus, school social workers emerged as school specialists with credentials established by state departments of education rather than by the profession of social work.

As qualified psychiatric social workers came to be employed by schools, school social workers represented two ends of the spectrum—from the psychiatrically oriented casework specialists to the educationally oriented teachers with a few courses in "school social work practice." In recent years the social work profession has developed training programs in school social work as a specialization within the profession, requiring intensive training and supervised experiences in a two-year graduate program.

In many respects the development of school social work parallels that of school psychology. The obstacles relative to the practice of school psychology—its emergence from the testing movement and its attempts to distinguish itself from clinical psychology—have their counterparts in the development of school social work.

Guidance counselors.   Guidance and counseling services are by far the most numerous and pervasive of the pupil personnel services. Their beginning is often attributed to the development of the Vocational Bureau in Boston in 1908 by Frank Parsons (Brewer, 1942), and the vocational guidance emphasis still dominates their activities. Guidance and counseling services are offered in some elementary schools, but they are predominantly secondary school services. They include such activities as course scheduling and advising, maintaining pupil records, and assisting students with college and occupational placement after graduation. The counseling function—working directly with pupils to help them make sensible and useful decisions and to solve problems—is seen as highly desirable by most guidance and counseling personnel. However, the maintenance functions of guidance, those that help keep the school functioning, have tended to occupy most of the guidance workers' time. Because the ratio of guidance counselors to pupils is more favorable than is true for any of the other pupil personnel workers, the potential is great for direct service to pupils by guidance counselors.

School health specialists. School health services include the procedures carried out by nurses, physicians, and dentists to protect and promote the health of pupils. In schools it is the nurse who offers the primary health service, and it is she who is most frequently considered to be the key health worker. Although responsible for the children's physical health, she is also actively concerned with their mental health. The nurse's office is likely to be the first stop for the anxious child. The school nurse, particularly in elementary school, is often the first to identify developing problems in children.

The learning disabilities specialist. The concern for children who have neurologically based difficulties or who have shown perceptual and visual-motor problems has produced a new pupil personnel worker called a learning disabilities specialist. His major concern is the assessment and remediation of learning problems attributable to specific disabilities. This specialist assists teachers in modifying and planning educational programs for children who have difficulty learning in the regular classroom. Training programs have begun to develop, but as yet the specialty must be considered in the process of formation.

THE PRINCIPLE OF SPECIALIZATION

Although distinct services are performed by the various specialties, pupil personnel service workers in actuality tend to function according to what might be called "the principle of specialization." Accordingly, the greater the number of different pupil personnel specialists employed by a school district, the more distinct the services they offer will be. The fewer the different kinds of specialists are in a school, the more likely each is to offer a variety of services, some typically carried out by others. The same principle applies to a physician practicing general medicine in a rural community as compared with medical specialists in group practice in a large urban hospital. If the only pupil personnel worker on the scene is a school psychologist, he will function in a variety of roles (depending on what is needed) within the limits of his competencies. Add a social worker, and the psychologist becomes the test specialist, the social worker the home specialist. Add a guidance counselor, and further division of labor becomes necessary.

The more each specialty narrows its focus and contribution, the less likely it is to help the school to improve its overall effectiveness. Over-specialization in pupil personnel services, as in medicine, may result in the inability of any one specialist to have a broad view of the problem under study. Under conditions of overspecialization, decisions have to be made by teams; somehow the pieces of a particular problem must be put together. Since schools employ a number of distinct specialists, each specialist contributes his particular expertise to the solution of the problem at hand. The pupil personnel specialists are usually designated the Child Study Team; and as the name implies, they must function as a unit to make decisions about a particular school problem.

The *necessity* for team decisions is quite different from the *desirability* of professional consultation and united action toward some goal. This is a crucial point in understanding how professional personnel, other than teachers, can help schools to solve problems. If the school psychologist or any other professional specialist is to serve at a level that allows him to help the school system to improve—to influence procedures, policies, and practices within the system—he must be free to function as a professional rather than as a technician responsible for only one small piece of the problem. He must have the opportunity to apply his background knowledge and skills to the school's problems as a whole.

How the pupil personnel services are organized to work together—the degree to which they can be helpful to one another, can tolerate over-lapping functions, yet offer specialized knowledge and expertise—will vary from school system to school system. In all cases, however, working together requires cooperation, sensitivity, and willingness to compromise.

Such considerations are at the very heart of school psychology and illustrate one of this book's central points—that content, as learned in a university classroom, cannot be separated from those factors that determine whether or not that content can be made applicable. The school psychologist's knowledge of how psychology and the behavioral sciences can serve the schools cannot be separated from the ways in which he goes about his business.

PROBLEMS IN TEAMWORK

To understand the problems created by the principle of specialization, an analysis of teamwork may be illuminating. Peter Kong-Ming New (1968), a sociologist, presented a concept of teamwork in community mental health work that is directly applicable to the problem at hand: what factors determine whether specialists, working together toward mutual goals, succeed or fail in their efforts.

New views teamwork as having two major axes. The first axis consists of a series of *assumptions*, and the second he terms the *cognitive dissonance* aspect, consisting of functional and substantive rationalities. According to his thesis, success or failure in teamwork is best explained by the degree of discord in the assumptions made by the team members.

A team is generally composed of members who have different backgrounds and experiences. It is in the nature of a team that each person offers something different and special; otherwise why bring the team together? Each member of the team operates on certain assumptions about what is happening in team efforts and what constitutes the relationships among those on the team. New emphasized six of the possible assumptions that can be made. Team members usually assume that they meet as *equals*. They assume that no one of them has all the knowledge needed to solve the problem for which the team has been assembled, that a reason for team action is to share the *knowledge* available, and that all team members are desirous of doing so. Further, each profession has certain, established *competencies* not shared by others that establish the boundary lines among professions. However, some professions are more solidly entrenched or established than others. Thus the issue of *marginality* of some specialties exists, especially those still in the process of emergence. The team members assume that they are all working on the same *task* and toward a common goal. Overriding the first five assumptions is that of *domain*; each specialty knows which areas it claims belong to it and is convinced that it has the best understanding of those areas and therefore contributes the best services.

New borrowed the concept of cognitive dissonance from Louis Festinger (1957) to explain that in each of the six assumptions there may be commonly accepted reasons that bind the team together (*the functional rationality of assembling a team*). At the same time there may be other reasons for action that do not coincide with the accepted reasons (*the substantive rationality*). When there is incongruence between the functional and substantive rationalities, cognitive dissonance occurs. In other words, unless the stated and the actual reasons for action are congruent, team members may act one way for stated reasons while realizing that other events, for actual but unstated reasons, may be transpiring that also influence team functioning and decision making. Under these circumstances, dissension and problems in team activity are bound to occur. The correct words may be said, and the team may operate by accepted procedures; but the team cannot satisfactorily resolve the problems before it.

Figure 9 presents a paradigm of cognitive dissonance in teamwork. An example of how it might work follows: The team members assume equality but recognize that some are more "equal" than others. The psychologist has a doctorate, whereas the social worker is a recently up-

Assumptions of teamwork	Cognitive dissonance or, incongruities in action	
	Functional rationality	Substantive rationality
Equality		
Knowledge		
Professions		
Marginality		
Task		
Domain		

FIGURE 9. A paradigm of cognitive dissonance in teamwork. Adapted from New, P. K. An analysis of the concept of teamwork. *Community Mental Health Journal*, 1968, *4*, p. 330.

graded visiting teacher. The learning disability specialist has been in the school for many years and knows all aspects of school functioning, but the school psychologist is an occasional consultant who hardly knows his way around the building. Ostensibly, the team members may assume each is there to share knowledge, but knowledge is also power; and one or another team member may actually be using his knowledge to upstage a fellow participant. Each professional specialty supposedly has some clear areas of competency; but in fact it could happen that the school nurse on the team is a better counselor than the guidance counselor or that the school social worker is a better diagnostician than the school psychologist. Although all may claim that they are concerned about the welfare of the child they are discussing, the meeting in which the child's problem is being discussed may become the vehicle for jockeying for the dominant position by one specialty over the others.

By no means is this analysis confined to pupil personnel service workers. It applies to all kinds of groups of different personnel meeting together to achieve a goal. It offers an example of the kinds of behaviors that need to be understood when professionals meet to solve problems. The school psychologist, concerned with how his services might best be used to help the school district, must be aware of the dynamics of team functioning, not only when he is serving as a consultant but when he is himself part of the team. Being able to stand aside from one's own involvement and to take an objective stand toward one's own behavior are

qualities much desired in any professional person and of crucial importance to the successful functioning of the school psychologist.

Research in the Schools

It is not by chance that this section comes late in the book. The school
psychologist who engages in research activity as a major part of his work
is a rare individual. The school psychologist is a practitioner of applied
psychology employed primarily as a problem solver and an information
giver. School administrators, teachers, boards of education, and taxpayers do not typically think of research as problem solving, although it is.

It has been pointed out that schools are big business; forward-looking
industries will regularly spend 5 percent or more of their annual budget
on research and development. The research and development branch of
an industrial firm conducts ongoing evaluation of the company's product in terms of the projected needs and desires of its customers. Yet
schools, though also concerned with evaluation of their product, spend
considerably less than 1 percent of their budgets on research and development [Gray, 1963].

The conflict of interest between school and community on one side
and research investigators on the other relates in part to mutually exclusive goals and methods of achieving these goals. As Susan Gray (1963)
put it:

> Ability to do research on problems of human behavior seems to be the
> *sine qua non* of the psychologist's role as impressed upon the psycholo-
> gist-to-be in graduate school. Yet the school psychologist, going out
> upon the job, is likely to have a rude awakening. Accustomed in gradu-
> ate school to seeing research as a veritable Holy Grail, he is dismayed
> to see that the public, including the parents and the teachers in the
> schools where he works, fails to share his reverence. Indeed, research
> is sometimes an ugly word, looked upon with downright suspicion or
> dislike [p. 56].

Martin Kohn and Jerome Beker (1964) of the Bank Street College of
Education mentioned some of the ways school personnel and research
investigators differ:

> Teachers and school administrators, especially, are beset by so many
> pressures and problems that they are driven to look for concrete results
> immediately applicable to the practical situation in which they operate.
> In addition, if they have had no previous contact with research and are
> therefore unaware of the complicated and often drawn out processes of
> data collection and analysis, they find themselves more and more in a

situation of being asked to honor something which they feel is suspect. To them, as practitioners, research is a detour. To the research investigator, on the other hand, laboriousness and uncertainty are part of life [p. 32].

To school personnel, even those who are willing to tolerate research or related activity and who are interested in what might be learned, research in the school is of dubious value, of suspect ethics, and is potentially a nuisance. In addition to all the daily considerations that are part of school life, research causes work and problems. Schedules must be disrupted, cutting into teaching time; rooms must be found; children must be taken from class. Teachers may be asked to implement procedures that differ from their established and comfortable teaching methods. Parents must be informed of what is happening. Means must be found to respond satisfactorily to those parents who see such use of their child as an intrusion into their private affairs or who object to a new "experimental" method of teaching. If teachers are observed or asked questions, anxiety and resistance may be engendered. Researchers coming to the school too often are perceived by school personnel as haughty, conveying the impression that research is more important than practice and that the school is a laboratory, the staff and children merely subjects. Although principals, parents, children, and teachers may be asked to give time and effort, they may get little in return.

It is not surprising that schools give a low priority to the research role of the school psychologist. Nevertheless, as Marcia Guttentag (1968) succinctly stated, "School psychologists are constantly exhorted to more research and blamed for doing so little" [p. 254].

Schools demand much of their school psychologists, expecting them to be privy to a vast amount of validated information on psychology and on other behavioral sciences. When answers are not forthcoming, the school psychologist is held responsible. In addition, with the influx of federal funds to public schools since 1965, schools have had to assess the effectiveness of programs financed by federal funds. *Accountability* is a new word for school personnel and one to which they are sensitive. Since assessment of effectiveness demands research, schools turn to their psychologists to do the job. Of all school personnel, the psychologist has had the most training in research methodology and in scientific inquiry. He also has developed respect for objectivity and for conclusions inferred from data. He is aware that although school personnel have long experimented with curricula, trying this method and that, they lack the rigorous training in statistical techniques and experimental design needed to evaluate the effectiveness of their innovations. Lacking such training, other school personnel are likely to think that opinion ("The children seemed to learn better"; "I liked using the technique") is sufficient evidence of effectiveness. As Susan Gray (1963) reminds us, "Research . . . is seldom urgent. Service always is. It takes a strong commitment to research to prevent the school psychologist from completely bogging down in service demands. Research, then, is a function the school psychologist will find extremely hard to carry out effectively" [pp. 57–58].

Most school psychologists and other practitioner psychologists tend to resolve these dilemmas by making a choice. They distinguish between practice and research, attributing certain roles to one and other roles to the other. Practitioners continue to read research literature in their field and use their training in methods of scientific inquiry as the base for practice. However, they do not ordinarily initiate investigations beyond the immediate concerns of their practice. Researchers do not ordinarily attempt to solve immediate problems for their own sake. Whether this dichotomy is necessary has been one of the major battlegrounds of American psychology for at least a quarter of a century. The concept of a scientist-practitioner is still thought by many psychologists to be the most desirable model for practitioners to follow. The difficulties, however, in resolving the stresses created by trying to mesh practice with research training and orientation have promoted interest in greater autonomy between the two.

RESEARCH: SCHOOLING AND SCHOOLS

A distinction should be made between research *about schooling* (basic research) and research *for schools* (ad hoc or applied research). More knowledge is needed about the processes of teaching and learning and the effects of the school setting on children.[1] Much of the background necessary for adequate functioning of the school psychologist and other school personnel has yet to be learned. Eli Bower (1964) listed some of the crucial problems to be solved through research about schooling. Research is needed to help schools to identify crisis points in children's lives and to find ways to use such times to increase the child's cognitive and affective resources. We have yet to find adequate means to provide successful school experiences for lower-class children. We do not know how best to go about minimizing those aspects of schooling that are damaging to children. Research is needed to develop approaches to early school interventions to reduce educational casualties. Knowledge is

---

[1] A book in this series, *Educational Psychology* by Donald Ross Green, presents an excellent overview of some of the research findings related to teaching and learning in schools.

needed about how to improve teacher competence to serve as "a provider and planner of mediating experiences for children" [p. 10]. Ways need to be found to help children use language for "a variety of purposes and to recognize language for what it is: an object through which other objects and events are seen" [p. 10]. Education as a primary institution needs assessment and evaluation. To Bower's list could be added a multitude of unsolved problems having to do with schooling.

Research *for schools* refers to attempts to solve problems in specific schools in which the problems of schooling are issues of immediate concern to a limited number of people trying to solve real problems in their particular school situation. At one level, each of the areas delineated by Bower can be personalized as the kind of question asked a school psychologist about individual children. As a practitioner, the school psychologist attempts to answer the questions raised by Bower using whatever conclusions can be made from the research literature. He makes his decisions and bases his judgments, however, on what he can learn about the particular child and the factors influencing his life. At this level, Bower's list of problems might be translated to the following questions: What serious problems are plaguing Jimmy, and how can we use his present vulnerability to improve his ability to function? Since Jimmy has little background for understanding or handling what we present to him in school, how can we improve what we are doing to teach him? How can we prevent those aspects of school experience we have identified as harmful for Jimmy from further hurting him? Since Jimmy is only in the first grade, what can we do now that might improve his chances of succeeding later on? Is there some way to make Jimmy's teacher more responsive to his needs and better able to help teach him? How can we help Jimmy to learn better what we have to teach him?

At another level, research *for schools* involves studying and changing the conditions in the school that affect not only Jimmy but all the other children as well. If we can raise questions about Jimmy, can we not also raise questions about how to systematically and deliberately alter what happens in the school to improve the lives of all who work and live there? This kind of research stems from problems of importance to the school. The likelihood that the school psychologist will be able to engage in such investigation is considerably greater than that of his engaging in research *about schooling*. The school system can see a "pay-off" from having its school psychologist devote time to research *for schools* (activities that directly concern school administration, staff, and parents).

Not all school psychologists work in schools. A person trained in school psychology working in a university, clinic, or research organization may come to a school district, as would any other researcher, requesting permission to engage in research *about schooling*. From this the school district can expect only the most indirect benefit: the know – ledge that it is contributing to a better understanding of phenomena that are important to all concerned with schools. Under these circumstances the psychologist's sensitivity to the operations of the school and his understanding of how his research efforts might be disruptive should stand him in good stead in planning how to conduct his research.

The school psychologist who is employed by a school and who engages in research of interest to that district must operate in a very different way. In many respects his activities can be compared to those of applied researchers in industry, especially in market research. Bernard Berelson (1969), in "The Researcher as a Man of Action," cogently presented some of the differences between applied social research and more traditional research approaches. He pointed out that traditional (basic) research concentrates on contributing to the theory or techniques of a discipline whereas applied social research concentrates on contributing to the solution or amelioration of a problem. According to Berelson, pure research is directed toward finding generalizations; action research is directed toward finding a satisfactory solution to a particular problem. Pure research leads to the understanding of basic processes, whereas action research tries to discover whatever might make a desirable difference, even though that difference may appear to be relatively superficial. Pure research is concerned with the precision of technical methodology. Action research, in addition to techniques, requires pragmatic judgment about the usefulness of the findings in a particular situation. In action research, an effort is made to answer such questions as: Can change be introduced effectively, given the personalities involved in a situation? Is the desired change economically feasible? Will the change lead to important situational differences (rather than merely statistically significant differences)?

The findings from pure research are assumed to lead to action, but action research is not conducted unless the collected facts have a direct relationship to a specific, identified problem.

Pure research usually is directed toward the publication of an article, a monograph, or a book; it is designed to enlighten the entire professional field. Action research, since it is directed toward a specific problem in a particular setting, may result only in an inter-situation memorandum. In fact, the results from a particular action research project may not be generalizable to other situations. The publication based on the pure research project will probably be couched in the jargon of the discipline; the brief report on action research will be written in language understandable to those who will be taking action on the results in the setting in which the research was conducted. As Berelson put it, pure research looks for the *why*. Action research looks for the *how*. "The one, in short, aims at coming to conclusions; the other aims at reaching decision—and the two are not the same" [p. 19].

Research for schools may not have all the attributes and differences mentioned by Berelson, but his distinctions between action research and other kinds of research are highly descriptive of the difference. School psychologists engaged in action research may even be perceived, by school administrators and others, as not engaged in research at all but rather as helping with problem solving in schools. The difference is that school personnel are not accustomed to having research activity work for them in direct fashion.

RESEARCH METHODOLOGY IN
APPLIED RESEARCH FOR SCHOOLS

Some of the procedures followed in well-designed research studies are difficult, if not impossible, to carry out in schools. For example, a school district wants to introduce a recently developed method of perceptual-motor coordination training in first grade, since there seem to be many children who by second or third grade have difficulties in reading that may be related to perceptual-motor skills. The training method has been used by one first-grade teacher who reports that she believes it has been helpful. However, the questions, "How helpful?" "Helpful to which children?" "Helpful in what way?" are not answered.

To answer these questions, the training's effects on reading progress might be objectively measured by comparing the reading progress of a group of trained children with that of children who have received no training. In other words, an experimental (treatment) group is compared with a control (nontreatment) group.

If first grade A is assigned to be the experimental group, and first grade B the control group, the researcher has to be sure that extraneous or *intervening variables* are also controlled. If first grade A consists mainly of children who are "fast learners" from educationally oriented homes, then their reading progress is likely to exceed that of first grade B with or without the training program—if first grade B consists of a large number of children who are relatively "slow learners." Intervening variables are all those factors related to reading progress other than the experimental variable (the training method).

Another intervening variable is the teacher. If teacher A is an excellent, experienced teacher who motivates all her classes well and who is enthusiastic and eager to use the new method, the chances are that group A's reading progress will exceed that of group B. If teacher B is convinced that the reading methods she has used for years are the best, and she knows her group is part of an experiment, she may succeed in having her class's reading progress exceed that of the treatment group.

The general characteristics of experimental and control classrooms should be equalized, meaning assignment of children to first grades A and B in random fashion. In addition, a number of other first grades should be assigned to experimental and control groups to take into account the teacher variable.

These considerations have deliberately been oversimplified; there are many more. Parents react because Jimmy was assigned to classroom B, the control group; but they have heard of the new technique (in classroom A) and want Jimmy perhaps to profit from it. Such projects must be conducted at least for an entire school year; children move into and out of the district, causing the introduction of new subjects and the loss of other subjects.

A number of pretest and post-test instruments must be administered to the experimental and control groups, that is, prior to treatment and again after the treatment method has been used for some time. Teaching is disrupted by the loss of time consumed in the administration of such tests.

It is impossible to have a controlled situation that is an exact facsimile of the experimental condition unless the researcher is fortunate enough to have at least fifty sets of identical twins in the first grades, with identical twins as teachers (matched subjects—subjects identical on every cogent variable). Even the closest possible approximation of matched subjects is not available without considerable manipulation of school programming and activities. Experimental designs that require different treatments presented in a uniform manner to large numbers of children may interfere with the ordinary organization of schools. Perfect control of extraneous and intervening variables is never possible. Educational psychologists often resort to simulation of school experiences, isolation of those variables under study, and experimental examination in a laboratory setting. Long, hard work to arrange situations that provide the conditions necessary to understand the phenomena under consideration is another alternative.

In applied school psychological research, the intervening and extraneous variables that operate to obfuscate exactly how certain factors influence others cannot be eliminated. One approach is to randomize the subjects as much as possible (taking large numbers of subjects and selecting them according to a table of random numbers) on the presumption that the extraneous variables involved are operating equally among treatment and control groups. Perhaps Joe, in the treatment group, does not score as well as he could on a post-test because he is upset about a fight he had on the way to school; perhaps Jill, in the control group, does not score as well as she might because she is about to succumb to a virus.

School psychological research involves trying to understand what the school is like *as it is* and how improvements can be made *under existing conditions.* Attempts at changing the school, distorting its operations, to find out how it might function under new and different conditions will interfere with school operation and will be allowed only if the school system is already seriously considering such a change.

Unobtrusive measures. Marcia Guttentag (1968), a social psychologist, has mentioned a number of techniques she believes highly suitable for research conducted in schools. They offer minimum inconvenience for the schools yet provide useful information for and about the school. She called attention to a distinction made by Roger G. Barker (1965) between the psychologist as "operator" and the psychologist as "transducer." The "operator" contrives events to produce data, as in a laboratory. The "transducer" is a translator of psychological phenomena into data. The transducer observes and codes events that occur naturally, organizing coded observations into data suitable for analysis.

Guttentag called particular attention to unobtrusive measures, the noting of behavior patterns without any direct manipulation of events. *Archival methods* can be used to collect various data available from school records that can be used for comparison purposes.

> Suppose the school psychologist collects figures on the number and characteristics of all children who have referred themselves to the nurse's office every month for a period of time. Suddenly there is a significant rise in the number of self-referrals during one month [p. 256].

Using this change to test hypotheses (tentative statements to explain the change), the school psychologist can check other kinds of information to try to determine what is happening in the school so that the problem can be handled. There may also have been an increase in referrals to other pupil personnel workers. Perhaps the absentee rate has risen. Checking possible reasons may result in understanding the effects of important changes in the school, the seriousness of which has not been recognized by the staff. A change in the grading system, for instance, may have resulted in undue pressure on children. The pace of a new scheduling system may be too difficult for some pupils. Further analysis of archival information about children who were self-referred or absent might give clues to the kinds of pupils most detrimentally influenced by the changes.

There are less spectacular but equally effective ways to use archival data for school research. A variety of group tests are administered in most schools each year. The publishers of group tests provide national norms, data indicating how pupils perform on the tests nationwide. School psychologists can assist schools in developing local norms so that pupil progress may be assessed realistically in terms of characteristics of the district.

Simply describing the students and staff, including ethnic, socio-economic, racial, and sex composition and distribution, can lead to a better understanding of how the school system works and perhaps to changes in policy.

In addition to archival data, data can be collected unobtrusively through the use of *physical traces*. Noting withdrawals of a certain kind from the library might help the school to understand the effects of a new science program. Guttentag, noting unobtrusive measures used by other researchers, mentioned that the position of chairs after a group meeting might be used to discover characteristics of the group's behavior. A study earlier mentioned (Autry & Barker, 1970) indicated that pupils whose last names begin with the first letters of the alphabet tend to score higher on achievement tests than do pupils whose names begin with the last letters of the alphabet. The study is an example of unobtrusive measurement. A clue to racial attitudes can be gained by observing where black and white pupils sit in the cafeteria. The effects of a smoking ban in the high school could be studied by counting the accumulation of cigarette butts in different parts of the building. Harold Hodgkinson (1971) suggested rating schools by what janitors have to say. Bulletin boards provide interesting information about school activities, and an analysis of graffiti on basement walls is another unobtrusive measure.

Program evaluation. Evaluation of school programs represents the kind of research that schools have recently been supporting more whole-heartedly than in the past. This may be due to greater sophistication on the part of personnel, pressure by federal funding agencies for account-ability, or the publicity about the efficacy of commercial reading pro-grams with "guaranteed success or you don't pay for it." A school dis-trict may want to compare several publishers' methods of teaching arithmetic or reading. If the school is sufficiently concerned about which method will do the best job, it may permit a semester or more and some flexibility in programming to allow the school psychologist to assess the effect of different systems on learning, the difficulty of using the systems, and the relative costs. In the long run such investigations can also save school districts money and demonstrate the relative effectiveness of alternate educational programs.

A school district may want to determine how to improve its guidance department or its psychological services. Systems analysis methods have recently been used for such purposes. Lane Roosa (1972), a school psychologist, completed a thorough analysis of the psychological services of a school district using systems analysis methodology. He developed procedures that can be used by other school psychologists to determine the effectiveness of various units of a school district and to make recommendations for improvement. Systems analysis involves a systematic and careful analysis of a system or of a subsystem, based on the premise that an understanding of how to improve a system requires knowledge as to how the system functions and the factors that influence it. Roosa quoted Pilecki (1970):

> This process is accomplished through the documentation of information regarding the system, analysis of the data into small segments which receive individual assessment, and synthesis of all the information inductively, from the individual to the complex whole which the system represents [p. 54].

School psychologists can conduct quasi-longitudinal studies on children. It is no great problem to collect information about children during a period of time and describe changes in their behavior. Children are in school for at least twelve years, and post-high-school information is often available from guidance department records. Questions can be answered relating to early problem behavior and later adjustment, to changes in performance as a result of guidance services, to retention and acceleration practices, or to the effects of special educational programs.

INTERPRETING RESEARCH FINDINGS

A special role for which the school psychologist is especially well prepared is that of the research interpreter. Teachers and school administrators do not always have the training or the time to read research studies related to school behavior. Yet new information and reevaluations of old ideas are constantly published in research journals. The school psychologist is in an ideal position to help school personnel to understand new findings, to assess their validity, and to guage the applicability of research data to school practice. The task is not an easy one. Technical language sometimes defies translation; laboratory studies may not have immediate applicability to practice; conflicting findings may make it all but impossible to report anything with conviction. Still it is possible to apprise school personnel of the state of knowledge in some areas and sometimes, tentatively, to adapt some research-based knowledge to school practice.

Stephen L. Yelon (1969) gave an example of how empirical evidence, stated as a probabilistic, hypothetical principle, can be translated into understandable language. It then can be restated operationally so that a teacher can develop a plan of action based on the principle.

Yelon presented a fairly well established psychological principle taken from a book on behavior modification by Ullman and Krasner (1965):

> Many research studies with humans and animals have shown that extinction of operant behavior is a function of noncontingent withdrawal of positive reinforcers. The probability of change in the dependent variable is very high. We might expect a gradual reduction of the operant behavior with an initial rise in rate over and above the present rate and possible "emotional behaviors" [p. 156].

Yelon translated this principle as follows:

> If you wish to decrease the frequency or rate of a behavior which is now controlled by some of its consequences, set up the situational conditions so that the consequences which you believe are serving to increase the number of responses, are not presented. When this procedure is first instituted, beware; for the behavior may increase in number and intensity, but will gradually decrease. Some crying or tantrum behaviors may be expected [p. 156].

Finally, the teacher is helped to apply the principle. First she would have to assess the behavior she wanted changed. She must make sure that her objective has the same characteristics as the behavior described by the dependent variable in the principle.

> The teacher's goal is to find the reason for the crying and by manipulating the causative stimuli, reduce the crying . . . If the teacher guesses that this behavior is an effort to gain the expected consequences of adult attention or some material goods, then this principle may be applied. The teacher can refer to knowledge gained from observing the child in the past and from observing present parent-child interaction or present teacher-child interactions, i.e., presenting and withdrawing possible consequences. If it were determined that adult attention was the consequence that was increasing the frequency, then this consequence would not be presented when the crying is emitted. This can be done because all the relevant stimuli are available and manipulable. The teacher can expect things "to get worse before they get better" and can expect further emotional outbursts such as statements like "I hate you" to occur. She may also expect more crying on the first few days than ever encountered before [p. 157].

Research as described here offers only some of the ways school psychologists can serve as modifiers of the school system. That most have not done so to this date is a function of the limited expectations held by school administrations and staff of what school psychologists have to offer. Even more importantly, it is a function of the limited expectations school psychologists hold of the services they can offer. The school psychologist of the future need not be so constrained.

Training
for School Psychology
and Prospects for the Future

chapter seven

In previous chapters we attempted to show how school psychology differs from other psychological specialties and how the school psychologist approaches the multitudinous problems he is asked to help solve. What kind of preparation will produce the kind of school psychologist we have described?

School psychology is only one of the professional subspecialties in psychology: like medicine, professional psychology encompasses an ever-growing, ever-changing body of knowledge in a variety of subspecialties that cannot possibly all be absorbed in a "reasonable" amount of time. Therefore, graduate training programs in professional psychology are usually directed toward one subspecialty or toward a combination of particular subspecialties: clinical, community, counseling, industrial, or school psychology. Regardless of the emphasis on the subspecialty, all these varieties in training must succeed in producing a graduate who is and thinks of himself as a *psychologist*.[1]

---

[1] Two leaders in school psychology, Susan Gray (1963) and Norma Cutts (1955), have cited the Spaulding Lecture at Yale by Charles W. Cole (1953) as pertinent to training for school psychology. Cole made the point that medical knowledge has long exceeded the point at which a student in medical school

What Determines Professional Training?

Training for school psychology has its roots in training for psychology, which shares many of the aspects of professional training in general.

Wilbert E. Moore (1970), in his definition of a professional, clearly indicated the impact that professionalism has on the kind of training that produces a professional.

> The professional practices a full-time *occupation*, which comprises the principal source of his earned income. . . . A more distinctly professional qualification is that of commitment to a *calling*, that is, the treatment of the occupation and all of its requirements as an enduring set of normative and behavioral expectations. Those who pursue occupations of relatively high rank in terms of criteria of professionalism are likely to be set apart from the laity by various signs and symbols, but by the same token are identified with their peers—often in formalized *organization*. Organization presupposes a distinctive occupation with a common commitment by those engaged in it to protect and enhance its interests.
>
> An important next step in professionalism is the possession of esoteric but useful knowledge and skills, based on specialized training or *education* of exceptional duration and perhaps of exceptional difficulty [pp. 6–7].

Moore explained that "useful" knowledge implies that the professional has a service orientation; that he perceives the needs of others that are relevant to his competence and is indeed competent in attending to those needs. The final aspect of professionalism is that the professional proceeds to use his knowledge autonomously; he proceeds by his own judgment and authority.

THE ORGANIZATION: THE AMERICAN
PSYCHOLOGICAL ASSOCIATION (APA)

The APA is concerned with the occupation of psychology, with a common commitment by those engaged in it to define, protect, and enhance the occupation. Like other professional organizations, the APA also protects the public that the profession serves. If an individual meets the standards and criteria for membership in the organization, then the public knows that he has certain qualifications. Although APA does not

---

can possibly master sufficient knowledge in four years to practice as a physician. Instead, the emphasis in training must shift to teaching the medical student to think like a physician.

equate membership with competence, membership does imply some minimum level of training and/or experience. Similarly, professional organizations set up internal safeguards by accrediting training programs and, through their participating state organizations, by setting the standards for license to practice.

The good aspect of professional organization is that it sets standards that are relatively uniform and that define the profession. The drawback is that once standards are set, the development of new and creative training programs tend to become stultified because written guidelines are not easily changed. This issue has long been debated in the APA.

Membership in the professional organization is the point of entry to the profession, and APA's criterion for full membership is "the doctoral degree based in part upon a psychological dissertation, or from a program primarily psychological in content, and conferred by a graduate school of recognized standing" [APA, 1970, p. xii]. The requirement of a doctoral degree may change in the future as pressure is brought to bear on APA for inclusion of nondoctoral psychologists as full participants in APA affairs. The point we wish to make at this time is that the APA, in large part, determines what the training for psychology shall be.

"A graduate school of recognized standing" means a graduate school that someone, somewhere, has evaluated in terms of its curriculum, its supervised experiences, the caliber of its students, and the quality of its faculty. The "someone" may have been APA's own accrediting agency of psychology programs, but accreditation most certainly was granted by one of the geographical subcommittees of the National Council on Accreditation, which accredits both undergraduate and graduate programs in various specialties.

In psychology the typical model for any practitioner specialty has come to be known as the "Boulder Model." After Warld War II, a conference on training held in 1949 in Boulder, Colorado, (Raimy, 1950), defined the practicing psychologist as a "scientist-practitioner"; a scientist in the sense that he should be a competent researcher and contributor of new knowledge as well as a careful evaluator of previous knowledge; a practitioner in that he is exercising his profession. The guidelines set by the Boulder Conference became the basis for the four-year doctoral program that incorporated training in research as well as a practical internship.

Post-World War II's psychology had close ties with medicine, since most practicing psychologists were working in psychiatric settings. Medical terminology still is pervasive in psychology, e.g., "diagnosis" and "therapy." During the 1960s in particular, graduate training in practitioner psychology, in an effort to develop as an autonomous rather than an ancillary profession (to medicine), emphasized academic and scientific training and deemphasized professional training. University support for some clinical practitioner programs was lessened, and in some instances practitioner programs were eliminated or transferred to other departments.

Since psychology grew in popularity as an undergraduate major and became accessible as a profession only to those with graduate degrees, graduate programs in psychology attracted an ever-increasing number of applicants. A rigorous array of admission tests began to be required along with evidence of high undergraduate grades. Certain cutoff points in graduate programs were devised to weed out the unworthy. How to offer a comprehensive and adequate curriculum, how best to offer supervised experiences, how to select students who are committed professionally and are academically superior, what criteria to use to choose faculty to implement the program—all of these have been issues of vigorous and emotional debate among psychologists.

Carl Rogers (1965), in his "Passionate Statement" for a revision of graduate training in psychology, deplored the use of the examinations commonly used to judge professional promise, questioning whether high scores on Graduate Record Examinations and the Miller Analogies Tests predict creative thinking. Rogers further suggested that the supervision, guidance, and evaluation of students inhibits their freedom to pursue learning on their own. Learning, says Rogers, is not equivalent to hearing a lecture; nor does knowledge accumulate from brick upon brick of content and information. Learning takes place primarily and significantly when it is directly related to the meaningful purposes and motives of the individual student. Passive learners who simply absorb and deliver on the many examinations in graduate school do not become creative scientists upon graduation. Rogers also commented on the tendency to look upon method as science, a point of view that he says seems to revere rigorous scientific procedures more than the ideas that the procedures purport to investigate.

Much of what Rogers has to say represents issues that permeate all graduate (and for that matter undergraduate) programs in all fields. Violent and emotional discussions rage among students, faculty, and commentators (expert or otherwise) on the value of grading systems, objective evaluation of student progress, and formal didactic courses; on student-versus-faculty determination of programs, requirements that penalize lower socioeconomic groups, "relevance," and a multitude of other topics that reflect the current social unrest.

Not all psychologists, college professors, students, or even society at large want a revision of training, especially if "revision" is interpreted as completely laissez-faire: "Let the student do his own thing" and "Anyone who *wants* to go to college and/or graduate school should be admitted." The man on the street has summed up the attitude of the "traditionalists" with his statement, "I'm not sure I want a surgeon removing my appendix if he didn't think the study of anatomy was relevant."

Many training programs are adopting a middle ground and are experimenting with new and different models of training. Perhaps psychology training programs have been among the first to experiment, some drastically, some cautiously.[2] The subject matter of psychology is, after all, the modification of behavior via learning.

Influences on School Psychology Training

The various state certification standards for school psychologists influence training programs very directly—a psychologist whose training does not include whatever state certification requires is not employable. If we hold that the school psychologist is first a psychologist, then the standards of the professional organization, APA, and the licensing laws of the various states define what his basic training must include. These taskmasters with predetermined standards may ensure minimum competency, but they may also inhibit innovation in training.

The school psychologist we have described enacts many roles that are not spelled out in the laws or certification requirements of the states. He fulfills roles for which he may not have had extensive training in graduate school. The magic number of four years has been adopted as "reasonable" for doctoral training, usually with an allowance of up to three more years to complete the dissertation. A training program that required a thorough series of courses plus sufficient supervised experience to ensure competency in all the roles we have described would far exceed the four-year limit.

The Division of School Psychology, Division 16 of APA, has published suggested *Standards and criteria . . .* (1971–72) for training programs as has the National Association of School Psychologists, an organization devoted to the enhancement of the professional status and functioning of school psychologists [1972]. On the nondoctoral level Division 16 suggested a minimum of two years of university training plus a year of supervised experience; the National Association of School Psychologists recommended that training programs meet the certification standards established by the education department of the state in which the program is located and that a year of full-time, supervised experience be provided. Emphasis at the nondoctoral level is on training the school

[2] The National Council on Graduate Education in Psychology has published a monograph entitled *The revolution in professional training*, a review of innovative programs for the training of professional psychologists [Norman J. Matulef, Ed., Washington, D.C., 1970].

psychologist to become a competent practitioner with sufficient research knowledge to take advantage of the literature. At the doctoral level of training, Division 16 suggested a four-year program that recognizes different models of training. Emphasis is on a curriculum that provides for basic knowledge in psychology, an organized sequence of courses and experiences, and in general a program in keeping with the scientist-practitioner model. These guidelines imply that students shall be recruited from candidates presenting strong indications of academic competence and that they shall work with a faculty that is firmly identified with school psychology—faculty that has demonstrated its leadership in both the university setting and in the professional field of school psychology.

These standards exert a strong influence on school psychology training, but they do not necessarily represent what always *is* nor what all school psychologists *believe* training should be.

Aspects of Rogers's aforementioned "Passionate Statement" are reflected in many school psychology training programs, some of which have already integrated course work with experiences in the schools to make basic knowledge in psychology relevant to the goals of the student (and the program). Some school psychology programs are experimenting with action research, viewing the methods and procedures of research as tools, not as goals in and of themselves. The emphasis on research in training programs varies widely, since school psychologists (like most practitioner psychologists) are urged to conduct research but have difficulty in finding time and facilities to do so. The demands for practice are immediate and great, and most state certification standards *require* the practice component but minimize the research component. Training programs, then, frequently emphasize the "intelligent consumption of research" rather than the production of research findings.

Differences in emphasis in school psychology programs are often reflective of and contingent upon the point of view adopted by the department of psychology or of education that houses the program. For example, in a university wherein the psychology program in the graduate school of arts and sciences has become strictly academic (nonpractitioner), the school psychology program in a graduate school of education may be the only practitioner-oriented program in that particular university. In some universities the school psychology program may be part of a department of psychology, and it may not differ very much from the programs of the other psychological specialties. In still other universities, the school psychology program may be an adjunct to the counseling and guidance program offered by the school of education.

The identification of school psychology as an autonomous subspecialty of psychology and the strength of the program offered depend largely on how it is perceived by the university that houses it. If the university perceives school psychology as an important offering, it will supply the necessary funds for quality faculty, student stipends, facilities, and equipment. If the university takes a dim view of school psychology, the program may consist of one junior faculty member struggling to maintain adequate supervision and advisement of students whose work is done primarily in other programs within the university.

Programs are greatly influenced by support that augments university funds. The National Institute of Mental Health has provided funds that help to support some school psychology programs; the United States Office of Education has also provided limited (relative to the total amount expended) support to a very few programs. NIMH support generally has gone to programs whose graduates are psychologists in the scientist-practitioner model. Funding from the U.S. Office of Education may be limited because school psychologists are usually viewed as part of the general group of pupil personnel workers, ancillary to education per se. As such, school psychology becomes only one part of the broad, comprehensive programs sponsored by the Office of Education. The programs are in a complex of educational centers consisting of schools, communities, and universities operating on a number of levels to improve the quality of education.

MASTER'S VERSUS DOCTORAL TRAINING

A broad issue within all psychology is the level of training. Although psychologists agree that we need and should recognize subdoctoral or nondoctoral training, there are dissenters. The dissension is exemplified by the fact that APA and most of its state affiliates require the doctorate for full membership and restrict nondoctoral psychologists to associate membership. Current qualifications for associate membership are (*a*) having two years of graduate training in psychology and full-time devotion to work or graduate study that is psychological, or (*b*) having the master's degree in psychology plus one full year of professional work in psychology and full-time devotion to work or graduate study that is primarily psychological in character.

Until 1971 only full members could vote or hold office. However, APA has modified its requirements so that associate members may vote or hold office after five years of associate membership. In 1972 the Council of Representatives, APA's official governing body, began considering a proposal to admit master's degree psychologists to full membership. These changes and considerations indicate a recognition of the importance and the contribution of the nondoctoral psychologist.

As long ago as 1955 at the Thayer Conference on "School psychologists at mid-century" (Cutts, 1955), there was general agreement that school psychology training could be at two levels, doctoral and non-doctoral. The participants of this conference did not agree completely on the appropriate nondoctoral level of training, although two years of graduate training were generally considered to be the minimum acceptable.

Diversity of Training Programs

More important than a discussion of how many courses in which subjects, how many credits accumulated, how many supervised hours, how much emphasis on research, and how many years of graduate training leading to what degree is a consideration of what kind of training will produce the professional previously described: someone who thinks like a psychologist and who utilizes psychology as an approach to solving the problems of the schools.

Thinking like a psychologist means learning the basic tools and knowledge of the profession, even if some of this is discarded later. Part of training is learning that what is learned today may be outdated tomorrow. A school psychologist learns approaches to problem solving: the niceties of objective reasoning, a sensitivity to the impact of emotion upon cognitive processes. He acquires a humble but positive skepticism that reflects an understanding of the imperfections of his knowledge and tools. He develops a critical, cautious approach to the assessment of his own findings and deliberations. To cope with his continuous assignment to learn what is new and to participate in creating what is new, he must be flexible in his approach.

Within this framework of thinking like a psychologist, the school psychologist is primarily involved with real-life situations. He must care about what happens to people. He must be capable of genuine identification with different kinds of people and their modes of behavior, including those whose cultural backgrounds, ethnic origins, and basic beliefs may be very different from his. He must have a sincere and positive attitude toward humanity that will enable him to try new approaches and to persist, even in the face of discouragement, lack of results, and frustrations.

We hold that the school psychologist can function in many different ways and that learning from specific courses is not necessarily the best or the only way to learn. Some of the insights and understandings gleaned from course work are part of becoming a psychologist; but course work is made meaningful only when the psychologist learns how to assess and to develop new knowledge through real-life experiences, and when he learns to integrate this new knowledge with his basic psychological background. The real-life experience that makes psychology meaningful for and applicable to its future functional setting is experience in the school concomitant with academic learning. Research activities are meaningful if they are based on inquiry into the real and pragmatic questions that schools ask and need answered.

School psychology training programs should provide diversity among the kinds of professionals who work with students and who, therefore, serve as role models and provide a major source of professional identification—faculty members who think like psychologists and who are school psychologists.

Characteristic of school psychology training programs is their lack of a single, identifiable model. The standards set forth by Division 16 of APA specifically mention and make provision for differing models of training. Some programs place more emphasis on research training, others on practitioner skills. Some include many hours of supervised experiences, other relatively few. Some require previous experience in education, others do not. Some require undergraduate psychology as preparation for graduate training, others do not.

This diversity among training programs in content, in supervised experiences, and in goals inevitably presents problems. The graduate of Training Program A may be employed by a school district that expects the kind of graduate produced by Training Program B. Neither A nor B produces a graduate with all the competencies implicit in the functions outlined in this book.

Yet the very diversity of types of training is an asset to school psychology as a still-developing specialty within psychology. The authors of this book are of course subject to bias; but it seems that school psychology, among all the professional subspecialties, has served as a model for experimentation and innovation in graduate training in psychology. The fact that the role of the school psychologist is not fixed by tradition and that it is moving away from the constraints of the medical model permits experimentation in the training programs for that role. No definitive evidence exists as to the effectiveness of various kinds of psychological services in the schools, and no program can claim that it alone provides training the "right way." Susan Gray, speaking of school psychology training, said:

> Probably more than any other thing, what we need is the development of different kinds of training programs, ones that are imaginative, that take cognizance of the best psychology has to offer to the schools, that exploit the potentials of a given university center . . . University departments have upon them a demand—an opportunity—not only to devise new and better methods of training. They also have a responsibility to evaluate these new approaches as their worth is revealed in the performance of the graduates of these new programs [p. 285].

Although Susan Gray wrote in 1963, her charge to training programs is applicable today.

Prospects for the Future

We have tried to present a realistic view of how school psychology serves the schools while attempting to suggest how its service might be improved. No other specialty in psychology, in our view, illustrates so well the problems and promise presented when specialists trained in the behavioral sciences try to serve a particular segment of society. To apply knowledge and skills to the problems of others is a hazardous undertaking and an impure one at best. It is as dependent on how applications are made as it is on what is applied. College students should know about these problems as they study the subject matter. Otherwise they will be sorely disappointed and disillusioned when the practical contingencies of application of knowledge are first faced. Students should also know that the very problems that make the application of knowledge so difficult offer in and of themselves challenging opportunities for the development of further knowledge and for the solution of important societal problems.

Another purpose of this book has been to convey a view of the school as a social setting different enough from other societal institutions to deserve independent study and analysis. Further, we have tried to show that going to school involves considerably more than learning subjects in classes. In fact it is our view, shared we believe by most pupils who think about it, that more schooling takes place on the way to the building, in the halls, and in extracurricular activities than is usually acknowledged. It is our view that this is true because of the dynamics of pupil-pupil, pupil-teacher, teacher-teacher, and teacher-administrator interactions. Without downgrading subject matter teaching, we hold that the influences of schooling, as we define it, are probably comparatively greater than the influence of education as commonly defined: what one learns is important, but what is happening to the pupil while subject matter is taught and learned is also very important. Current dissatisfaction with schools is in large measure dissatisfaction with the school as a place in which to learn and work. What is criticized most often can be described as atmosphere—ways of interacting, expectations pupils have of teachers, and those that teachers have of pupils. Earlier we compared the school to the home. Both are places in which learning takes place. Both involve child-adult interaction of great importance to the child. When the home fails to do its job, society's response has most often been to try to improve the home or to provide a substitute home. When the school fails to do its job, society has not bolstered it as well; nor has it provided acceptable alternatives.

The school psychologist is that psychologist who has chosen to work in this most difficult and important setting. In the past he was primarily concerned with helping individual children to adjust to the setting or to profit from its efforts. His methods and point of view typically have been those of clinical psychology, concerned with diagnosis and recommendation, sometimes with treatment. Until fairly recently it had not been possible to expand very much on this relatively narrow conception of school psychological service. Until state laws mandated the use of psychologists and until training programs developed, the number of psychologists employed by schools was too small to matter. What schools asked for could adequately be handled by clinically trained psychologists.

THE CHANGING SCENE

The situation has changed. There are training programs for school psychologists; schools are asking—even demanding—more from psychologists. Educators in general are better trained than they were and have more sophisticated expectations both of themselves and of psychological knowledge. The idea of a school as a distinct, complex setting, different from other schools and from other kinds of community facilities is better appreciated. Schools, like most other aspects of our culture, are in turmoil and will continue to be in turmoil for many years to come. As discussed in Chapter Four, periods of crisis are periods that produce change for better or worse, depending on what is done. If one can conceive of a school as a client, then the potential for school psychology's impact upon society can best be seen.

The school psychologist of the future cannot adequately be described or predicted. Especially if we are correct, he will be doing different things in different schools expressly because he has viewed the school as his client and because he has attended to those problems that lend themselves to his background in psychology and to his knowledge of schooling and schools. His orientation is more likely to relate to education than to mental health.

THE MEDICAL-MODEL APPROACH

Traditional psychological services have taken what has been called a medical-model approach. When this approach is applied to psychological services, it usually refers to one or more working hypotheses deeply embedded in the value system of the professional offering the service. Among these hypotheses are the following:

Adult disorders have their genesis in pathological events occurring during the preschool years. Therefore, it is important to help children early in their lives to prevent their becoming mentally ill as adults. It is legitimate to talk about working with children to prevent adult problems, since prevention looks to the future. The child is important for what he will become even more than for what he is. Helping children means gathering information about the nature and extent of pathological or aberrant behavior, then evaluating the behavior either on some normative scale of adjustment-maladjustment or according to one's understanding of the personality and interrelational dynamics of one of the major personality theories. Gathering information this way is diagnosis, and diagnosis is essential to understanding psychological problems. If lay persons (anyone who is not a mental health professional) are provided with correct diagnostic information, they will understand the child better and will be more helpful to him in that they will be able to act in ways that will keep him from becoming mentally ill.

Help is best defined as certain qualities of behavior toward children that are best exemplified in a treatment method called psychotherapy. Whatever form psychotherapy takes, it is really "essence of ideal relationship" as seen by the mental health professional. If others can act toward the child as mental health professionals do, the child will be on the road to "mental health."

The goal of the mental health professional with children is to "work his way out of a job." He hopes to be so influential that others can take over, and his services will no longer be needed. This utopia will arrive when everyone else is behaving toward children exactly as the mental health professional would behave if he were present.

This view, presented deliberately in an exaggerated form, clearly is present in some parts of this book. It does describe in part how school psychologists have functioned in the past and still do—as mental health professionals in the schools.

THE DEVELOPMENTAL-EDUCATIONAL APPROACH

There are other sets of beliefs that can be used equally well by professional psychologists, beliefs that might better fit the kinds of activities in which school psychologists may engage during the next decade or two.

Growing up involves solving certain crucial developmental tasks. These tasks are both cognitive and affective and are cumulative in nature: if early tasks do not get solved, later tasks become more difficult. Helping children to move through their developmental periods successfully is the major task for any adult who rears or educates them.

Success or failure experiences are important byproducts of development. Solving problems—experiencing failure and turning it into success

—is even more helpful than having only successful experiences; but both are better than uncorrected failure. The crucial element in the balance between success and failure is mastery. Perhaps the best single predictor of adult success is not the absence of pathological symptoms but the presence of resources for problem solving.

The influential determinants of a child's success-failure index and the key to his growing up successfully are the various social systems in which he functions. These include his family, his neighborhood, his peer group, and his school. If schooling is a part of his life, it becomes a potent force for good or for harm. Schooling is not merely preparation for some future life; what the child does *now* is important in its own right. The child is not only father to the man. He is a person, now.[3]

This developmental-educational view of children and of the influences on their lives is in accord with the way schools function and with how school personnel think. If the psychologist can help the school to improve its efficiency, create a better atmosphere for learning, devise ways to improve success and minimize failure, and permit sufficient failure to occur so that coping behavior can be rewarded, he can become an essential professional rather than a peripheral, occasional consultant. That is why it is so difficult to say what he should or will do in the future. He should do whatever his training has helped him to do that will improve the school's ability to help children grow and learn. In some school systems, undoubtedly, the school psychologist will be child-centered in his activities, working with teachers to understand how a child learns and helping to devise programs based on his psycho-educational assessment of the child's learning style and of the factors influencing his school behavior. In other instances management and organization of classroom behavior and practices will be the major concern. Increasingly, school psychologists will engage in applied research in the schools, working on the kinds of problems that affect how the school delivers its services and appraising the effectiveness of the school's efforts. There will be intimate school psychologists working on a one-to-one ratio with pupils, teachers, and administrators, helping them solve pressing, everyday problems including their interactions with each other. There will also be technologically oriented school psychologists who will work primarily on curricular and organizational matters. Some will best be described as entrepreneurial school psychologists. These will locate unmet needs and will ini-

---

[3] We are indebted to James Glidewell for his excellent summary of the issues involved in community mental health endeavors. We have borrowed his ideas liberally, but he is not responsible for the interpretations we have placed on them. [Glidewell, J. Priorities for psychologists in community mental health. In G. Rosenblum (Ed.), *Issues in community psychology and preventive mental health*. New York: Behavioral Publications, 1971.]

tiate, develop, organize, and implement programs in schools to meet those needs.

Although it is fashionable to talk about psychologists as change agents, it is perhaps better to consider the future school psychologist as a facilitative agent who works to get others to do better what they want to do or need to have done.

Chris Argyris of Yale University (1970) said that change is not the primary task of the interventionist:

> The interventionist's primary tasks are to generate valid information, to help the client system make informed and responsible choices, and to develop internal commitment to these choices. One choice that the clients may make is to change aspects of their system. If this choice is made responsibly, the interventionist may help the client to change. However . . . change is not a priori considered good and no change considered bad [pp. 21–22].

Obviously, the better educated our future school psychologist is, the more likely he is to have the multiple skills needed to fulfill the broad roles we have briefly described. Although school psychologists with master's degree level training have served and will continue to serve the schools with distinction, it is our view that a college student planning a career in school psychology should plan to complete graduate study through the doctorate.

The problems of the school are great. Psychology has not yet provided the solutions necessary to school problems. It is our hope that through the efforts of that psychological practitioner called the school psychologist, knowledge from the behavioral sciences can be translated into help for our troubled schools.

References

AMERICAN PSYCHIATRIC ASSOCIATION. *Diagnostic and statistical manual of mental disorders.* Washington, D.C.: American Psychiatric Association, 1968.

AMERICAN PSYCHOLOGICAL ASSOCIATION. *Bibliographical directory.* Washington, D.C.: American Psychological Association, 1970.

ANASTASI, A. *Psychological testing.* New York: Macmillan, 1957.

ANDERSON, C. *New media for instruction I: Technology in American education, 1650–1900.* Washington, D.C.: U.S. Department of Health, Education, and Welfare, OE–34018, 1962.

ANDREWS, J. K. The results of a pilot program to train teachers in the classroom application of behavior modification techniques. *Journal of School Psychology,* 1970, *8,* 37–42.

ANDRONICO, M. P., & GUERNEY, B., JR. The potential application of filial therapy to the school situation. *Journal of School Psychology,* 1967, *6,* 2–7.

ARCISZEWSKI, R. A. Perception training in the first grade. *The Reading Instruction Journal,* 1968, *11,* 48–51.

ARGYRIS, C. *Intervention theory and method: A behavioral science view.* Reading, Mass.: Addison-Wesley, 1970.

AUTRY, J. W., & BARKER, D. G. Academic correlates of alphabetical order of surname. *Journal of School Psychology,* 1970, *8*(1), 22–23.

BANKS, G., & CARKHUFF, R. R. Sensitivity training: A brief annotated bibliography, *Professional Psychology*, 1972, *3*, 93–95.

BARKER, R. G., Explorations in ecological psychology. *American Psychologist*, 1965, *20*, 1–14.

BARKER, R. G., & GUMP, P. V. *Big school, small school: High school size and student behavior*. Stanford: Stanford University Press, 1964.

BATEMAN, B. Implication of a learning disability approach for teaching educable retardates. *Mental Retardation*, 1967, *5*, 23–25.

BEERS, C. *A mind that found itself*. New York: Longmans, Green, 1908.

BELLAK, L., & SMALL, L. *Emergency psychotherapy and brief psychotherapy*. New York: Grune & Stratton, 1965.

BERELSON, B. The researcher as a man of action. In L. BOGART (Ed.), *Current controversies in marketing research*. Chicago: Markham, 1969.

BERENSON, D. H. The effects of systematic human relations training upon classroom performance of elementary school teachers. *Journal of Research and Development in Education*, 1971, *4*, 70–85.

BERSOFF, D. N. School psychology as "institutional psychiatry." *Professional Psychology*, 1971, *2*, 266–70.

BERSOFF, D. N., & GRIEGER, R. M. II. An interview model for the psychosituational assessment of children's behavior. *American Journal of Orthopsychiatry*, 1971, *41*, 483–93.

BESSELL, H., & PALOMARES, U. *Methods in human development: Theory manual, 1970 revision*. San Diego: Human Development Training Institute, 1970.

BINET, A., & SIMON, T. Methodes nouvelles pour le diagnostic du niveau intellectuel des anormaux. *Annie psychologie*, 1905, *11*, 191–244.

BIRNBAUM, P. *A treasury of Judaism*. New York: Hebrew Publishing Co., 1962.

BLUESTEIN, V. W., & MILOFSKY, C. A. Certification patterns and requirements for school psychologists. *Journal of School Psychology*, 1970, *8*, 270–77.

BOWER, E. M. Psychology in the schools: Conceptions, processes and territories. *Psychology in the Schools*, 1964, *1*, 3–11.

BOWER, E. M. The school psychologist's role in the identification and adjustment of socio-emotionally handicapped children. In J. F. MAGARY (Ed.), *School psychological services*, Englewood Cliffs, N. J.: Prentice-Hall, 1967.

BOWER, E. M. *Early identification of emotionally handicapped children in school*. Springfield, Ill.: Charles C. Thomas, 1969.

BOYER, W. H., & WALSH, P. Are children born unequal? *Saturday Review*, October 19, 1968, 61–63, 77–79.

BREWER, J. *History of vocational guidance*. New York: Harper, 1942.

BROTEMARKLE, R. A. (Ed.) *Clinical psychology: Studies in honor of Lightner Witmer*. Philadelphia: University of Pennsylvania Press, 1931.

CAPLAN, G. Opportunities for school psychologists in the primary prevention of mental disorders in children. *Mental Hygiene*, 1963, *47*, 525–39.

CAPLAN, G. *The theory and practice of mental health consultation.* New York: Basic Books, 1970.

CARKHUFF, R. R. *The development of human resources: Education, psychology, and social change.* New York: Holt, Rinehart & Winston, 1971.

CASON, E. Some suggestions on the interaction between the school psychologist and the classroom teacher. *Journal of Consulting Psychology,* 1945, *9,* 132–37.

CHAREN, C. L. *The effect of systematic tangible reinforcements on reading skill development for retarded readers in an urban school setting.* Unpublished doctoral dissertation, Rutgers—the State University, New Brunswick, N.J., 1971.

CONNECTICUT SPECIAL EDUCATION ASSOCIATION. *History of special education for mentally deficient children in Connecticut.* New Haven, Conn.: The Association, 1936.

CONTI, A. P. A follow-up study of families referred to outside agencies. *Psychology in the Schools,* 1971, *8,* 338–40.

CONTI, A. P. A follow-up study of families referred by the school psychologist to resources outside of the schools. Unpublished doctoral dissertation, Rutgers—the State University, New Brunswick, N.J., 1972.

COWEN, E. L. Coping with school adaptation problems. *Psychology in the Schools,* 1971, *8,* 322–29.

CUTTS, N. (Ed.) *School psychologists at mid-century.* Washington, D.C.: American Psychological Association, 1955.

DENO, E. Special education as developmental capital. *Exceptional Children,* 1970, *37*(3), 229–37.

DINKMEYER, D. The "C" group: Integrating knowledge and experience to change behavior—an Adlerian approach to consultation. *The Counseling Psychologist,* 1971, *3,* 63–72.

DINKMEYER, D., & MURO, J. *Group counseling: Theory and practice.* Itasca, Ill.: Peacock Publishers, 1971.

ENGLISH, H. B., & ENGLISH, A. C. *A comprehensive dictionary of psychological and psychoanalytical terms.* New York: Longmans, Green, 1958.

EYSENCK, H. J. (Ed.) *Behavior therapy and the neuroses.* London: Pergamon Press, 1960.

FERGUSON, D. G. *Pupil personnel services.* Washington, D.C.: The Center for Applied Research in Education, Inc., 1963.

FESTINGER, L. *A theory of cognitive dissonance.* Stanford: Stanford University Press, 1957.

FIFIELD, M. The role of school psychology in public education. *Psychology in the Schools,* 1967, *4,* 66–68.

FLEMING, E. S., & ANTTONEN, R. G. Teacher expectancy or my fair lady? *The School Psychology Digest,* 1972, Spring, 17–21.

FROSTIG, M., & HORNE, D. Assessment of visual perception and its importance in education. *American Association of Mental Deficiency Education Reporter,* 1962, *2,* 11–12.

GLASSER, W. *Reality therapy: A new approach to psychiatry*. New York: Harper & Row. 1965.

GLASSER, W. *Schools without failure*. New York: Harper & Row, 1969.

GLIDEWELL, J. Priorities for psychologists in community mental health. In G. ROSENBLUM (Ed.), *Issues in community psychology and preventive mental health*. New York: Behavioral Publications, 1971.

GORDON, J. W. The psychologist as a consultant in an in-service program of child and youth study. *Journal of School Psychology*, 1967, *6*, 18–21.

GRAY, S. W. *The psychologist in the schools*. New York: Holt, Rinehart & Winston, 1963.

GREEN, D. R. *Educational psychology*. Englewood Cliffs, N.J.: Prentice-Hall, 1964.

GREENE, M. *The public school and the private vision*. New York: Random House, 1965.

GUERNEY, B., JR. Filial therapy: Description and rationale. *Journal of Consulting Psychology*, 1964, *28*, 304–10.

GUERNEY, B. G., JR., & FLUMEN, A. B. Teachers as psychotherapeutic agents for withdrawn children. *Journal of School Psychology*, 1970, *8*, 107–13.

GUERNEY, B. G., JR., & MERRIAM, M. Toward a democratic elementary school classroom. *The Elementary School Journal*, 1972, *72*, 372–83.

GUTTENTAG, M. Research is possible: New answers to old objections. *Journal of School Psychology*, 1968, *6*, 254–60.

HALL, C. S. *Primer of Freudian psychology*. New York: Mentor, 1962.

HALL, C. S., & LINDZEY, G. *Theories of personality*. New York: John Wiley, 1965.

HANDLER, L., GERSTON, A., & HANDLER, B. Suggestions for improved psychologist-teacher communication. *Psychology in the Schools*, 1965, *2*, 77–81.

Harvard Educational Review: Environment, Heredity, and Intelligence. Series No. 2, 1969.

HODGKINSON, H. Unobtrusive measures. Reported in *Behavior Today*, November 22, 1971, *2*(47), 2.

HOEDT, K., & FARLING, W. *National survey of school psychologists*. Washington, D.C.: U.S. Department of Health, Education, and Welfare, 1971.

JENSEN, A. R. How much can we boost IQ and scholastic achievement? *Harvard Educational Review*, 1969, *39*, 1–123.

JOINT COMMISSION ON MENTAL HEALTH OF CHILDREN. *Crisis in child mental health: Challenge for the 1970's*. New York: Harper & Row, 1970.

JONES, M. C. A laboratory study of fear: The case of Peter. *Pedagogical Seminary*, 1924, *31*, 308–15.

KAMII, C. K., & RADIN, N. L. The retardation of disadvantaged Negro preschoolers: Some characteristics found from an item analysis of the Stanford-Binet test. *Psychology in the Schools*, 1969, *6*, 283–88.

KOHN, M., & BEKER, J. Special methodological considerations in conducting field research in a school setting. *Psychology in the Schools*, 1964, *1*, 31–46.

KORNRICH, M. Deadend: The rejection of a recommendation for psychotherapy. *Psychology in the Schools*, 1965, *2*, 275–78.

KOUNIN, J. S. An analysis of teachers' managerial techniques. *Psychology in the Schools*, 1967, *4*(3), 221–27.

LEARY, M. E. Children who are tested in an alien language mentally retarded? *The New Republic*, May 1970, 17–18.

LEVINE, M., & LEVINE, A. *A social history of helping services: Clinic, court, school, and community.* New York: Appleton-Century-Crofts, 1970.

LINDSLEY, O. R. The beautiful future of school psychology: Advising teachers. In M. C. REYNOLDS (Ed.), *Psychology and the process of schooling in the next decade.* Washington, D.C.: Bureau for Educational Personnel Development, U.S. Office of Education, 1971.

LUBORSKY, L., AUERBACH, A. H., CHANDLER, M., COHEN, J., & BACHRACH, H. M. Factors influencing the outcome of psychotherapy: A review of quantitative research. *Psychological Bulletin*, 1971, *75*, 145–85.

MANN, L. Psychometric phrenology and the new faculty psychology: The case against ability assessment and training. *The Journal of Special Education*, 1971, *5*, 3–15.

Manual of mental disorders. Washington, D.C.: American Psychiatric Association, 1968.

MASLOW, A. H. *Motivation and personality.* New York: Harper, 1954.

MATULEF, N. J. (Ed.) *The revolution in professional training.* Washington, D.C.: National Council on Graduate Education in Psychology, 1970.

MOORE, W. E. *The professions: Roles and rules.* New York: Russell Sage Foundation, 1970.

MORSE, W. C. Crisis intervention in school mental health and special classes for the disturbed. In N. J. LONG. W. C. MORSE, & R. G. NEWMAN (Eds.), *Conflict in the classroom: The education of children with problems.* Belmont, California: Wadsworth, 1971, 459–64.

MYRICK, R. D., & KELLY, F. D., JR. Group counseling with primary school-age children. *Journal of School Psychology*, 1971, *9*, 137–43.

NATIONAL ASSOCIATION OF SCHOOL PSYCHOLOGISTS. *Guidelines for training programs in school psychology.* Akron, Ohio: 1972.

NATIONAL EDUCATION ASSOCIATION. *NEA Research Bulletin: Would you teach again?* (Washington, D.C.) *NEA*, 1972, *50*, 35–36.

NEW, P. K. An analysis of the concept of teamwork. *Community Mental Health Journal*, 1968, *4*, 326–33.

NEWMAN, R. G., & KEITH, M. M. (Eds.) *The school-centered life space interview.* Washington, D.C.: Washington School of Psychiatry, 1963.

NEWMAN, S. A demonstration project in school consultation: A preventative approach, *Psychology in the Schools*, 1965, *2*, 70–76.

O'LEARY, K. D., & BECKER, W. C. The effects of the intensity of a teacher's reprimands on children's behavior. *Journal of School Psychology*, 1968–69, *7*(1), 8–11.

O'LEARY, K. D., & DRABMAN, R. Token reinforcement programs in the classroom: A review. *Psychological Bulletin*, 1971, *75*, 379–98.

PETER, L. J. *The Peter prescription: How to make things go right.* New York: Morrow, 1972.

PILECKI, F. J. Systems perspective and leadership in the educational organization. *Journal of Education*, 1970, *153*, 50–57.

PREMACK, D. Reinforcement theory. In D. LEVINE (Ed.), *Nebraska symposium on motivation.* Lincoln: University of Nebraska Press, 1965. Pp. 123–80.

PRESCOTT, D. *The child in the educative process.* New York: McGraw-Hill, 1957.

PRIBRAM, K. H. Education: An enterprise in language learning. In M. C. REYNOLDS (Ed.), *Psychology and the process of schooling in the next decade: Alternative conceptions.* Minneapolis, Minn.: Department of Audio-Visual Extension, University of Minnesota, 1972.

RAIMY, V. C. (Ed.) *Training in clinical psychology.* Englewood Cliffs, N.J.: Prentice-Hall, 1950.

REDL, F. The life-space interview—strategy and techniques. In *When we deal with children.* New York: Free Press, 1966. Pp. 35–67.

REYNOLDS, M. C. Categories and variables in special education. In M. C. REYNOLDS & M. D. DAVIS (Eds.), *Exceptional children in regular classes.* Minneapolis, Minn: Department of Audio-Visual Extension, University of Minnesota, 1971.

ROBERTS, R., & SOLOMONS, G. Perceptions of the duties and functions of the school psychologist. *American Psychologist*, 1970, *25*, 544–49.

ROGERS, C. R. *Client-centered therapy.* Boston: Houghton Mifflin, 1951.

ROGERS, C. R. Graduate education in psychology: A passionate statement. Unpublished manuscript, Western Behavioral Science Institute, La Jolla, California, 1965.

ROOSA, L. Planning the utilization of school psychological services: A systems approach. Unpublished doctoral dissertation, Rutgers—the State University, New Brunswick, N.J., 1972.

ROSENTHAL, R. *Experimenter effects in behavioral research.* New York: Appleton-Century-Crofts, 1966.

ROSENTHAL, R. & JACOBSON, L. *Pygmalion in the classroom: Teacher expectation and pupils' intellectual development.* New York: Holt, Rinehart & Winston, 1968.

ROSS, S. L., JR., DE YOUNG, H. G., & COHEN, J. S. Confrontation: Special education placement and the law. *Exceptional Children*, 1971, *38*, 5–12.

ROTTER, J. B. *Clinical psychology*. Englewood Cliffs, N.J.: Prentice-Hall, 1971.

Rules and regulations pursuant to title 18A, Chapter 46, New Jersey Statutes. Trenton, N.J.: State of New Jersey Department of Education, June 24, 1970. 21 pp.

RUZICKA, W. Working with parents and community agencies. In J. MAGARY (Ed.), *School psychological services*. Englewood Cliffs, N.J.: Prentice-Hall, 1967.

SALTEN, D. G. Reactions to the conference. In J. I. BARDON (Ed.), Problems and issues in school psychology—1964: Proceedings of a conference on new directions in school psychology. *Journal of School Psychology*, 1964–65, *3*, 26–32.

SARASON, S. B. *Psychological problems in mental deficiency*. (2nd ed.) New York: Harper, 1953.

SARASON, S. B. *The culture of the school and the problem of change*. Boston: Allyn & Bacon, 1971.

SCHEIN, E. H. *Organizational psychology*. (2nd ed.) Englewood Cliffs, N.J.: Prentice-Hall, 1970.

SCHIFFER, M. The therapeutic group in the public elementary school. In M. KRUGMAN (Ed.), *Orthopsychiatry and the school*. New York: American Orthopsychiatric Association, Inc., 1958.

SCHWEBEL, A. Physical and social distancing in teacher-pupil relationships. Unpublished doctoral dissertation, Yale University, New Haven, Conn., 1969.

SCHWEBEL, M. *Who can be educated?* New York: Grove Press, 1968.

SKINNER, B. F. *Science and human behavior*. New York: Macmillan, 1953.

SKINNER, B. F. Contingencies of reinforcement in the design of a culture. *Behavioral Science*, 1966, *11*, 159–66.

Standards and criteria for the accreditation of doctoral training programs in school psychology. *The School Psychologist*, 1972, *26*, 14–25.

Standards and criteria for non-doctoral training programs in school psychology. *The School Psychologist*, 1971, *26*, 2–11.

STARKMAN, S. The professional model: Paradox in school psychology. *American Psychologist*, 1966, *21*, 807–8.

STEPHENS, J. M. *The process of schooling: A psychological examination*. New York: Holt, Rinehart & Winston, 1967.

STEPHENS, T. M. Psychological consultation to teachers of learning and behaviorally handicapped children using a behavioral model. *Journal of School Psychology*, 1970, *8*, 13–18.

SYMONDS, P. J. The school psychologist—1942. *Journal of Consulting Psychology*, 1942, *6*, 173–76. Cited by S. GRAY, *The psychologist in the schools*. New York: Holt, Rinehart & Winston, 1963.

TERMAN, L. M., & MERRILL, M. A. *Stanford-Binet Intelligence Scale*. Boston: Houghton Mifflin, 1960.

THOMAS, A., HERTZIG, M. E., DRYMAN, I., & FERNANDEZ, P. Examiner effect in IQ testing of Puerto Rican working-class children. *American Journal of Orthopsychiatry*, 1971, *41*, 809–21.

THORNDIKE, R. L., & HAGEN, E. *Measurement and evaluation in psychology and education.* New York: John Wiley, 1960.

TOLBERT, E. L. *Introduction to counseling.* New York: McGraw-Hill, 1959.

TROW, W. C. What should be expected of psychologists in educational reform? *Journal of School Psychology*, 1968–69, *7*(4), 64–69.

TRUAX, C. B., & CARKHUFF, R. R. *Toward effective counseling and psychotherapy: Training and practice.* Chicago: Aldine Press, 1967.

ULLMAN, L. P., & KRASNER, L. *Case studies in behavior modification.* New York: Holt, Rinehart & Winston, 1965.

WALKER, L. The school psychologist as a preventive mental health consultant: The effects of in-service teacher education on teachers' attitudes and children's behavior. Unpublished doctoral dissertation, Rutgers—the State University, New Brunswick, N.J., 1972.

WALLACE, J. An abilities conception of personality: Some implications for personality measurement. *American Psychologist*, 1966, *21*(2), 132–37.

WATKINS, J. G. Psychotherapeutic methods. In B. B. WOLMAN (Ed.), *Handbook of clinical psychology.* New York: McGraw-Hill, 1965.

WATSON, J. B., & RAYNER, R. Conditioned emotional reactions. *Journal of Experimental Psychology*, 1920, *3*, 1–14.

WECHSLER, D. *The measurement and appraisal of adult intelligence.* Baltimore: Williams & Wilkins, 1958.

WHITE, M. A., & HARRIS, M. W. *The school psychologist.* New York: Harper, 1961.

WHITE, R. W. Ego and reality in psychoanalytic theory: A proposal regarding independent ego energies. *Psychological Issues*, 1963, *3*(3), Monograph 11.

WILLIAMS, D. L. Consultation: A broad, flexible role for school psychologists. *Psychology in the Schools*, 1972, *9*, 16–21.

WOHLKING, W. Management training: Where has it gone wrong? *Training and Development Journal*, 1971, *25*, 2–8.

WOLMAN, B. B. (Ed.) *Handbook of clinical psychology.* New York: McGraw-Hill, 1965.

WOLMAN, B. B. (Ed.) *Manual of child psychopathology.* New York: McGraw-Hill, 1972.

WOLPE, J. Reciprocal inhibition as the main basis of psychotherapeutic effects. *Archives of Neurology and Psychiatry*, 1954, *72*, 205–26.

WOOD, F. H. Behavior modification techniques in context. *Newsletter of the Council for Children with Behavioral Disorders*, 1968, *5*, 12–15.

YALOM, I. D., & LIEBERMAN, M. A. A study of encounter group casualties. *Archives of General Psychiatry*, 1971, *25*, 16–30.

YELON, S. L. Teachers as consumers of research. *Psychology in the Schools*, 1969, *6*, 155–57.

Index

Accountability, 158
Accreditation, 22
Adler, Alfred, 17, 99–100, 128
Adolescents, 102
American Psychological Association, 22, 96, 170–75 passim
American Psychologist, The, 22
Andrews, Joseph K., 123–124
Anttonen, R. G., 143
Anxiety, 32
Argyris, C., 182
Armed services, and need for psychologists, 17
Assessment, 60–61, 70
of disadvantaged children, 67–71
examples of, 49–51
group, 45–51
individual, 27–45
of learning disabilities, 39–40
personality, 40–45
psychosituational, 108–109
Association of Black Psychologists, 63
Attendance officer, 151
Auditory discrimination, 38

Beers, Clifford, 17
Behavior, 127
Behavior modification, 10, 123, 124
critique of, 83–87
with entire class, 81–83
with individual children, 75–81
Behavior rating scales, 28–29
Beker, Jerome, 157
Bender-Gestalt Visual Motor Test, 43
Berelson, Bernard, 161
Bersoff, Donald, 25–26, 108, 109
Bessell, Harold, 132
Binet, Alfred, 15–16
Boulder Conference, 171
Bower, Eli M., 102, 159–160
Boyer, William H., 67
Buck, Frank, 43

"C" group, 127–129
Caplan, Gerald, 104, 107, 116, 117
Carkhuff, Robert R., 129
Certification, 23, 173, 174
Charin, C. L., 84

Child (children), 18, 179–182
  auditorily handicapped, 53
  autistic, 81, 84
  black preschool, 63
  blind, 52
  chronically ill, 54
  deaf, 52
  disadvantaged, 62–71
  educable, 53, 60
  emotionally disturbed, 31–32, 52, 54, 60, 84
  learning disabilities in, 83
  mentally retarded, 51–53, 64, 83
  multiply handicapped, 55
  neurologically impaired, 52, 54, 60, 83
  orthopedically impaired, 54
  perceptually impaired, 54
  and reinforcers, 76, 77
  and Rorschach tests, 41
  socially maladjusted, 54–55
  trainable, 53
  visually handicapped, 53
Children's Apperception Test, 44
Child Study Association (England), 15
Child study groups, 119–120
Classroom, 4–5, 82–83, 87–91
Class size, 81
Cognitive functioning, 31
Cole, Charles W., 169n
Community attitudes, 100
Community services, 111–115
Comtois, Richard, 29
Confidentiality, 100
Consultations, 124–125
  defined, 116–118
  with teachers, 125–132, 135–139
Conti, Anthony, 113
Contingency management, 77
Controversial issues, 121–122
Counseling
  and community, 94–96
  defined, 91–93
  group, 100–105
  individual, 91–99
  models of, 93–94
  and school staff, 97–98
  vocational, 6
Cowen, Emory L., 145
Crisis intervention, 102–111
Cronbach, Lee, 67

Darwin, Charles, 14
Data, 5
Democratic Teacher Training Project, 130
Deno, Evelyn, 61
Dewey, John, 17n

Diagnosis, 56–57, 141
Dinkmeyer, D., 128
Draw-A-Person Test, 42–43

Education
  affective, 125–132
  in-service, 118–125
Ellis, Albert, 109
Empathy, 3
Encounter groups, 127
England, 14
Environmental modification, 87–91
Eysenck, Hans, 75

Family, 110
  See also Parents
Federal funds, 175
Festinger, Louis, 155
Fifield, Marvin, 140–141
Fleming, E. S., 143
France, 15–16
Freud, S., 13, 16–17, 41, 100

Galton, Sir Francis, 14
Gesell, Arnold, 16
Gesell Development Schedules, 38
Glasser, William, 130–131
Glidewell, James, 181n
Goals, psychologist's vs. teacher's, 134–135
Goodenough, Florence, 43
Gordon, Julia Weber, 119–120
Gray, Susan, 157, 159, 177–178
Grieger, Russell M., 108, 109
Guerney, Bernard, Jr., 129–130
Guidance counselors, 93, 152–153
Guttentag, Marcia, 158, 164–165

Handler, Leonard, 140
Harris, Myron, 147
Hawthorne Effect, 142
Health services, school, 153
Healy, William, 15
Human Development Program, 132
Human relations training, 129

Illinois Test of Psycho-Linguistic Abilities (ITPA), 38–39
Intelligence, 65, 66
Intelligence quotient (IQ), 33
Intelligence tests (*see* Tests, intelligence)
Interventionists, 182

Jacobson, L., 142–143
Jensen, Arthur, 66
Jones, M. C., 75

Kelly, Donald, Jr., 101–102
Kindergarten screening, 49
Kohn, Martin, 157–158
Kornrich, Milton, 113
Kounin, Jacob S., 82

Language facility and IQ scores, 63–64
Laws, on special education
    classification, 51–52
Learning ability and emotional
    adjustment, 18
Learning disabilities specialist, 153
Learning disability
    affective factors, 31–32
    assessment of, 39–40
Leiter International Performance Scale,
    35
Licensing, of psychologists, 22
Lieberman, Morton A., 127
Life-space interview, 106–108
Lindsley, Ogden, 123

Machover, Karen, 43
Magic Circle, the, 132
Make-A-Picture Test, 44
Mann, Lester, 39
Maslow, Abraham, 13n
Mental age, 33
Mental health, preventive approach,
    116
Mental health movement, 17–19
Mental illness, 17
Michigan Picture Test, 44
Minnesota Multiphasic Personality
    Inventory (MMPI), 48
Moore, Wilbert E., 170
Morse, William, 105
Motivation, theory of, 13n, 86
Murray, Henry, 43
Myrick, Robert, 101–102

National Association of School
    Psychologists, 173
National Committee for Mental
    Hygiene, 17
National Institute for Mental Health,
    175
New, Peter Kong-Ming, 154–155
New Jersey, 52–53, 119
Newman, Stanley, 138
New York City, 63
Nurse, school, 153

Observation, 28–30
Operant conditioning, 74
Organizational Psychology, 88

Palomares, Uvaldo, 132
Parents, 29, 86, 114
    and child's referral, 112–113
    and play therapy, 129
Parsons, Frank, 152
Pavlov, Ivan, 74
Pearson, Karl, 14
Personality, 104–105
    assessment, 40–45
Prescott, Daniel, 119
Pribram, Karl, 136
Principals, 149–151
Professionalism, 170
Professionals, licensing of, 21
Projective techniques, 41–45
Psychoanalysis, emergence of, 13–14
Psychological services, 179–182
Psychologists, 159
    and armed services work, 17
    clinical, 6, 9–10
    educational, 7, 9, 11
    military, 99
    and personality assessment, 40–45
    school, 1–8 *passim*, 18, 145–146
        approaches of, 179–181
        and behavior management, 73–87
        behavior modification, 85–87,
            123–124
        in child study groups, 120
        and community, 94–96
        as consultant, 132–143
        and controversial issues, 121–122
        and counseling, 93–94, 96, 100–105
        and crisis intervention, 105–111
        dissatisfaction with, 19
        and environmental modification,
            88–91
        examining style, 70
        goals, 134–135
        methods, 10–11
        overworked, 18–19
        and parents, 112–113
        personality characteristics, 2–4
        preparation, 2
        and principals, 149–151
        and professional autonomy, 25–26
        prospects for future, 178–182
        and referrals, 111–115
        and research, 157–168
        as school employee, 24–25,
            145–146
        and superintendents, 146–149
        and teachers, 72–73, 82, 116–143
            passim
        and testing, 34, 46, 47, 50–51,
            67–71, 120–121
        training of, 176–178

Psychologists (*cont.*)
  social, 8–9
  standards for, 22–23
  types of, 6–7, 11
Psychology, 14–15
  clinical, 6, 9–10, 15
  community, 7, 11
  ecological, 89n
  faculty, 40
  professional standards of, 22–23
  school, 8, 72
    current status, 21–26
    history of, 12–22
    prospects for future, 178–182
    specialties, 6–8
    training for, 169–178
Psychopathology, 6
Psychotherapy, 6
  defined, 91–93
  filial, 129–130
  group, 99–100
  play, 94, 101
  reality, 130–131
Punishment, 76
Pupil(s), and behavior modification, 77–81
Pupil personnel services, 151–157

Ravens Progressive Matrices, 35
Reading, testing for, 38–39
Redl, Fritz, 106–107
Rehabilitation, 6
Reinforcement, 74–76
Reinforcers, 76–77
Repression, 41
Research, 4
  in schools, 157–168
  in training programs, 174
Research studies, 142–143
Response capability, 3, 60
Response set, teacher's, 136–137
Reward, defined, 74
Reynolds, M. C., 56
Ripple Effect, 82
Rogers, Carl, 94, 172
Role playing, 110, 122
Rorschach, Hermann, 41
Rorschach technique, 41–42
Rosenthal, R., 142–143
Rotter, Julian, 91–93
Ruzicka, William J., 112

Salten, David G., 147–149
Sarason, Seymour, 55, 133–134
Schein, Edgar H., 88
Scholastic Aptitude Test, 46

School Apperception Test, 44
School psychologist (*see* Psychologists, school)
School psychology (*see* Psychology, school)
School(s), 87, 144–145, 178
  crisis intervention in, 105–111
  dissatisfaction with, 178
  group counseling in, 100–105
  New York City, 63
  personnel, 114–115
  psychological approaches in, 179–182
  and public, 92–93
  records, 30
  research in, 157–168
Schwebel, Milton, 65–66
Scientific approach, 14–15
Screening, 49, 55
Self-fulfilling prophesy, 3, 84
Sex education, 121–122
Simon, Theophile, 15–16
Skill training methods, 127–130
Skinner, B.F., 74
Slavson, S.R., 101
Social interaction, 100
Social worker, school, 152
Special education, 15, 51–62
Stanford-Binet Intelligence Scale, 16, 31–34, 63, 64, 68
Starkman, S., 26
Stephens, J.M., 142
Stephens, Thomas M., 123
Students, 49
Superintendents, 146–149
Symonds, P.J., 20

Teacher(s)
  and affective education, 126–132
  attitudes toward counseling, 97–98
  and behavior modification, 81–83, 84, 86, 123–124
  in child study groups, 119–120
  consultation with psychologist, 72–73, 116–118, 132–143
  and controversial issues, 121–122
  elementary school, 135
  and environmental modification, 88–91
  and filial therapy, 129–130
  goals of, 134–135
  and in-service education, 118–125
  as observers, 28–30
  public view of, 133–134
  and reality therapy, 130–131
  and research findings, 157–158
  and researchers, 158
  and testing, 70, 120–121